AR·TI·SAN·AL (är'ti-zən'əl)

MADE WITH PASSION, PRIDE, ENTHUSIASM, CARE, AND ATTENTION TO DETAIL

ARTISANAL COOKING

TERRANCE BRENNAN AND ANDREW FRIEDMAN

ARTISANAL COOKING

A CHEF SHARES HIS PASSION FOR HANDCRAFTING GREAT MEALS AT HOME

PHOTOS BY CHRISTOPHER HIRSHEIMER

JOHN WILEY & SONS, INC.

Photographs © 2005 by Christopher Hirsheimer
Published by John Wiley & Sons, Inc., Hoboken, New Jersey
Published simultaneously in Canada

Design by Vertigo Design NYC

For general information about our other products and services, please contact our Customer Care Department within the United States at (800) 762-2974, outside the United States at (317) 572-3993 or fax (317) 572-4002.

Wiley also publishes its books in a variety of electronic formats. Some content that appears in print may not be available in electronic books. For more information about Wiley products, visit our web site at www.wiley.com.

LIBRARY OF CONGRESS CATALOGING-IN-PUBLICATION DATA:

Brennan, Terrance.
Artisanal cooking : a chef shares his passion for handcrafting great meals at home /
by Terrance Brennan and Andrew Friedman.
p. cm.
Includes index.
ISBN-13 978-0-471-21061-0 (hardcover : alk. paper)
ISBN 0-7645-6822-1 (hardcover : alk. paper)
1. Cookery. I. Friedman, Andrew, 1967- II. Title.
TX714.B743 2005
641.5--dc22

2005000716

RECCA
SCIACCA . ITALY
ACCIUGHE SALATE
LAVORAZIONE
QUALITÀ SCELTA

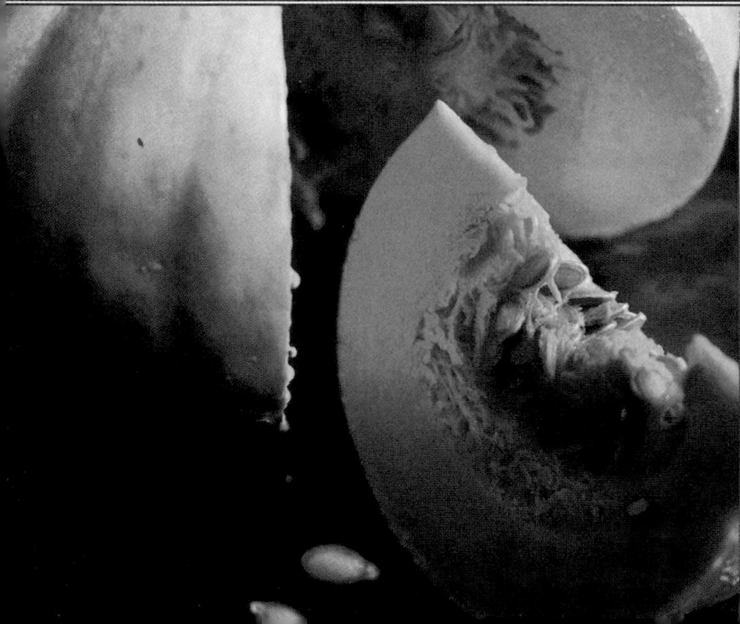

ACKNOWLEDGMENTS

This book reflects the efforts of many people who came together to help me produce my first cookbook. My heartfelt thanks to the following:

Andrew Friedman, my collaborator, who hounded me to pursue it in the first place, came up with the title and concept, and made it easy for me to write the book once we got going;

Linda Ingroia, my editor at Wiley, for her boundless enthusiasm, smart suggestions, and painstaking attention to detail, not to mention her patience for all the late-breaking changes;

The supportive and diligent Wiley team including Natalie Champan, the publisher; Diana Cisek, the production director; Jeffrey Faust, the cover art director; and Todd Fries and Michael Friedberg in marketing and Gypsy Lovett in publicity;

Vertigo Design who did a beautiful job designing this book;

Jessica Jaffe, who helped with several aspects of the book, dating back to the days of its inception, and was instrumental in coordinating the efforts of everyone involved;

The team of experts who tested, and retested (and in some cases triple- and quadruple-tested) the recipes: David Cox, the hard-working and incredibly passionate executive chef of Artisanal restaurant, who undertook the Herculean task of converting my restaurant dishes into "home size" versions; Keith Geter, one of Artisanal's sous chefs, and Craig Hopson, Picholine's chef de cuisine, who helped bring it all down the home stretch; Dan Rundell, Picholine's pastry chef, who vetted many of the dessert recipes; Valerie Broussard, who helped test the recipes and ensure their accuracy; and all the cooks at both restaurants for their help along the way, from rushing ingredients to us at the test kitchen on a moment's notice, to phoning in measurements and weights when we needed them;

My late father, Eugene, who was crazy enough to get into the restaurant business and introduced me to it, and my mother, Jean-Marie, who supported my decision to get into it, and has been my biggest fan;

Max McCalman and Daphne Zepos, my cheese-loving colleagues at Artisanal Premium Cheese, for sharing their wisdom and taste with me, both in this book and every day;

Christopher Hirsheimer, who makes taking great pictures look easy (though it isn't!), and her able assistant, Verity Liljedahl, who also happens to be her daughter; thanks also to Melissa Hamilton for securing the perfect props;

Angela Miller, my agent, for her guidance in developing the proposal and putting the idea in front of the good people at Wiley;

All of the employees of Artisanalcheese.com, and in the kitchens and the dining rooms, at both Artisanal and Picholine. It's a tough business we've chosen and there's not a day that goes by that I don't appreciate your tireless effort and professionalism;

Rob Patch, Ray Knox, and Peter Renfrey for helping me test the cooking times on our "grilling and chilling" weekend;

The farmers, purveyors, and artisanal cheesemakers that produce or supply all of the great ingredients we use at my restaurants; without you, we'd be only half the cooks you enable us to be;

Nach Waxman of Kitchen Arts and Letters, for his early words of advice, which led to many of the entries in the Artisanal Pantry chapter;

Ivy Ronquillo, for her countless hours of proofreading in the homestretch.

Marvin Numeroff, my business partner, for all of his longstanding support;

And to the guests of Picholine and Artisanal restaurants. Thank you for so many great years and memories. It is an honor and pleasure to serve you. I hope to continue doing so for many more years to come.

ARTISANAL COOKING

ARTISANAL COOKING
A PHILOSOPHY

NO WORD MEANS MORE TO ME PROFESSIONALLY, or better summarizes my view of food and cooking, than *artisanal*. Technically, *artisanal* means "handcrafted." But it connotes much more than that, namely a loving, almost obsessive attention to detail, and a sense of craftsmanship, tradition, and pride. It describes a concept so close to my heart that I took it for the name of one of my New York City restaurants, as well as my cheese company.

I'm not the only one who responds to *artisanal* this way. As our lives are increasingly defined by technology and commercialism, more and more Americans are looking for balance and seeking out artisanal food; for them, it signifies something that has been nurtured with great care, whether it's bread baked by a small, family-run bakery, produce painstakingly grown by farmers who sell it at green markets and roadside stands, or cheese that's been nurtured by passionate perfectionists. I also apply the word to certain ranchers, fishermen, and purveyors who have made it their lives' work to grow, or procure, and sell only the best that the earth and sea have to offer.

Artisanal also implies something that is especially reassuring in these fast-moving times—a methodical attention to detail and a pride that is unique to master craftspeople. The artisanal approach makes many of us imagine the pastoral charm of the French farmhouse or Italian villa, where ordinary people engage in artisanal pursuits every day, from growing their own fruits and vegetables to raising their own livestock.

As you might know, Artisanal Fromagerie and Bistro is best known for its cheese: we offer more than 250 varieties of it there and from our web site, and we participate in the artisan's process ourselves by acting as *affineur* (aging the cheeses in our own climate-controlled caves). But at Artisanal, and at my first restaurant, Picholine, I also use the word *artisanal* in that more all-encompassing way, to refer to just about every aspect of food and cooking, from the ingredients we procure to the integrity with which we transform them into meals for our guests.

Rare are the American chefs who have the real estate, time, or inclination to grow their own fruits and vegetables, raise their own livestock, or make their own cheese. But my colleagues and I revere those ingredients as much as those town and village dwellers who make their own foodstuffs, and we honor that sentiment by availing ourselves of the ever-growing list of artisanal foods available from farmers and small producers here and abroad, who have advanced American cuisine—ironically enough—by returning to generations-old production techniques and methods.

In the case of locally grown produce and locally raised livestock, availing oneself of these resources is, to my mind, an act of civic responsibility. When you buy from local farmers, you support your local or regional economy and enable those farmers to maintain and nourish natural resources, building an agricultural foundation for future generations. Taken as a whole, these concepts are commonly referred to as "sustainable agriculture," and the best part is that you can support it while availing yourself of the best possible ingredients.

This idea is so central to my culinary point of view that I think of what I do in the kitchen as "artisanal cooking," carefully considering every decision and task, from the selection of ingredients to the actual preparation of dishes. By the same token, the artisans of the world offer culinary role models to home cooks, just as they do to chefs. If every home cook approached making meals—whether preparing a simple weeknight family dinner or planning a Saturday evening feast for invited guests—with the enthusiasm of an artisan, there would be a lot more memorable meals served.

Artisanal cooking also facilitates one of my other great passions, one that might seem mutually exclusive with my fondness for cooking: I love spending time at the table, even when I'm the one responsible for the meal. I have always believed very strongly that a home cook should spend time with the person or people for whom he or she is cooking. I think this is truer than ever today, when we lead increasingly busy lives in times that are more troubled than any of us would like. There's no more potent antidote to the modern world, no sanctuary more qualified to restore one's sense of humanity and provide a means of connecting with others, than time spent around a dinner table with one's family and friends, enjoying the reassuring sounds of conversation and laughter, or even perhaps cooking together as a family.

One of the reasons I'm so enthusiastic about sharing my ideas in this book is that I've learned firsthand how much of a role cooking and eating can play in bringing a family closer together. When I sneak away to Vermont with my family for a weekend, dinners are always a highlight. We often plan theme dinners a week or more in advance, anticipating the time when the day's activities are done and we return to our house pleasantly exhausted and ravenously hungry. With a fire burning in the fireplace, we make and enjoy a meal that could be French-influenced or inspired by the food of another country, like my kids' favorite, Mexico.

People who know my European-leaning repertoire would probably be shocked to see me eating tacos, enchiladas, rice, and beans with my family and loving every minute of it. But when I think back on the most meaningful meals I've participated in, it's the ambiance of the table—the unique rhythm of a particular afternoon or evening, the people around me, the relaxed socializing before and after the dining itself—that abides in my memory.

In this book, I'm going to show you that conjuring this kind of atmosphere is more possible than you might think, if you follow my philosophy of turning to sound recipes founded in tradition, and making them with the best ingredients. We're going to discover together that when you begin with great ingredients and a concept rooted in tradition, creating and serving a memorable meal doesn't necessarily require a great deal of time and energy. (Though, of course, there are times when it does, and is worth it.)

My way of cooking is less about finding hard-to-procure ingredients than maintaining a devotion to a certain integrity and quality in every aspect of the cooking process, even just knowing what to look for when buying meats and produce. Armed with the information in this book, you'll be able to successfully accomplish your own brand of artisanal cooking, even if you do most of your shopping in a supermarket.

My repertoire is inspired by French cuisine. Unfortunately, to a lot of Americans that means rarefied dishes and unpronounceable terminology. But at the heart of French cooking is a reverence for fresh ingredients and simple presentations. (I'm reminded of a famous line from Escoffier, one of the forefathers of Western cuisine, which is stenciled like a mural across a wall at the French Culinary Institute in New York City: "The best dishes are also very simple dishes.") For every intimidating, complex French classic, there's a dish in the *grand-mère* style (the phrase literally means "grandmother," and refers to rustic preparations, often served in their cooking vessels) or a salad, soup, fish, or meat dish that celebrates a central, often seasonal, ingredient and requires very little effort to prepare, such as a tomato or asparagus salad, chicken cooked under a brick, fish cooked in parchment paper with vegetables, or a roast leg of lamb. These genres of food inspire most of the recipes you'll find in these pages, which I value for flavor above all else, including presentation.

I was fortunate to live and work in France while I was learning my craft. The time I spent in the three-star Michelin kitchens of Roger Verge's Le Moulin de Mougins, Taillevent, Le Tour d'Argent, and Gerard Boyer's Les Crayeres was priceless, as was the time I spent at La Gavroche in London. But I learned just as much from the French attitude toward the quality of time at the table.

Some of my most vivid memories of France occurred outside of these restaurants; for example, during the weekend I visited a friend's family's home outside Le Mans in the Loire Valley. It was one of the French farmhouses that I wrote about earlier, that few of us have ever actually experienced, let alone lived in on a daily basis. The family's larder—kept on shelves in a cool, stone-walled basement—would amaze even the most passionate American home cook or professional chef, with homemade pickled vegetables, duck confit, preserved porcinis, pâté, and a whole catalogue of condiments. Out back, they tended their own garden, where they grew salad greens and other vegetables, kept their own pigeon and duck coop, and retrieved trout from a rectangular fish-holding pen. They purchased cheese from nearby farms, and even foraged for their own porcini mushrooms in the nearby woods.

The quality of these culinary building blocks—ready to be picked from the garden or spooned from a jar on a moment's notice—was extraordinary. Needless to say, we had a number of wonderful meals that weekend; meals I treasured as much for the time we spent together as for the food itself. I still remember the sense of satisfaction and belonging that we all felt after a long, leisurely dinner one night as we lingered for one final hour over the cheese course, contentedly savoring the last of our wine and letting the night settle in around us before returning indoors and retiring for the evening.

I had many moments like this in France and it's an understatement to say that when it comes to food and dining I'm a Francophile, as much because of their regard for time at the table as for their passion for great ingredients like all of those resources my friend had in his backyard and cellar. In fact, it's the well-stocked pantry and the quality of the other ingredients that make the time at the table possible.

Take cheese, for example. One of the things I love about cheese is that the product itself contains all the flavor required to satisfy even the most sophisticated palate. A simple yet sublime lunch can be conjured from a few well-chosen pieces of cheese, a green salad, some crusty bread, a glass of wine, and fruit. Or consider late-summer tomatoes and how utterly perfect they are just drizzled with extra virgin olive oil, then seasoned with sea salt and a few grinds of black pepper.

Obviously, these are two examples that can be prepared with extreme ease and a minimum of time, just about 10 or 15 minutes. But I mention them to illustrate how making wise decisions, from how you select your ingredients to what dishes you decide to cook, can free you up to spend time at the table.

I think cooking is about giving pleasure, not showing off. And, as much as I love food, I don't think cooking is even ultimately about food taking center stage. In this book, I want to convey a philosophy of food and cooking that will satisfy your love of cooking, delight those for whom you are cooking, and afford you that precious table time.

This book brings together everything I love about food, cooking, and dining to offer you an attainable vision of being an artisan in your own kitchen, thoughtfully selecting and integrating the components of individual recipes and entire meals, and letting the ingredients shine as much as possible. The lesson of this book is that with a passionate mindset and some weekly planning, unforgettable meals can come together swiftly, turning the dinner table into a place for sustenance and socializing, nourishing body and soul in a way that only the great human tradition of dining with family and friends can accomplish.

WORKING SMART IN THE KITCHEN
GREAT COOKING IS EASIER THAN YOU THINK

WHEN I HAVE THE OPPORTUNITY TO MEET HOME COOKS, or to "talk shop" with guests of my restaurants, I often get the sense that they're making it more difficult than it has to be in the kitchen. It's a natural and noble mistake to make: If you want to make a great meal, some believe, you have to spend a lot of time, effort, and money.

Not necessarily. My motto in the kitchen isn't to work hard, but rather to work smart. There are a few basic rules I keep in mind whenever I plan to cook. Employing them as a decision-making template is at the heart of my cooking philosophy.

You'll see examples of these principles throughout the book, but I wanted to take a moment to spell them out in one place. They all have one thing in common: Each one involves respecting a force greater than yourself, which sounds potentially daunting, but in fact makes life easier. When you adhere to the following guidelines, you'll find that you have fewer decisions to make, that your food has a simplicity and order, and that you cook in harmony with the seasons.

USE THE BEST INGREDIENTS
There's a reason I put so much emphasis on the quality of raw ingredients: I want to taste each of them clearly in the finished dish. This means cooking with integrity, respecting each ingredient at each stage of the cooking process, selecting the best one available to you, then cooking and seasoning it with care, and surrounding it with compatible accompaniments.

RESPECT THE SEASONS
I encourage you to respect the role of nature in cooking. The rewards of using organic fruits and vegetables and free-range or wild animals is a prime example of why nature should be obeyed in the kitchen. As we come to certain recipes, I'll help you discover for yourself the superior quality of, say, wild salmon over the farm-raised alternatives. But the most essential advice I can offer, because it applies to everyday cooking, is the benefit of working with in-season ingredients. I use such seasonal touchstones as tomatoes, morels, figs, pomegranates, and chestnuts only when they are in season, and urge you to do the same.

HONOR TRADITION, THEN BE CREATIVE
Many of my recipes are founded in tradition, and for good reason: Time-honored dishes have been around for decades or centuries because they are structurally sound and produce delicious results. However, I truly believe that one can adhere to tradition in cooking and still find room to be creative and spontaneous. Throughout this book, I'll show you how to balance the two, whether by using the confit technique classically associated with duck to make preserved tomatoes, garlic, or lemon, or by making a daube (stew) with a popular cut of beef like short ribs rather than the traditional bottom round or shoulder.

HONE YOUR SKILLS

Technique can make or break your success in the kitchen just as surely as it can buoy or undo an artisan who produces cheese or other culinary products. This is not to suggest that you need to become a master chef to produce good food, but employing efficient, skilled technique will make meal preparation more enjoyable and yield consistently positive results. Throughout the book, I'll explain the principles behind techniques, focusing especially on how to select an appropriate heat level and the benefits and applications of steaming, sautéing, roasting, braising, and other cooking methods.

HOW TO USE THIS BOOK

I'M A TRADITIONALIST BY NATURE and this book is organized fairly traditionally, with chapters devoted to Hors d'Oeuvres, Salads and First Courses, Soups, Meats and Game, Desserts, and so on. But there are a few chapters and features that bear explanation:

The first recipe chapter, "The Artisanal Pantry," features recipes that show you how to become an artisan in your own home by making your own chutneys, pickled vegetables, condiments, and such. These are largely optional—most of the recipes that call for these ingredients give you the option of using store-bought versions—but I hope you'll try at least a few. Not only will you be amazed at how much better they taste when you make your own, but it will give you an appreciation of what goes into these ingredients in shops and restaurants.

This chapter features a subsection on cheese, the food with which I'm most closely associated. Think of it as a primer for purchasing, serving, and storing cheese. It also spotlights some of my favorite cheese combinations. I hope it inspires you to make cheese a part of your everyday life.

As for the recipes themselves, most are preceded by a headnote that talks about the recipe's inspiration, offers cooking advice, or describes a particular ingredient and how to shop for, handle, and cook it. In addition, many of the recipes are supported by one or more of the following recurring features:

TERMS AND TECHNIQUES Here I'll define or explain words and phrases that might be unfamiliar to you, such as *al dente* or *court-boullion,* or describe a basic method such as how to juice a pomegranate or a neat trick for rolling dough over a tart.

THE REASON In this feature, I'll detail why recipes call for taking certain steps, such as letting meat rest to give its juices a chance to redistribute after cooking or adding a dash of lemon juice to mushrooms to coax out all of their natural flavor.

VARIATIONS This is where I'll explain how to alter a dish to adjust for personal taste and ingredient availability, or to stay true to the current season. The Wild Mushroom and Duck Risotto (page 219), a perennial favorite at Picholine, is offered with the same adjustments we make at the restaurant: adding fava beans in the spring, corn in the summer, pumpkin in the fall, and squash in the winter. I even offer ways to adjust desserts for the seasons; for example, the Profiterole Sundae with Cherry Ice Cream and Cherry Compote (page 301), can be varied in the cooler months to incorporate pistachio ice cream and be finished with pecans or walnuts rather than fresh cherry compote.

EMBELLISHMENT This is where I'll show how to build on a recipe with additional ingredients, perhaps expanding a sauce with olives, capers, and diced tomatoes, or by adding another component, such as an oil or chutney, to the plate.

READING RECIPES

ONE OF THE BEST WAYS TO WORK SMART IN THE KITCHEN is to thoughtfully and thoroughly read every recipe before you begin cooking, then get your ingredients and equipment organized accordingly.

I'm a big proponent of the concept of *mise en place* (having everything in its place), so much so that I suggest cooks line up their ingredients and equipment in the order in which they'll be used so that they can focus all of their attention on the actual cooking process when they get down to it. I think this is one of the most important lessons home cooks can learn: to make yourself fully attentive to what is happening on the stovetop or in the oven so that you can be aware of the often infinitesimal changes in ingredients that are the cue to move on to the next step of a recipe; if you're looking around for, say, a strainer when it's time to move on in a recipe, you lose time and perhaps cause items to overcook.

ACCOMPANIMENTS, GARNISHES, SAUCES, AND OTHER FLOURISHES

THROUGHOUT THE BOOK, there are a number of condiments, dressings, sauces, side dishes, and other recipes that are presented as a component of a main recipe but which can be used to enhance many dishes in your own day-to-day cooking. Here's a guide to where to find them:

CHUTNEYS AND COMPOTES

(see also "The Artisanal Pantry," pages 10 to 49)

Apple-Walnut Chutney *(page 155)*

Cranberry Compote *(page 149)*

Mint Chutney *(page 167)*

CROUTONS, TOASTS, AND TUILLES

Anchovy Toasts *(page 96)*

Cheddar Croutons *(page 157)*

Parmesan and Black Pepper Croutons *(page 165)*

Parmesan Tuille *(page 100)*

DRESSINGS AND VINAIGRETTES

Basil Aïoli *(page 187)*

Citrus-Soy Vinaigrette *(page 111)*

Lemon Vinaigrette *(page 105)*

Harissa Vinaigrette *(page 115)*

Mustard Dressing *(page 130)*

Parsley Pistou *(page 248)*

Pomegranate Vinaigrette *(page 119)*

Sherry Vinaigrette *(page 100)*

Tahini Dressing *(page 133)*

Walnut Vinaigrette *(page 108)*

GARNISHES, MISCELLANEOUS

Marinated Scallops *(page 162)*

Parmesan Flan *(page 140)*

Raw Tomato Coulis *(page 187)*

Red Gazpacho Granité *(page 160)*

SAUCES

Béarnaise Sauce *(page 232)*

Horseradish Cream *(page 235)*

Morel Sauce *(page 128)*

Mustard Sauce *(page 195)*

Red Wine Butter *(page 189)*

SIDE DISHES

(see also Side Dishes and Accompaniments, pages 256 to 274)

Comté-Scallion Polenta *(page 212)*

Orange-Cumin Carrots *(page 239)*

Red Cabbage Confit *(page 253)*

Rutabaga "Sauerkraut" *(page 251)*

Vanilla Sweet Potato Puree *(page 227)*

Tabbouleh *(page 114)*

DESSERT TOPPINGS AND SWEET TOUCHES

Candied Almonds *(page 316)*

Chocolate Sauce *(page 315)*

Crème Chantilly *(page 299)*

Pecan Shortbread Cookies *(page 317)*

Raspberry Marshmallows *(page 280)*

THE ARTISANAL PANTRY

WHEN I SPEAK OF THE ARTISANAL PANTRY, I refer not only to the traditional pantry of dry goods such as spices, oils, pastas, legumes, and so on, but also to those staples kept in the refrigerator and freezer, many of which you might make yourself, such as stocks, infused oils, pickled vegetables, chutneys, and marmalades.

A well-stocked pantry offers variety, enabling the cook to select the best ingredient for any given recipe. Just as certain meats are better for braising than for grilling and certain vegetables are better roasted than poached, certain oils are best used for sautéing, certain salts are more suited to raw preparations than cooked ones, and certain peppers complement different dishes to greater and lesser effect.

A pantry gives you a wide range of options, from embellishments for sweet and savory dishes, to go-to items such as pasta and rice that can become the centerpiece of a quickly prepared recipe. Accordingly, one's pantry should be replenished regularly, with items being replaced as they are depleted. Maintaining a pantry is like giving yourself an open invitation to cook, minimizing the number of ingredients you need to procure at the last minute to dive into a given recipe or to satisfy whatever craving might overtake you as the lunch or dinner hour approaches.

This chapter is divided into two parts. The first, "What to Buy," offers my suggested list of the real fundamental basics that no kitchen should be without. The second, "What to Make," earned this chapter its name: I use the term "artisanal pantry" because you can prepare many of the items yourself. This section includes recipes for mayonnaise, stocks, compound butters, and other essentials that you can call on in all kinds of cooking.

> It should be noted that the pantry items in this chapter do not constitute an exhaustive pantry. Rather, they are the items I call on most often and therefore the ones called for or suggested most frequently throughout the book. Another chef's pantry might include a selection of, say, Asian staples, and your own pantry should be tailored to suit your own culinary leanings.

If you're wondering when to make pantry items in the midst of your busy schedule, the best approach is to look at them as part of your everyday cooking. I've found two strategies to be very effective at home: One is to periodically schedule a "pantry day" when you make a number of these recipes, then use one as part of your dinner that night, perhaps serving a marmalade alongside a simple roast or creating a soup from one of the stocks, and saving the rest for another time. The other strategy is to make one or two pantry items while doing unrelated cooking. For example, if you're roasting poultry or meat, use the waiting time to make a few pantry items or, on the other hand, if you're preparing a quick meal, stay in the kitchen a little longer (or start a little earlier) and make something you'll call on another day.

A small amount of time can leave you with your own homemade basics for weeks or months to come; most of these recipes don't require many ingredients or much attention. You could, of course, purchase readymade versions of them instead, but there's nothing like making your own to really put your imprint on everything that comes out of your kitchen.

WHAT TO BUY

ANCHOVIES I love using anchovies as a seasoning agent in sauces and stews. If you can, purchase salt-packed anchovy fillets rather than those stored in olive oil. Soak them for 15 minutes in warm water or milk, rinse them, and pat them dry with paper towels before using.

BAY LEAVES These aromatic leaves are used throughout Western cooking to deliver pungent flavor to stocks, sauces, soups, and stews. We all know them in their dried form, but fresh bay leaves are increasingly available, even in supermarkets, and transmit a cleaner, more subtle flavor. By all means use fresh and dried bay interchangeably whenever bay leaves are called for. One note: bay leaves should always be removed from any preparation that won't be strained.

BEANS Dried beans turn up in a wide range of recipes, from salads to soups to stews. In this book, I call for white beans and chickpeas. Though I personally don't use them very often, other legumes such as (dried) peas and lentils are also well worth stocking at home.

BREAD Add a large loaf of country bread (boulle) to your weekly shopping list. You'll use it for sandwiches and serving at the table. One of my favorite times to enjoy bread is at breakfast, toasted, spread with butter, and drizzled with honey. If you don't use bread within a day or two, freeze it wrapped in plastic. If you wait too long and it goes stale, you can make bread crumbs or toast, or revive it with this method: Set the bread on a sheet of aluminum foil, sprinkle it with cold water, wrap the foil loosely around it, and bake in the oven for 7 to 10 minutes. Remove the foil and bake another 5 minutes. The bread will come out crispy on the outside and soft on the inside.

Space here doesn't allow for a responsible lesson in bread-baking, but if you're inclined to make your own, I encourage you to plow ahead. Many cooking schools now offer courses in bread baking, and there are many helpful books and bread machines on the market.

BUTTER (SALTED AND UNSALTED) Though both salted and unsalted (sweet) butters are widely available, salted butter is really an anachronism of sorts, originally turned to as a means of preservation. Unsalted butter is the only butter I use for cooking, because it gives you more control over the salt content in a dish. When seeking a butter, take an artisanal attitude and select a distinctive, creamery butter with a fat content of 80 percent or higher.

(As a "table butter" I do love a good salted butter; ones with sea salt that hail from Brittany are the best.)

CAPERS Grown in warm climates all over the world, capers—the preserved flower buds of a shrub—are indigenous to Asia. I prefer the smaller nonpareil variety to larger caper berries because they integrate effortlessly into dishes and sauces whereas the larger ones need to be chopped, asking another step of the cook and producing a less attractive ingredient. Capers turn up over and over in the foods of my favorite French regions, especially in fish dishes. They should be drained, rinsed, and drained again before using.

CHEESE See Cheese section, pages 50 to 61.

CHOCOLATE Splurge for a premium brand and stock a variety such as milk, bittersweet, and semisweet. My two favorite brands are Valrhona and Michel Cluizel, both of which have a clarity of flavor without too much sweetness, that brings nuance to desserts.

CORNSTARCH Once a popular means of thickening sauces and soups, cornstarch isn't called on in many modern recipes. In this book, however, you'll discover that it's a crucial component of one of the most famous and beloved of all cheese preparations in the world: fondue.

DAIRY PRODUCTS (ALSO SEE BUTTER AND CHEESE) Obviously eggs, milk, and cream have limited lifespans, but it's worth keeping a fresh supply of all of them in your refrigerator at all times if you cook on a regular basis.

FLOUR (ALL-PURPOSE, CAKE, SEMOLINA) True to its name, (unbleached) all-purpose flour can be used in most recipes that call for flour. But certain pastas and pasta-like preparations require semolina. If you bake at home, also make some room for a box of cake flour as well as more specialized items such as almond flour and hazelnut flour.

HERBS You won't keep fresh herbs in your pantry, but they are a staple in most cooking, so here's some important background information: I either snip (yes, with scissors) or carefully slice fresh herbs rather than chopping them. Treating them more gently preserves their natural flavor and character by keeping the membrane and water cells intact. Chopping herbs can turn them soggy or, in the case of basil, black. To slice herbs (as for the Garlic-Herb Butter, page 24), use a very sharp knife and a back-and-forth slicing motion rather than chopping them.

I also believe that herbs should never be used for color alone. All herbs, even the vastly overused parsley, should be selected for flavor, not as a garnish, and should be as thoughtfully incorporated as all other ingredients in a dish.

HONEY Honey isn't just something for sweetening tea: It's delicious drizzled over cheeses, and it brings new life to yogurt or toast. It can also round out a simple dessert of fresh farmer's cheese, fruit, and nuts. Seek out honey produced from a single floral source. I'm partial to chestnut, lavender, orange blossom, and the Sicilian carob honey.

MEATS, CURED Made to be stored for weeks or months, cured meats can be included in an hors d'oeuvres platter along with cheese and olives, dipped in fondues, used to add flavor to cooked dishes, or simply snacked on, whether on their own or as part of a charcuterie plate (featuring cured meats and accompaniments such as cheese, paté, and cornichons). Bacon is the only truly essential one, but prosciutto, salami, and soppressata all have unique charms of their own.

MUSTARDS (DIJON, GRAIN) Dijon and grain mustards turn up over and over again in recipes for vinaigrettes and sauces, not to mention ranking as great sandwich condiments in their own right. As you'll see in this book, I often use these two mustards in tandem to create a complex, composite flavor marrying the sharp flavor of Dijon mustard with the mellower, creamier qualities of grain mustard.

Also worth keeping on hand is Colman's Dry Mustard Powder (which is the key ingredient in the Mustard Oil on page 28). It's also a quick way to add zip to dressings and sauces, and can be a powerful player in dry rubs and marinades.

NUTS In both sweet and savory dishes, nuts are a quick way to add texture. I always toast nuts to release their natural oils, which are their greatest source of flavor; it's generally a good idea to do this before using them in a recipe, even if the nuts will be cooled and served cold or at room temperature. At a minimum, you should always have a cup or two of almonds and walnuts on hand. I also make it a point to keep pecans in the house.

If not using nuts in the very near future, freeze them in airtight plastic bags to keep them from turning rancid.

OILS Understanding which oils to select for which uses is important. Here are my suggestions:

Extra virgin olive oil The easiest way to think of extra virgin olive oil is as a condiment to be drizzled over finished dishes, though it is occasionally used in mayonnaises, aïoli, and other emulsions when a truly special flavor is desired. (I also occasionally employ it in vinaigrettes when they won't be competing with other strong flavors like, say, curry.) There are many extra virgin olive oils on the market, with flavors ranging from fruity (which I prefer for vegetables and other relatively light ingredients) to peppery (which I like for steak), though it must be said that these preferences are largely subjective and personal. I suggest you keep at least one oil from both ends of the spectrum on hand and that you explore the world of extra virgin olive oils, tasting new ones whenever possible and keeping as wide a selection as possible on hand. If you really get to know them, you may find that you prefer one as a dip for breads, one for drizzling on hot soups, and one as a finishing touch for blanched and chilled spring vegetables. Generally speaking, the lighter, fruitier ones are most appropriate to delicate dishes; heavier, spicier ones suit hearty dishes.

There are also many affordable extra virgin olive oils that you might find useful for cooking, and well worth the small incremental expense for the extra flavor they impart.

Olive oil Despite its name, olive oil isn't generally used to obtain an olive flavor. Rather it imparts additional character to dishes. I also use it in salad dressings when the flavor of the olives themselves will be a welcome addition.

Canola oil For searing poultry and meats, sautéing vegetables, and other cooking, canola oil is as close as it gets to a reliable all-purpose oil. Its neutral flavor lets the other ingredients shine, and it has a relatively high smoking point, meaning it can be heated considerably before scorching becomes a concern, which recommends it as the most healthful choice for frying because it's also lower in saturated fats than most other oils. It can be replaced by grapeseed, soybean, and other vegetable oils. As you'll see in the book, I often use canola oil in tandem with butter (for flavor), unless cooking a Provençal dish that calls exclusively for olive oil.

Grapeseed oil A rare, relatively expensive, neutral-flavored oil, grapeseed is often my choice for dressings and vinaigrettes that focus on a particular flavor other than the oil itself. It offers a bit more body than canola oil, but not so much that it can't stand in for canola oil for cooking. Whenever I call for canola oil in the book, grapeseed oil can be substituted.

OLIVES Having olives in your refrigerator means you'll always have something to put out for guests, not to mention a versatile ingredient that can embellish more salads and sauces than you might think. Keep a variety of hand; Kalamata and Picholine are two of my favorites.

PASTA, RICE, AND GRAINS Always have a good assortment of pasta and rice on hand. They are called for in many recipes and are also good mediums for improvising and whipping up quick meals on short notice. At a minimum you should have a selection of dried pastas (long strands like spaghetti, spaghettini, or linguine; shorter, extruded shapes like farfalle, rigatoni, and penne; and the ear-shaped pasta called orecchiette), some variety of risotto rice (Arborio, Carnaroli, Vialone Nano), basmati rice, and brown rice. As for grains, pearl barley and bulgur or cracked wheat are good, versatile ones to keep stock.

PEPPERCORNS You should always have both white and black pepper in your kitchen, and they should always be freshly ground. I suggest keeping them in two separate mills and grinding them when cooking. Black pepper is more widely used, but white is often important for its less pungent flavor and for its camouflage-like ability to disappear into predominantly white dishes such as those featuring cauliflower and cheeses.

Most books suggest seasoning with pepper "to taste." While I agree with this in principle, I find that many home cooks, and cookbooks for that matter, use pepper on everything when it's not really needed. For example, many fresh vegetables are overwhelmed by pepper and only need to be seasoned with salt to bring out their natural flavor.

I also feel that pepper should be used judiciously so as not to become too distracting in a dish. To that end, I've adopted two courses in this book: In many cases I indicate the number of grinds of the mill in the recipe; in others I call for a specific measurement in the ingredient list. You may need to adjust these quantities slightly to taste, but they should be useful guidelines in helping you know how much pepper to add in each situation.

Always have extra peppercorns in your pantry, both to replenish your mills, and also because some recipes call for whole or crushed peppercorns.

In addition to black and white peppercorns, having other peppercorns gives you one more resource to draw on in your cooking. I call for pink peppercorns in a few recipes in this book, and you might also think about making room in your cupboard for additional ones such as tellicherry (the largest, most flavorful black peppercorns, from India), green peppercorns (often packed in brine), and grains of paradise (actually the seed of an African fruit plant; these pack an exotic, citrus punch).

There's another pepper worth mentioning: I don't use crushed red pepper flakes very often, but they are a staple in Italian cooking and a quick way to add heat to pasta sauces.

SAFFRON Saffron has a unique flavor associated with many Mediterranean and Provençal fish and seafood dishes, such as bouillabaise and steamed mussels. Though expensive, a few threads can imbue an entire potful of soup with golden-yellow color.

SALT If you were to ask me what the most important ingredient in the kitchen is, I wouldn't even have to think about the answer: salt.

It's impossible to overstate the importance of salt in cooking. Salt bridges the gap between our taste buds and the foods we eat. Salt amplifies the natural flavor of each ingredient it touches. I even use it in some desserts.

For seasoning in day-to-day cooking, I prefer kosher salt. The shape of the grains makes it easy to control between your fingertips, allowing you to moderate the amount of salt in each dish.

There are also many times when you want to taste salt itself, to feel its crystals on your tongue, hard for a moment, then melting like raindrops, dissipating their gentle salinity. Those are the times to reach for sea salt. My four favorites are:

Fine sea salt Unlike most other types of salt, which are coarse, fine sea salt has the unique ability to dissolve into recipes. For that reason, I use it in many pastries and desserts, where it heightens other flavors without altering the texture.

Fleur de sel These little light crystals are sprinkled on everything from fish to meats to add a last-second crunch and salinity. Fleur de sel is sweet and delicate as snow, the perfect condiment for salads, seafood preparations, carpaccios, and ceviches.

Sel gris (Brittany sea salt) This salt gets its gray tint from the natural color of the clay in salt beds, as well as the plentiful minerals there. Tinged with the flavor of residual sea water, it comes alive over beef, poultry, and grilled meats. I like to sprinkle sel gris over foods after they've been cooked and suggest having a small bowl of it on your table for guests to draw from as they see fit.

Malden sea salt These large, fluffy salt crystals from southern England have a distinct pyramid shape and a crunch. I love the way they register on the palate. Use this salt on salads, fish dishes, and uncooked ingredients like vegetable crudité, or carpaccios.

Steer clear of iodized or table salt, which rather than coaxing out the flavors of other ingredients, as salt should, only contributes an unpleasant and artificial-tasting salty flavor.

SPICES Dried spices are a quick way to add intense and often exotic flavor to a dish. They're increasingly important in U.S. kitchens as we become enamored of the foods of different cultures. To cook foods inspired by the cuisine of places like India, Morocco, and Spain, you need to have ground spices such as allspice, cardamom, coriander seed, whole chile powder, cinnamon, cumin, curry, fennel seed, paprika, saffron, and star anise available.

SUGARS Granulated sugar will get you through most cooking scenarios, but if you do much baking, superfine and confectioners' sugar come up quite a bit as well. I prefer to bake with superfine sugar because its finer texture blends more quickly and easily into batters and creams.

TOMATOES (CANNED) Although I'm devoted to cooking seasonally, meaning I only use tomatoes in the mid- to late summer and early fall, when they are at their peak, there are times when peeled, canned tomatoes are necessary flavoring agents in a sauce, braising liquid, or stew. The best are San Marzano tomatoes from Italy, but if you can't get these select an American organic brand.

VANILLA The sweet fragrance of vanilla is a valuable and frequent addition to desserts. I sometimes call on it in savory dishes, where its perfume is unexpected and beguiling. Keep a small bottle of pure vanilla extract—it will last you a long time—and a half-dozen or so beans in your pantry. The best way to store vanilla beans is in an airtight jar, covered with sugar; a happy by-product is the vanilla-flavored sugar you're left with afterward.

WINE (FOR COOKING) Don't draw on your own precious wine cellar for cooking. In almost all cases, moderate dry white and full-bodied, but not-too-tannic red wine are all you need for cooking. Identify one, purchase a case, and keep it in your kitchen. By all means ask your wine merchant for a suggestion. Do not buy so-called cooking wines in the supermarket.

VINEGARS

Red- and white-wine vinegar Red- and white-wine vinegars are frequently called on to brighten the flavor of, and give a much-needed acidic boost to, vinaigrettes, sauces, and braising bases.

Sherry vinegar My favorite vinegar, kissed with sweetness and riding in on a complex wave of flavor, it adds a one-of-a-kind base to dressings and sauces. Along with Banyuls vinegar, this is always just a reach away in my home kitchen.

Balsamic vinegar As vastly celebrated as this vinegar is, I find it to be a bit overused. There are times when I appreciate a true, aged balsamic as much as the next chef (for example, drizzled over Parmigiano-Reggiano cheese, tiny wild strawberries, or even ice cream), but for the most part I find that it's an attention grabber that makes it hard to concentrate on other flavors in a dish, adding excessive sweetness and not much complexity. Beware imitation balsamic, purchasing only those bottles that bear the designation "Aceto Balsamico Tradizionale di Modena."

Banyuls vinegar Made from a sweet wine from the southwest region of France, this fruity and complex vinegar gives a select group of dressings and vinegar sauces (such as the one used in the classic chicken with vinegar) their distinct flavor. It can often stand in for sherry vinegar in recipes that call for the latter. Banyuls is one of my favorites, but can be difficult to find; it is worth the effort, even if it means mail ordering (see Sources, page 318).

WHAT TO MAKE

Here's a list of great staples to prepare at home and have on hand. The recipes are on the pages that follow.

FLAVORED SALTS
Celery Salt
Cumin Salt
Fennel Seed Salt
Garlic Salt
Lemon Salt

COMPOUND BUTTERS
Garlic-Herb Butter
Blue Cheese Butter
Anchovy Butter
Orange-Olive Butter
Black Truffle Butter

FLAVORED OILS
Citrus Oil
Provençal Oil
Mustard Oil
Autumn Spice Oil
Black Truffle Oil

AÏOLI
OVEN-DRIED TOMATOES
MAYONNAISE
TAPENADE
GREEN OLIVE-ALMOND TAPENADE
DRIED ORANGE PEEL
GARLIC CONFIT
PICKLED VEGETABLES

COMPOTES, CHUTNEY, AND MARMALADES
Cherry Compote
Fig Chutney
Grape Compote
Lemon Marmalade
Orange Marmalade
Rhubarb Marmalade

STOCKS
White Chicken Stock
Dark Chicken Stock
White Beef Stock
Veal Stock
Vegetable Stock

FLAVORED SALTS

THESE ESSENTIALLY TURN FLAVORFUL INGREDIENTS such as garlic and lemon into a variety of salt. Use them as a quick way to add extra flavor to dishes as you're seasoning them.

You'll see that these and other recipes in the book call for using a spice or coffee grinder. I strongly recommend obtaining a dedicated grinder, since it can be difficult to keep the lingering coffee taste out of your spices, and vice versa, but if you use your coffee grinder, clean it before and after grinding spices with a combination of kosher salt and vinegar or lemon juice. Grind the mixture, then empty and wipe out the grinder.

CELERY SALT

MAKES ¼ CUP

USE this salt in vinaigrettes and sauces, fish and tomato dishes, or to up the celery's presence in a Bloody Mary.

2 TABLESPOONS CELERY SEED   ¼ CUP KOSHER SALT

PUT the celery seeds in an 8-inch sauté pan and toast over low heat, shaking constantly, until lightly fragrant, 2 to 3 minutes. Remove the pan from the heat and let the seeds cool.

PUT the salt in a spice or coffee grinder. Add the seeds and finely grind. Transfer to an airtight container, cover, and store at room temperature for up to 1 month.

FACING PAGE, CLOCKWISE FROM TOP: Cumin Salt, Celery Salt, Lemon Salt, Fennel Seed Salt, Garlic Salt

CUMIN SALT

MAKES ¼ CUP

SPRINKLE this salt on lamb or chicken after cooking, or use it to season couscous and curry dishes.

1 TABLESPOON CUMIN SEEDS

¼ CUP KOSHER SALT

PUT the cumin seeds in an 8-inch sauté pan and toast over low heat, shaking constantly, until fragrant but not browned, 2 to 3 minutes. Remove the pan from the heat and let the seeds cool.

PUT the salt in a spice or coffee grinder. Add the seeds and finely grind. Transfer to an airtight container, cover, and store at room temperature for up to 1 month.

FENNEL SEED SALT

MAKES ¼ CUP

USE this anise-flavored seasoning to bring a Provençal flourish to fish, lamb, and vegetables.

2 TABLESPOONS FENNEL SEED

¼ CUP KOSHER SALT

PUT the fennel seeds in an 8-inch sauté pan and toast over low heat, shaking constantly, until lightly toasted, 2 to 3 minutes. Remove the pan from the heat and let the seeds cool.

PUT the salt in a spice or coffee grinder. Add the seeds and finely grind. Transfer to an airtight container, cover, and store at room temperature for up to 1 month.

GARLIC SALT

MAKES ¼ CUP

THIS salt knows no boundaries; sprinkle it over any dish that would benefit from a garlicky punch. It is especially useful at those times when you realize, at the last second, that your fresh garlic has gone bad.

2 CLOVES GARLIC, MINCED   **¼ CUP KOSHER SALT**

PREHEAT the oven to 200°F. Spread the garlic out on a nonstick cookie sheet and bake until dry and golden-brown, approximately 40 minutes. Remove the sheet from the oven and let the garlic cool.

PUT the salt in a spice or coffee grinder. Add the garlic and finely grind. Transfer to an airtight container, cover, and store at room temperature for up to 1 month.

LEMON SALT

MAKES ¼ CUP

GIVE an acidic lift to poultry and seafood dishes or bean stews, especially those of Provençal heritage, by seasoning before or after cooking with this salt.

PEELS OF 4 LEMONS (USE A VEGETABLE   **¼ CUP KOSHER SALT**
PEELER; REMOVE ALL PITH)

PREHEAT the oven to 225°F. Put the lemon peels on a baking rack. Set the rack on a cookie sheet and bake in the oven until the peels are dry but not browned, approximately 40 minutes. Remove the dish from the oven and let the peels cool.

PUT the salt in a spice or coffee grinder. Add the peels and finely grind. Transfer to an airtight container, cover, and store at room temperature for up to 1 month.

COMPOUND BUTTERS

COMPOUND BUTTERS, the traditional name for flavored butters, are made by softening butter at room temperature, enhancing it with herbs, aromatics, and other flavoring agents, and firming it up in the refrigerator or freezer where it can be held for weeks, or even months. They offer a powerful illustration of the merits of a well-stocked artisanal pantry. Invest a few minutes to make one, and you have a secret weapon in your refrigerator or freezer. The butters can be sliced and served over meats, vegetables, and fish, and tossed with hot pasta. As the butter melts, its flavors are unlocked, essentially transforming itself into a sauce. In fact, you can make compound butter itself into a quick sauce: Use water, stock, or wine to deglaze a pan in which you've seared or roasted fish, poultry, or meat, and whisk in a few tablespoons of compound butter to form an emulsion, or simply melt them in a tablespoon or so of hot water and whisk.

TERMS AND TECHNIQUES *Deglazing* Deglaze means to remove the tasty bits of food (flavorful protein particles) cooked onto the bottom of a cooking surface, usually by adding a liquid (e.g., water, stock, wine, or liquor) and loosening the bits with a wooden spoon or wire whisk.

GARLIC-HERB BUTTER

MAKES ABOUT ½ CUP

ONE of the classic bistro toppings for grilled steak, this butter—also know as maitre d'hotel butter—is also a natural for fish and poultry.

8 TABLESPOONS (1 STICK) UNSALTED BUTTER, SLIGHTLY SOFTENED AT ROOM TEMPERATURE

1 TABLESPOON MINCED GARLIC

1 TABLESPOON FINELY SLICED FLAT-LEAF PARSLEY

1 TABLESPOON FINELY SLICED CHIVES

½ TABLESPOON FINELY SLICED TARRAGON

½ TABLESPOON FRESHLY SQUEEZED LEMON JUICE

¼ TEASPOON KOSHER SALT

PUT all ingredients in a bowl and combine well with a wooden spoon or rubber spatula, making sure all ingredients are well incorporated.

WRAP the butter and refrigerate for at least 2 hours, or up to 1 week, or freeze for up to 3 months. (See Terms and Techniques, page 23.)

BLUE CHEESE BUTTER

MAKES ABOUT ½ CUP

FOR an indulgent treat, top grilled steaks with a slice or two of this butter. It's also wonderful tossed with hot pasta, diced roasted beets, and crushed walnuts.

¼ CUP (½ STICK) UNSALTED BUTTER, SLIGHTLY SOFTENED AT ROOM TEMPERATURE

¼ CUP CRUMBLED ROQUEFORT CHEESE OR OTHER BLUE CHEESE (FROM ABOUT 1 OUNCE CHEESE), AT ROOM TEMPERATURE

½ TABLESPOON FRESHLY SQUEEZED LEMON JUICE

¼ TEASPOON KOSHER SALT

BLACK PEPPER IN A MILL

PUT the butter in a bowl and add the Roquefort and lemon juice. Combine well with a wooden spoon or rubber spatula. Season with the salt and 6 grinds of pepper, or to taste.

WRAP the butter and refrigerate for at least 2 hours, or up to 1 week, or freeze for up to 3 months. (See Terms and Techniques, below.)

TERMS AND TECHNIQUES *Rolling and storing compound butter:* Transfer the butter to the center of a 12- by 12-inch piece of wax paper, arranging it in a cigar-like shape about 4 inches long and the diameter of a 50-cent coin. Roll the paper over the butter and use the edge of a sheetpan to push the butter back to one end of the folded-over paper. Then tautly roll the paper over the butter. Turn the ends of the wrap over and over until they coil up, sealing the butter within. Refrigerate until firm or for up to 1 week, or wrap in aluminum foil, turning and twisting the ends until they coil up and seal the log, and freeze for up to 3 months. (Foil can be wrapped right over the wax paper.) If frozen, let thaw before using.

ANCHOVY BUTTER

MAKES ABOUT ½ CUP

ANCHOVIES' salty character adds complexity to a dish by amplifying the flavors of other ingredients. This butter is especially appropriate to fish, poultry, beans, haricots verts, and shell beans. It's also surprisingly good over lamb and beef.

8 TABLESPOONS (I STICK) UNSALTED BUTTER, SLIGHTLY SOFTENED AT ROOM TEMPERATURE

2 TABLESPOONS FINELY DICED SHALLOTS

I TABLESPOON MINCED GARLIC

2 TABLESPOONS (PACKED) FINELY CHOPPED ANCHOVY FILLETS (FROM 8 FILLETS, SOAKED, DRAINED, AND PATTED DRY; SEE PAGE II)

¼ CUP FINELY SLICED FLAT-LEAF PARSLEY

I TEASPOON FRESHLY SQUEEZED LEMON JUICE

I½ TEASPOONS FINELY GRATED LEMON ZEST

¼ TEASPOON KOSHER SALT, PLUS MORE IF NECESSARY

PUT all ingredients in a bowl or the bowl of a mortar and pestle. Stir well with a rubber spatula or the pestle until evenly incorporated. Taste and season with additional salt, if necessary.

WRAP the butter and refrigerate for at least 2 hours, or up to 1 week, or freeze for up to 3 months. (See Terms and Techniques, page 23.)

ORANGE-OLIVE BUTTER

MAKES ABOUT ½ CUP

SERVE this over seafood, poultry, or lamb, to add a Provençal flavor.

8 TABLESPOONS (I STICK) UNSALTED BUTTER, SLIGHTLY SOFTENED AT ROOM TEMPERATURE

¼ CUP PITTED, MINCED NIÇOISE OLIVES

I TABLESPOON FINELY GRATED ORANGE ZEST

2 TABLESPOONS THINLY SLICED CHERVIL (OPTIONAL)

½ TEASPOON FRESHLY SQUEEZED LEMON JUICE

½ TEASPOON KOSHER SALT

I TEASPOON MINCED GARLIC

I TABLESPOON GRAND MARNIER (OPTIONAL)

PUT all ingredients in a bowl and combine well with a wooden spoon or rubber spatula, making sure all ingredients are well incorporated.

WRAP the butter and refrigerate for at least 2 hours, or up to 1 week, or freeze for up to 3 months. (See Terms and Techniques, page 23.)

TERMS AND TECHNIQUES *Microplane zester:* If you don't already own a Microplane zester, do yourself a favor and get one. Now sold as a kitchen implement, the zester originated as a woodworking tool. It makes it very easy to remove citrus zest and grate cheese in light, snowy fashion.

BLACK TRUFFLE BUTTER

MAKES ABOUT ½ CUP

ARRANGE slices of this butter over seared and roasted fish, poultry, or beef, or toss it with cooked pasta (fresh or dried) such as fettuccine or pappardelle.

8 TABLESPOONS (1 STICK) UNSALTED BUTTER, SLIGHTLY SOFTENED AT ROOM TEMPERATURE

2 CANNED BLACK TRUFFLES, 2 OUNCES EACH, DRAINED AND MINCED

1 TEASPOON MINCED GARLIC

1 TEASPOON FRESHLY SQUEEZED LEMON JUICE

¼ TEASPOON KOSHER SALT

PUT the butter in a bowl and add the truffles, garlic, and lemon juice. Combine well with a wooden spoon or rubber spatula. Season with the salt.

WRAP the butter and refrigerate for at least 2 hours, or up to 1 week, or freeze for up to 3 months. (See Terms and Techniques, page 23.)

FLAVORED OILS

EACH OF THESE OILS ADDS its own signature flavor to a dish. Use them for searing poultry and meats, drizzle them over vegetables or soups, or make them the basis for vinaigrettes.

Flavored oils are a dramatic example of how decorative pantry items and other foods can be. Keep them in a cool place in your kitchen, away from direct sunlight, and they become a culinary ornament.

CITRUS OIL

MAKES ABOUT 1 CUP

ENLIVEN seafood and poultry dishes with the sunny flavor this oil delivers.

PEELS OF 2 LEMONS (USE A VEGETABLE PEELER; REMOVE ALL PITH)

PEEL OF 1 ORANGE (USE A VEGETABLE PEELER; REMOVE ALL PITH)

1 CUP EXTRA VIRGIN OLIVE OIL

2 BAY LEAVES

PREHEAT the oven to 225°F. Spread out the lemon and orange peels on a cookie sheet and bake in the oven until dried and shriveled, approximately 40 minutes; do not let them brown. Remove the sheet from the oven and let the peels cool.

MEANWHILE, pour the oil into a small pot and warm over low heat.

PUT the peels in a spice or coffee grinder and grind to a powder. Remove the pot with the oil from the heat and add the ground peels and the bay leaf. Let cool, then transfer to an airtight container and let infuse for 24 hours.

COVER and keep at room temperature for up to 1 week or refrigerate for up to 1 month.

FACING PAGE FROM LEFT TO RIGHT: Autumn Spice Oil, Provençal Oil, Citrus Oil

PROVENÇAL OIL

MAKES ABOUT 1 CUP

SERVE this with fish, shellfish, poultry, meat, and summer vegetables.

1 CUP EXTRA VIRGIN OLIVE OIL

3 SPRIGS THYME

2 SPRIGS ROSEMARY

1 TABLESPOON FENNEL SEEDS

2 CLOVES GARLIC, PEELED

PUT the fennel seeds in an 8-inch sauté pan, and toast over medium heat, shaking constantly, until fragrant, 2 to 3 minutes. Remove the pan from the heat and let cool.

POUR the oil into a 1-quart pot and heat it over medium-low heat until warm. Remove the pot from the heat and add the thyme, rosemary, fennel seeds, and garlic. Cover and let infuse for 24 hours at room temperature, then transfer to a container, cover, and refrigerate for up to 1 week. Or discard the garlic and store, in a decorative jar, if desired, at room temperature for up to 2 weeks.

MUSTARD OIL

MAKES ABOUT 1 CUP

JUST what the name says: the essence of mustard captured in a drizzle-able oil. Use it on fish, poultry, meats, and vegetables.

3 TABLESPOONS COLEMAN'S DRY MUSTARD

2 TABLESPOONS WATER

1 CUP CANOLA OIL

PUT the mustard and water in a bowl and stir together to make a paste.

POUR the oil into a sauté pan and warm it over medium heat until warm. Pour the warm oil into the mustard paste, whisking vigorously, until well incorporated. Transfer into a tall, narrow container. Keep the container at room temperature, agitating it periodically over 3 days. Then, spoon the oil into another container and discard the paste.

COVER and keep at room temperature for up to 1 week or refrigerate for up to 1 month.

AUTUMN SPICE OIL

MAKES ABOUT 1 CUP

DRIZZLE this oil over pork, game, and fall squashes and fruits; use it as a cooking medium for any of those foods; or use it as the oil in vinaigrettes for autumn salads. (For a moderately spiced vinaigrette, use half canola oil and half Autumn Spice Oil.)

4 STAR ANISE

½ TABLESPOON JUNIPER BERRIES

1 TABLESPOON PLUS 1 TEASPOON CARDAMOM

1 TEASPOON ALLSPICE

1 MEDIUM CINNAMON STICK, CRUSHED, OR 1 TEASPOON GROUND CINNAMON

1 TEASPOON WHOLE CLOVES

⅓ VANILLA BEAN, SPLIT LENGTHWISE, SEEDS SCRAPED

2 PIECES DRIED ORANGE PEEL (PAGE 35; OPTIONAL)

PUT the star anise, juniper berries, cardamom, allspice, cinnamon, and cloves in an 8-inch sauté pan and toast over medium heat, shaking constantly, until fragrant, 2 to 3 minutes. Remove the pan from the heat and let cool.

TRANSFER the spices to a spice or coffee grinder and pulse for a few seconds.

TRANSFER the spices to a bowl, add the vanilla bean and orange peel, if using, and set aside.

POUR the oil into a small pot and heat it over medium-low heat until warm. Pour the oil over the spices and vanilla. Cover and let infuse at room temperature for 24 hours, periodically mixing the bowl. Do not strain.

COVER and keep at room temperature for up to 2 weeks or refrigerate for up to 1 month.

BLACK TRUFFLE OIL

MAKES ABOUT 1 CUP

2½ OUNCES CANNED BLACK TRUFFLES (SEE SOURCES, PAGE 318)

1 CUP PLUS 2 TABLESPOONS CANOLA OIL

REMOVE the truffles from the can and reserve the juice for another use.

POUR the oil into a small pot and heat over medium heat until warm. Transfer the oil to a blender, add the truffles, and blend. Transfer the mixture to a bowl and let cool.

COVER and keep at room temperature for up to 24 hours or refrigerate for up to 1 month.

AÏOLI

MAKES ABOUT 1½ CUPS

THIS is a fairly traditional version of the Provençal condiment made from garlic and olive oil and served with fish, vegetables, and brothy soups.

2 LARGE EGG YOLKS, AT ROOM TEMPERATURE

1 TABLESPOON FRESHLY SQUEEZED LEMON JUICE, ROOM TEMPERATURE

1 TABLESPOON BALSAMIC VINEGAR

2 TEASPOONS MINCED GARLIC

1 TEASPOON KOSHER SALT

1 CUP FRUITY EXTRA VIRGIN OLIVE OIL

PUT the yolks, lemon juice, vinegar, garlic, and salt in the bowl of a food processor fitted with the steel blade. With the motor running, slowly add the oil in a thin stream to form a thick emulsion. Transfer to a container.

COVER and refrigerate the aïoli for up to 1 week.

THE REASON *My aïoli features balsamic vinegar:* Lemon juice can sometimes register as excessively acidic in aïoli. Adding balsamic vinegar smoothes out the flavor, and softens the character of the olive oil.

OVEN-DRIED TOMATOES

MAKES ABOUT 1 CUP

DRYING tomatoes in a low oven concentrates their flavor, enabling you to add them to sauces, stews, and other recipes without the fruit's liquid. If you must use tomatoes out of season, this is a way to get the most from them.

6 PLUM TOMATOES (APPROXIMATELY 1 POUND)

2 TABLESPOONS OLIVE OIL

2 CLOVES GARLIC, VERY THINLY SLICED

2 TEASPOONS THYME LEAVES

½ TEASPOON KOSHER SALT

PREHEAT the oven to 200°F. Cut the tomatoes in half lengthwise and gently squeeze out the seeds. Cut the tomatoes in half again lengthwise. Put the tomatoes in a bowl and toss them with the olive oil, garlic, thyme, and salt. Set a wire cooling rack on a baking sheet, place the tomatoes on the rack, and bake until dry but still a bit supple, about 2½ hours. The tomatoes toward the outer part of the rack might cook more quickly, so remove them earlier with tongs, if necessary.

When the tomatoes are cool enough to handle, remove the peels with a paring knife and discard them. The tomatoes can be refrigerated for up to 1 week if you put them in an air-tight container and cover them with olive oil.

EMBELLISHMENT If you store the tomatoes, add additional fresh herbs such as basil leaves to the container to heighten their presence.

MAYONNAISE

RICH and creamy, homemade mayonnaise bears little resemblance to the supermarket variety. On its own, or dressed up with herbs and other additions (see the Embellishment), it's a useful condiment to make on a regular basis.

2 LARGE EGG YOLKS, AT ROOM TEMPERATURE

½ TABLESPOON DIJON MUSTARD, AT ROOM TEMPERATURE

2 TABLESPOONS WHITE-WINE VINEGAR

⅛ TEASPOON CAYENNE

½ TABLESPOON SEA SALT

1¼ CUPS CANOLA OIL

PUT the yolks, mustard, vinegar, cayenne, and salt in the bowl of a food processor fitted with the steel blade. With the motor running, slowly add the canola oil in a thin stream to form an emulsified mixture. Transfer to an airtight container.

COVER and refrigerate for up to 1 week.

TERMS AND TECHNIQUES *Emulsification: Emulsify* means to suspend the ingredients in a mixture until it becomes thick and viscous. Emulsifications require at least one ingredient that binds the others, such as mustard or an egg yolk. They are generally made by very slowly drizzling the primary liquid (usually an oil) into the mixture as it is whipped by a blender or food processor, or by hand using a whisk.

EMBELLISHMENTS Add whatever herbs (up to ¼ cup) or ground spices (up to 1 teaspoon) you like to mayonnaise. If using large-leaved herbs such as basil, thinly slice them.

To make a Niçoise mayonnaise, the perfect condiment for tuna and other fish, steamed and/or sautéed vegetables, and chicken sandwiches, stir in any or all of the following just before serving: 1 teaspoon minced garlic, 1 tablespoon chopped capers, and/or a total of ¼ cup diced tomato, diced olives, and/or chopped thyme.

TAPENADE

MAKES ABOUT 1 CUP

THERE'S little doubt in my mind that one of the reasons this popular Mediterranean olive paste has endured for so long, and become popular around the Western world, is its ease of preparation and its multiple applications. It's wonderful as a dip, and stirred into mayonnaise it becomes a spread for sandwiches or a topping for vegetables. Make it with whatever olives you like, such as Kalamata or Picholine.

1 CUP PITTED NIÇOISE OLIVES (FROM ABOUT 2½ OUNCES PITTED OLIVES), OR 4 OUNCES UNPITTED OLIVES

2 (PREFERABLY SALT-PACKED) ROUGHLY CHOPPED ANCHOVY FILLETS, SOAKED, DRAINED, AND PATTED DRY (SEE PAGE 11)

2 TEASPOONS CAPERS, RINSED AND DRAINED

2 SMALL GARLIC CLOVES, ROUGHLY CHOPPED

1 TEASPOON FINELY GRATED ORANGE ZEST

¾ CUP EXTRA VIRGIN OLIVE OIL

1 TABLESPOON COGNAC (OPTIONAL)

BLACK PEPPER IN A MILL

PUT the olives, anchovies, capers, garlic, and orange zest in a blender. With the motor running, add the oil in a thin stream, stopping to scrape the sides down periodically with a rubber spatula if necessary. Continue to puree until mostly smooth but a bit pulpy.

TRANSFER the tapenade to a container, stir in the cognac, if using, and season with 4 grinds of pepper, or to taste.

COVER and refrigerate the tapenade for up to 1 month.

EMBELLISHMENT To make tapenade creamier and more spreadable, add 1 tablespoon mayonnaise to this recipe. For a richer version that achieves the same result, add an egg yolk to the food processor along with the anchovies when making the tapenade.

GREEN OLIVE-ALMOND TAPENADE

MAKES ABOUT 1 CUP

THIS is especially delicious over fish and vegetables, and as a dip.

¼ CUP PICHOLINE OLIVES, OR OTHER OLIVES, PITTED

1 TABLESPOON CAPERS, RINSED AND DRAINED

½ TABLESPOON MINCED GARLIC

½ TABLESPOON (PREFERABLY SALT-PACKED) CHOPPED ANCHOVY FILLETS (FROM ABOUT 4 FILLETS, SOAKED, DRAINED, AND PATTED DRY; SEE PAGE 11)

½ CUP PEELED, SLICED ALMONDS

¾ TEASPOON FINELY GRATED ORANGE ZEST

1½ CUPS EXTRA VIRGIN OLIVE OIL

BLACK PEPPER IN A MILL

PUT the olives, capers, garlic, anchovies, almonds, and orange zest in the bowl of a food processor fitted with the steel blade. Process until smooth. With the motor running, add the oil in a thin stream, stopping to scrape the sides down periodically with a rubber spatula if necessary. Continue to puree until mostly smooth but a bit pulpy. Transfer the tapenade to a container, and season with 6 grinds of pepper, or to taste.

COVER and refrigerate the tapenade for up to 1 month.

EMBELLISHMENT To make tapenade creamier and more spreadable, add 1 tablespoon mayonnaise to this recipe. For a richer version that achieves the same result, add an egg yolk to the food processor along with the anchovies when making the tapenade.

DRIED ORANGE PEEL

MAKES ABOUT ¼ CUP

STIR this peel into soups and stews to impart a bright citrus flavor. It makes an especially effective impact on the Daube of Beef on page 237, or ground into a citrus salt following the recipe on page 21.

PEELS OF 6 ORANGES (USE A VEGETABLE PEELER; REMOVE ALL PITH)

PREHEAT the oven to 225°F. Put the orange peels on a baking rack. Set the rack on a cookie sheet and bake in the oven until the peels are dry but not browned, approximately 1 hour. Remove the peels from the oven and set aside to cool.

STORE the peels in an airtight container at room temperature for up to 1 month.

GARLIC CONFIT

MAKES 2 CUPS

I LOVE having garlic confit on hand. The name is a playful reference to the classic confit technique in which duck and other meats are preserved in their own fat. Garlic confit is made for its mellow garlic flavor, not preservation, though it can be refrigerated for a few weeks. It's a potent addition to soups and sauces, and helps vinaigrettes and sauces emulsify, adding body.

6 CUPS COLD WATER

2 CUPS PEELED GARLIC CLOVES

1½ CUPS EXTRA VIRGIN OLIVE OIL

POUR 2 cups water into a 2-quart pot, add the garlic, and bring to a simmer. Strain the garlic and repeat 2 more times.

RETURN the garlic to the pot, and add the oil. Bring to a simmer over medium heat and let simmer until the garlic is very tender but retains its shape, approximately 15 minutes. Remove the pot from the heat and let cool.

TRANSFER the contents of the pot, including the oil, to an airtight container and refrigerate for up to 2 weeks.

PICKLED VEGETABLES

MAKES ABOUT 3 CUPS

SERVE these vegetables with smoked and cured meats, as an accompaniment to Fondue (pages 87 to 91) or Râclette (page 122), or set them out alongside sandwiches or for snacking. They're also a great way to elevate a burger at home.

- 1 TABLESPOON CORIANDER SEEDS
- 1 TABLESPOON BLACK PEPPERCORNS
- 1 TABLESPOON DRIED THYME
- 4 BAY LEAVES
- ¾ CUP WHITE-WINE VINEGAR
- 12 CUPS WATER
- 1 HEAD GARLIC, SPLIT HORIZONTALLY, EXCESS PAPERY SKIN REMOVED

- 1 TABLESPOON PLUS 2 TEASPOONS KOSHER SALT
- ½ CUP PEELED PEARL ONIONS
- ½ CUP CAULIFLOWER FLORETS
- 8 BABY CARROTS, PEELED
- 8 MEDIUM WHITE MUSHROOM CAPS
- 4 BABY GOLDEN BEETS, PEELED

PUT the coriander, peppercorns, thyme, and bay leaves in a piece of cheesecloth. Gather up the ends and tie it into a sachet.

PUT the vinegar, 4 cups of water, the garlic, 1 tablespoon of salt, and sachet in a 4-quart saucepan and bring to a boil over high heat. Lower the heat and let simmer for 30 minutes. Remove the pan from the heat and set aside. (This is your pickling liquid.)

MEANWHILE, pour 8 cups of water into a 4-quart saucepan and bring to a boil over high heat. Add the remaining salt. Cook the vegetables, one type at a time, in the liquid, removing them with a slotted spoon, gathering them in a bowl, and letting the water return to a boil between vegetables. Cook the onions for 6 minutes, the cauliflower for 6 minutes, the carrots for 8 minutes, the mushrooms for 4 minutes, and the beets for 8 minutes.

DISCARD the cooking liquid.

WHILE it's still warm, pour the pickling liquid over the vegetables. Let cool, then transfer to a mason jar or other type of glass jar with a lid, and refrigerate overnight, or for up to 1 week.

VARIATION Omit any type of the vegetables and add more of the others to compensate.

COMPOTES, CHUTNEY, AND MARMALADES

CHERRY COMPOTE

MAKES 2 CUPS

SERVE this with savories such as game and foie gras, or with ice cream and other desserts such as the profiteroles on page 301 or the chocolate terrine on page 282.

2 POUNDS (4 CUPS) CHERRIES, PITTED

4½ TABLESPOONS UNSALTED BUTTER

¼ CUP SUGAR

1 CINNAMON STICK

1 TABLESPOON FRESHLY SQUEEZED LEMON JUICE

1 TABLESPOON KIRSCH (OPTIONAL)

2 TABLESPOONS FINELY SLICED MINT OR HYSSOP

PUT the cherries, butter, sugar, and cinnamon in a 2-quart pot and heat over medium heat. Cook for 40 minutes. Remove the pot from the heat and stir in the lemon juice and Kirsch, if using. Let cool to room temperature. Add the mint, cover, and refrigerate for up to 5 days.

TERMS AND TECHNIQUES *Hyssop:* Hyssop is a fuzzy, leafy herb with an anise (licorice) flavor.

FACING PAGE: Lemon Marmalade (foreground left); Orange Marmalade (foreground right); Cherry Compote (background top); Fig Chutney (background bottom); Rhubarb Marmalade (background right)

FIG CHUTNEY

MAKES 1 ½ CUPS

SERVE this alongside lamb and game, as a surprisingly apt accompaniment to pork, or with cheese.

1 ½ CUPS RED WINE

½ CUP PORT

¼ CUP SUGAR

2 STAR ANISE

1 POUND 4 OUNCES BLACK MISSION FIGS, STEMS REMOVED, CUT IN HALF LENGTHWISE

1 ½ TABLESPOONS FRESHLY SQUEEZED LEMON JUICE

KOSHER SALT

PUT the wine, port, star anise, and sugar in a 2-quart pot and set over medium heat. Bring to a simmer, then lower the heat and let simmer until reduced by half, approximately 15 minutes. Stir in the figs and star anise. Let simmer until syrupy, approximately 1 hour 20 minutes more.

REMOVE the pan from the heat, stir in the lemon juice, and season with salt. Let cool, transfer to an airtight container, and refrigerate for up to 5 days.

GRAPE COMPOTE

MAKES 2 ½ CUPS

GRAPES have their place at the table in wine, but are often overlooked as an ingredient in cooking. Serve this compote with foie gras, game, poultry, fish, cheese, and/or fruits.

3 POUNDS SEEDLESS GREEN GRAPES, HALVED LENGTHWISE

½ CUP FINELY DICED SHALLOTS

1 CUP VERJUS (AVAILABLE IN SPECIALTY AND GOURMET SHOPS AND BY MAIL ORDER; SEE SOURCES, PAGE 318)

½ CUP SUGAR

½ CUP WATER

KOSHER SALT

PUT the grapes, shallots, verjus, sugar, and water into a 3-quart saucepan and bring to a boil over medium heat, stirring frequently. Lower the heat, cover, and simmer until the mixture thickens, approximately 1 hour. Remove the pan from the heat and season to taste with salt.

LET cool, then transfer to an airtight container and refrigerate for up to 5 days.

LEMON MARMALADE

MAKES ABOUT 1 CUP

SERVE this as a condiment for fish, or anything that would benefit from an acidic boost, or make it the basis of a vinaigrette.

3 SMALL LEMONS, PEEL AND ALL, CUT INTO ½-INCH DICE, SEEDS DISCARDED

6 CUPS COLD WATER

¾ CUP SUGAR

½ TEASPOON KOSHER SALT

PUT the lemon dice into a saucepan and cover with 1½ cups cold water. Bring to a boil for 3 minutes.

POUR off the hot water and re-cover the lemon with fresh cold water. Bring back to a boil for a further 3 minutes. Repeat this process one more time.

USING the same saucepan after discarding the water for the third time, cover the lemon dice with 1½ cups of fresh water, the sugar, and the salt.

BRING to a simmer and cook for 1 hour 30 minutes until the marmalade takes on a syrupy consistency. Let the mixture cool, then transfer to an airtight container and refrigerate for up to 7 days.

ORANGE MARMALADE

MAKES ABOUT 1 CUP

BOTH sweet and bitter, this marmalade cuts the richness of such foods as duck, foie gras, quail, and stewed beef.

- 1 ORANGE, PEEL AND ALL, CUT INTO ½-INCH PIECES, SEEDS DISCARDED
- 1 CUP WHITE-WINE VINEGAR
- ¾ CUP SUGAR
- 1 TEASPOON KOSHER SALT
- 3 CUPS COLD WATER
- 2 TABLESPOONS PLUS 2 TEASPOONS FRESHLY SQUEEZED LEMON JUICE

PUT the orange dice, vinegar, sugar, salt, and water in a saucepan and set over medium-high heat. Bring to a boil, then lower the heat and let simmer until it takes on a syrupy consistency, approximately 1 hour 30 minutes.

REMOVE the pan from the heat and stir in the lemon juice. Let the mixture cool to room temperature, then transfer to an airtight container and refrigerate for up to 5 days.

RHUBARB MARMALADE

MAKES ABOUT 1 CUP

THIS tart marmalade puts one of the most unique flavors of spring at your fingertips, allowing you to enjoy it on a moment's notice. It's especially good with duck, over ice cream, or alongside fresh farmer's cheese.

½ TEASPOON GROUND ALLSPICE, PREFERABLY FRESHLY GROUND

½ TEASPOON GROUND CARDAMOM

1 TEASPOON GRATED FRESH GINGER

½ CUP WATER

1 CUP RHUBARB, 2-INCH DICE (FROM 6 OUNCES RHUBARB, 1 TO 2 PEELED STALKS)

¼ VANILLA BEAN, SPLIT LENGTHWISE, SEEDS SCRAPED

¼ CUP SUGAR

1 TEASPOON KOSHER SALT

IN a 2-quart saucepan combine the spices, ginger, water, rhubarb, vanilla, sugar and salt. Bring to a boil over high heat, then lower the heat and simmer until the mixture is dry, approximately 20 minutes.

COVER and refrigerate the marmalade for up to 5 days. Reheat before serving.

STOCKS

STOCKS ARE ONE OF THE GLUES that hold French culinary tradition together. With all of the conveniences of modern supermarkets, the very notion of making stocks might seem quaint or even antiquated. And, I must admit that there *are* many high-quality stocks on the market. Nevertheless, personally, I find stock-making to be a relaxing, meditative pursuit that fills the home with wonderful aromas and leaves you with a product that will take your sauces and soups to a level you simply cannot achieve with store-bought alternatives.

The thing that separates good stocks from great ones is the patient extraction and removal of any and all impurities and solids, specifically the coagulated proteins that rise to the surface as foam, resulting in a pure flavor base for sauces, soups, and other dishes. This means careful and constant skimming and, at the end of the process, ladling the stock through a strainer to ensure it's as clean, clear, and clarified as possible. It sounds like a lot of effort, but it really isn't, and the payoff is very satisfying.

Stocks are a good reason to plan one of those "pantry days" I mentioned in the introduction to this chapter; get several stocks going at once and you'll be supplied for months to come.

With the exception of the Veal Stock, which is reduced to a demi-glace, all of these recipes produce 8 cups of stock. You can divide them into smaller containers, freeze them, and thaw and use them as needed. For a quick sauce, swirl some butter into hot stock, add sliced fresh herbs, and season to taste with salt and pepper.

WHITE CHICKEN STOCK

WHITE chicken stock and dark chicken stock are more different than their names might suggest. White chicken stock is probably the most used stock in American kitchens; dark chicken stock, which derives its rich flavor from roasting the bones, should be used much more selectively, in dishes that almost demand a heartier stock to stand up to other big flavors.

3 POUNDS CHICKEN BACKS AND NECKS, EXCESS FAT TRIMMED, RINSED IN COLD WATER

6½ QUARTS COLD WATER, PLUS ADDITIONAL WATER, AS NEEDED

1 TABLESPOON KOSHER SALT

¼ CUP LEEKS, WHITE AND LIGHT GREEN PARTS, WELL RINSED, LARGE DICE

⅔ CUP ONION, LARGE DICE

¼ CUP PEELED CARROT, LARGE DICE

2 STALKS CELERY, LARGE DICE

3 GARLIC CLOVES, CRUSHED

4 SPRIGS FLAT-LEAF PARSLEY, WITH THEIR STEMS

2 BAY LEAVES

1 TABLESPOON WHITE PEPPERCORNS

5 SPRIGS THYME

PUT the chicken pieces in a stockpot. Pour in enough cold water to cover them by 2 inches and set the pot over medium heat. Bring the water to a simmer and let simmer for 5 minutes, skimming any impurities and foam that rise to the surface. Drain the chicken pieces, rinse them, and return them to the pot.

POUR the 6½ quarts cold water into the pot, add the salt, and bring to a boil slowly over medium heat, then lower the heat and let simmer. Skim any impurities that rise to the surface and continue to skim until their production subsides, approximately 10 minutes.

CONTINUE to simmer the stock for 1 hour, then add the leeks, onion, carrot, celery, and garlic. After another 30 minutes, add the parsley, bay leaves, peppercorns, and thyme. Simmer for another 30 minutes, for a total simmering time of 2 hours, skimming any impurities and foam that rise up during this time. If at any time the liquid falls below the level of the solids, add enough cold water to cover them again.

REMOVE the pot from the heat and let rest for 15 minutes so all solids and residue sink to the bottom of the pot. Gently ladle the stock through a fine-mesh strainer set over an airtight container. Use the stock right away, or let the stock cool, refrigerate for up to 3 days, or freeze for up to 3 months. (If you are in a hurry, cool the stock faster by filling a large bowl halfway with ice water and setting the bottom of the container in the ice water. Swirl the stock with a ladle to cool it as quickly as possible. It will cool even faster if in a stainless steel vessel.)

DARK CHICKEN STOCK

MAKES 8 CUPS

3 POUNDS CHICKEN BACKS AND NECKS, EXCESS FAT TRIMMED, RINSED IN COLD WATER

2 TABLESPOONS CANOLA OIL

¼ CUP LEEKS, WHITE AND LIGHT GREEN PARTS, WELL RINSED, LARGE DICE

⅔ CUP ONION, LARGE DICE

I HEAD GARLIC, SPLIT HORIZONTALLY, EXCESS PAPERY SKIN REMOVED

2 ROMA TOMATOES, LARGE DICE

¼ CUP PEELED CARROT, LARGE DICE

2 STALKS CELERY, LARGE DICE

2 TABLESPOONS TOMATO PASTE

ABOUT 6½ QUARTS WHITE CHICKEN STOCK (PAGE 45) OR WATER, PLUS MORE AS NEEDED

2 BAY LEAVES

5 SPRIGS THYME

I TABLESPOON BLACK PEPPERCORNS

PREHEAT the oven to 375°F. Put the chicken pieces in a stockpot. Pour in enough cold water to cover them by 2 inches and set the pot over medium heat. Bring the water to a simmer and let simmer for 5 minutes, skimming any impurities and foam that rise to the surface. Drain the chicken pieces, rinse them, and transfer them to a roasting pan.

DRIZZLE the chicken with the oil and toss to coat. Roast in the oven for 35 minutes, periodically turning the bones with tongs or a wooden spoon to help them turn golden-brown all over. Add the leeks, onions, garlic, tomatoes, carrots, and celery, toss to coat them with oil, and roast, stirring occasionally, until caramelized, another 20 minutes. Add the tomato paste.

RINSE and wipe out the stockpot. Transfer the contents of the roasting pan to the stockpot and pour in 6½ quarts stock or water, or enough to cover the bones by 4 inches, and 1 tablespoon salt. Bring to a boil over high heat, then lower the heat and let simmer for 90 minutes, frequently skimming any impurities that rise to the surface. Add the bay leaves, thyme, and peppercorns. Simmer for another 30 minutes, for a total simmering time of 2 hours, skimming any impurities that rise up during this time. If at any time the liquid falls below the level of the solids, add enough cold water to cover them again.

REMOVE the pot from the heat and let rest for 15 minutes so all solids and residue sink to the bottom of the pot. Gently ladle the stock through a fine-mesh strainer set over an airtight container. Let the stock cool; use it right away, refrigerate for up to 3 days, or freeze for up to 3 months. (If you are in a hurry, cool the stock faster by filling a large bowl halfway with ice water and setting the bottom of the container in the ice water. Swirl the stock with a ladle to cool it as quickly as possible. It will cool even faster if in a stainless steel vessel.)

EMBELLISHMENT For richer flavor, use half White Chicken Stock (page 45) and half Veal Stock (page 48).

WHITE BEEF STOCK

MAKES 8 CUPS

8 POUNDS BEEF SHANK BONES, CUT CROSSWISE INTO 3- TO 4-INCH PIECES BY YOUR BUTCHER

6½ QUARTS WATER, PLUS MORE AS NEEDED

¼ CUP LEEKS, WHITE AND LIGHT GREEN PARTS, WELL RINSED, LARGE DICE

¼ CUP ONION, LARGE DICE

¼ CUP PEELED CARROT, LARGE DICE

¼ CUP CELERY, LARGE DICE

2 HEADS GARLIC, SPLIT HORIZONTALLY, EXCESS PAPERY SKIN REMOVED

4 PLUM TOMATOES, LARGE DICE

4 WHITE BUTTON MUSHROOMS, QUARTERED

4 BAY LEAVES

5 SPRIGS THYME

1 TABLESPOON BLACK PEPPERCORNS

6 SPRIGS FLAT-LEAF PARSLEY, WITH THEIR STEMS

1 TABLESPOON KOSHER SALT

RINSE the bones and put them in a stockpot. Pour in enough cold water to cover them by 2 inches and set the pot over medium heat. Bring the water to a simmer and let simmer for 10 minutes, skimming any impurities and foam that rise to the surface. Drain the bones, rinse them, and return them to the pot.

POUR in the 6½ quarts water, or enough to cover the bones by 4 inches. Bring to a boil over high heat, then lower the heat and let simmer for 5 hours, frequently skimming any impurities that rise to the surface.

ADD the leeks, onions, carrots, celery, garlic, tomatoes, and mushrooms. Simmer for another 30 minutes, then add the bay leaves, thyme, peppercorns, parsley, and salt and simmer for 30 minutes more, for a total simmering time of 6 hours, skimming any impurities that rise up during this time. If at any time the liquid falls below the level of the solids, add enough cold water to cover them again.

REMOVE the pot from the heat and let rest for 15 minutes so all solids and residue sink to the bottom of the pot. Gently ladle the stock through a fine-mesh strainer set over an airtight container. Use it right away, or let the stock cool and refrigerate it for up to 3 days. It can also be frozen for up to 3 months. (If you are in a hurry, cool the stock faster by filling a large bowl halfway with ice water and setting the bottom of the conatiner in the ice water. Swirl the stock with a ladle to cool it as quickly as possible. It will cool even faster if in a stainless steel vessel.)

VEAL STOCK

MAKES 4 CUPS

THE natural gelatin in the veal bones give this stock its body and viscosity. This is the only stock in the book that's reduced to a demi-glace, ensuring rich and potent flavor.

8 POUNDS VEAL BONES, NECKS AND BACKS, CLEANED

1 CALF'S FOOT, SPLIT (OPTIONAL; AVAILABLE FROM THE BUTCHER)

¼ CUP CANOLA OIL

½ CUP ONION, LARGE DICE

½ CUP LEEKS, WHITE AND LIGHT GREEN PARTS, WELL RINSED, LARGE DICE

½ CUP CELERY, LARGE DICE

½ CUP PEELED CARROTS, LARGE DICE

2 HEADS GARLIC, SPLIT HORIZONTALLY, EXCESS PAPERY SKIN REMOVED

4 ROMA TOMATOES, LARGE DICE

3 TABLESPOONS TOMATO PASTE

6½ QUARTS WATER, PLUS MORE AS NEEDED

4 BAY LEAVES

5 SPRIGS THYME

2 TABLESPOONS BLACK PEPPERCORNS

5 SPRIGS FLAT-LEAF PARSLEY

PREHEAT the oven to 350°F. Put the bones in a 3-gallon pot. Pour in enough cold water to cover them by 2 inches and set the pot over medium heat. Bring the water to a simmer and let simmer for 10 minutes, skimming any impurities and foam that rise to the surface. Drain the bones, rinse them, and transfer them to a roasting pan.

DRIZZLE the bones with the oil and toss to coat. Roast in the oven for 40 minutes, periodically turning the bones with tongs or a wooden spoon to help them turn golden-brown all over. Add the onion, leeks, celery, carrots, garlic, and tomatoes, toss to coat them with oil, and roast, stirring occasionally, until caramelized, another 20 to 25 minutes. Add the tomato paste, and stir.

TRANSFER the contents of the roasting pan to a stockpot and pour in the 6½ quarts water, or enough to cover the bones by 4 inches. Bring to a boil over high heat, then lower the heat and let simmer for 5½ hours, frequently skimming any impurities that rise to the surface.

ADD the bay leaves, thyme, peppercorns, and parsley. Simmer for another 30 minutes, for a total simmering time of 6 hours, skimming any impurities that rise up during this time. If at any time the liquid falls below the level of the solids, add enough cold water to cover them again.

REMOVE the pot from the heat and let rest for 15 minutes so any lingering impurities sink to the bottom of the pot. Gently ladle the stock through a fine-mesh strainer set over a clean pot. You should have 8 cups of stock. Gently raise the heat to a simmer and let simmer until reduced by half and thick enough to coat the back of a wooden spoon.

Let the stock cool; use it right away, refrigerate for up to 3 days, or freeze for up to 3 months. (If you are in a hurry, cool the stock faster by filling a large bowl halfway with ice water and setting the bottom of the pot in the ice water. Swirl the stock with a ladle to cool it as quickly as possible. It will cool even faster if in a stainless steel vessel.)

VEGETABLE STOCK

MAKES 8 CUPS

THIS stock provides a light and balanced base that focuses exclusively on the vegetables that often fade into the background of meat-based stocks. It's a good all-purpose stock for vegetarian dishes and recipes for which you want the flavor of other ingredients to be front and center.

2 TABLESPOONS CANOLA OIL

¼ CUP WHITE MUSHROOMS, LARGE DICE

¼ CUP FENNEL, LARGE DICE

½ CUP PEELED CARROTS, LARGE DICE

½ CUP LEEKS, WHITE AND LIGHT GREEN PARTS, WELL RINSED, HALVED LENGTHWISE AND CUT CROSSWISE, LARGE DICE

½ CUP CELERY, LARGE DICE

½ CUP ONION, LARGE DICE

3 GARLIC CLOVES, CRUSHED

4 SPRIGS FLAT-LEAF PARSLEY WITH THEIR STEMS

3 BAY LEAVES

3 SPRIGS THYME

1 TABLESPOON KOSHER SALT PLUS A PINCH

12 CUPS WATER

POUR the oil into a 6-quart stockpot and heat over medium heat. Add the mushrooms, fennel, carrots, leeks, celery, onion, garlic, parsley, bay leaves, thyme, and a pinch of salt. Cook, stirring, until the vegetables are softened but not browned, 6 to 7 minutes.

POUR in the water, add the tablespoon of salt, and bring to a boil. Lower the heat and let simmer for 1 hour. Strain the liquid though a fine-mesh strainer set over an airtight container.

USE the stock right away, or cool, cover, and refrigerate for up to 2 days, or freeze for up to 3 months. (If you are in a hurry, cool the stock faster by filling a large bowl halfway with ice water and setting the bottom of the container in the ice water. Swirl the stock with a ladle to cool it as quickly as possible. It will cool even faster if in a stainless steel vessel.)

TERMS AND TECHNIQUES *Aromatics:* Leek, onion, celery, and garlic are often referred to as aromatics in this context because they contribute a fragrant flavor to cooking. Plants (herbs and spices) used in cooking are also referred to as aromatics.

CHEESE

MY PASSION FOR CHEESE BEGAN during my time working and living in Europe in my early twenties. There, cheese has been a part of daily life for ages, just as fine wine has. Cheese making goes back centuries, longer than the United States has been around, and I have no trouble seeing why: From my first exposure to great cheese, I've been fascinated by it.

My profession has given me the pleasure of meeting and getting to know many artisanal cheese makers. Consequently, I'm intimately familiar with how much work goes into producing cheese. But despite the countless human hours required to bring it to life, I find there to be something almost divine about cheese, something seemingly effortless and altogether gorgeous that, for me, takes it beyond the category of foodstuffs.

About 12 years ago, this personal fascination—obsession, really—inspired me to make it one of the missions of my career to help make artisanal cheese as much a fact of daily life here in my home country as it is throughout Europe. Most of you reading this can remember how, just a few decades ago, cheese divided Americans into two camps: those who enjoyed sublime cheeses while traveling abroad and rarely, if ever, bothered with what was available stateside, and those who served inferior supermarket cheese—mass-produced and shrink-wrapped in undistinguished factories—at home.

The gap between these groups has been steadily closing over the past decade as more and more Americans have developed an insatiable appetite for world-class cheese. They don't just eat it in restaurants; they actually take the time to learn about it and seek it out from gourmet markets and mail-order companies. And the high-protein, low-carbohydrate diet being adopted by millions of Americans adds considerably to the intense and ever-growing interest.

Americans have also begun turning out some world-class artisanal cheeses, enough that several restaurants here now offer exclusively American cheese selections, which would have been unimaginable and impossible just 10 years ago. I'm very proud of the cheesemakers of America and their constant effort to improve and expand their offerings.

This burgeoning sophistication has made cheese the millennial counterpart to the big culinary developments of the 1980s and 1990s. Those decades ushered in the eras of fine wines, gourmet coffees, and organic foods in the United States, and now the current decade is fast becoming the time for cheese for many of you reading this. Just as many of you who once knew only Chardonnay and Merlot can today distinguish between a world of varietals, and coffee drinkers who only knew caffeinated and decaffeinated now know the difference between Guatemalan and Sumatran beans, so too can today's cheese aficionados detail the differences among the cheeses of different countries and distinguish among different styles such as washed rind, bloomy rind, and so on. You continue to learn about cheese for the same reason you continue to learn about wine and coffee: Your curiosity is rewarded with aromas and flavors that delight the senses and linger in the memory.

Cheese has been the subject of a number of books. Space here doesn't allow for a comprehensive discussion of the topic, but no artisanal pantry should be without cheese (nor, dare I say, should any day go by without cheese). So, here are some general musings and advice about one of my favorite topics.

WHEN TO SERVE CHEESE

THERE WAS A TIME, NOT SO LONG AGO, when the extent of most Americans' experience with cheese was limited to eating it on crackers during cocktail parties or on a sandwich or hamburger. The percentage of us who had tasted fine European cheeses, let alone savored them after a meal, was infinitesimal.

Every culture has its own place for cheese. For example, the French prefer, insist on really, having it between a main course and dessert, while the Italians and Spanish are less finicky, happy to nibble on cheese before or after dinner.

I have my own very modest proposition about when to serve and eat cheese: any time you feel like it.

On its own or in recipes, cheese fits into almost any time of day, from the sunrise omelet to the midday salad or sandwich to the post-dinner punctuation that brings your day of dining to an end. I love making cheese the focus of my lunch; accompanied by fruits, nuts, and greens, it's a satisfying and efficient way to get energy without filling up excessively. There are recipes throughout this book that can help you enjoy cheese at various times and occasions, from fondues to salads to soups to cheese in place of dessert.

Despite my French culinary leanings, at home I'm apt to set out a selection of cheeses as part of an hors d'oeuvres offering. For more formal dinners, I usually put a big platter in the center of the table and let everyone serve himself or herself, rather than making a big production of carving the cheeses and arranging individual portions on everyone's plate. I think it makes people more comfortable, and makes the cheese more accessible, when they serve themselves. It's also more visually exciting and, simply put, fun.

PURCHASING CHEESE

BUY YOUR CHEESE FROM A RELIABLE CHEESE MONGER, either in person or via the Internet. (I can't resist directing you to my own company, www.artisanalcheese.com.) Try to buy artisanal cheeses that are cut to order rather than precut and prewrapped, to ensure maximum freshness. If possible, buy raw-milk cheeses; contrary to popular belief, raw-milk cheeses are available in the United States, provided they are at least 60 days old. While this means that you cannot avail yourself of the best brie and camembert, you can discover a whole new level of cheese appreciation. All of that said, there are plenty of excellent pasteurized cheeses available; a few favorites are Stilton, Pierre Robert, Mount Tam, and Red Hawk.

CARE AND HANDLING

STORE YOUR CHEESE IN A COOL, DRY PLACE. A wine cellar or wine refrigerator would be an optimal location, but the vegetable drawer of your refrigerator is also a suitable place to store cheeses. The best way to store each variety of cheese is as follows.

YOUNG CHEESES (e.g., soft goat's-milk cheeses, mascarpone) should be kept in a plastic container with holes poked in the lid, or in a ceramic bowl, loosely covered with plastic wrap.

SEMI-SOFT, BLOOMY-RIND (semi-soft cheeses such as Camembert and Brie whose rinds are covered with *Penicillium candidum*, allowing them to ripen from the outside in), and washed-rind cheeses (cheeses such as Epoisses and Munster d'Alsace, whose rinds are periodically washed with a liquid solution—salt and water or perhaps cider or spirits—to keep the cheese moist and infuse it with flavor) should be tautly wrapped in wax or parchment paper.

SEMI-HARD CHEESES (e.g., Comte, Cheddar, Gruyère) should be wrapped in wax paper or parchment paper.

HARD-RIND CHEESE (e.g., Roomano, Parmigiano-Reggiano) should be wrapped in parchment paper, then loosely in plastic.

FIRM BLUE CHEESE (e.g., Roquefort, Stilton, Great Hill) should be wrapped in wax or parchment paper, then in plastic. Wet (soft and moist) blues such as Westfield Farm should be stored in a plastic container, or wrapped in plastic wrap, then aluminum foil.

HOW TO SERVE CHEESE

SERVE A TOTAL OF THREE TO SIX OUNCES OF CHEESE PER PERSON. When serving cheese before dessert, lean toward the lower end of that scale; if not serving dessert, then err toward the higher. Also lean toward the high end of the spectrum if the cheese will be part of a lunch or dinner buffet.

Arrange cheese in a clockwise, circular pattern, with the order determined first by mild to strong flavor, and then by soft to hard texture. In other words, flavor trumps texture, so a soft and stinky cheese would come after a firm and sharp cheese because its flavor is stronger.

Set out an individual knife for each cheese (or a spoon for particularly runny or potted ones) to keep from getting bits of one cheese on another.

Bring cheeses to room temperature before serving. Remove them from the refrigerator 1½ to 2 hours ahead of time, depending on size, setting them out in a cool area in their wrapping. Unwrap and plate them just before bringing them to the table.

If desired, artfully arrange a few pieces of greenery such as fig leaves or lemon leaves around the cheese and scatter some nuts around the plate.

Serve cheese with crusty artisanal bread or walnut bread. If cheese is part of a buffet, or will not be followed by dessert, serve it with dried and fresh fruits, nuts, quince paste, and/or fig cake. If fresh figs are in season, serve them with cheese for a sublime combination.

To make cheese more of a meal, serve it with salad, cured meats, olives, and raw vegetables.

By the way, I often get asked what one should do with leftover cheese. My advice is to wrap it, store it overnight, and simply eat it again the next night, treating yourself to an encore presentation of the same cheese course.

THE CHEESE COURSE

MANY PEOPLE FIND COMPOSING A CHEESE COURSE CHALLENGING. It's actually not all that difficult. I'd even go so far as to say that there are no bad cheese courses, just degrees of goodness and greatness.

Here are a few guidelines for cheese courses:

The gateway to a great cheese course is selecting high-quality cheeses. (By the same token, I find one superior cheese accompanied by a condiment to be a perfectly respectable cheese course in its own right.). Once you decide how many cheeses you'll feature—the prevailing wisdom is that one to six cheeses is acceptable, but I prefer a minimum of three—try to achieve some variety among the following considerations.

There are three milk types: cow, goat, and sheep. Choose a variety.

Try to procure cheeses from different countries, unless deliberately focusing on one country.

Pick an assortment of textures, such as runny, soft, hard, and so on.

Whenever possible, make the selection interesting to the eye with cheeses of different shapes and colors.

Feature varying ages of one cheese variety (months or years apart).

SOFT AND MILD: **8** Mont d'Or **9** Pierre Robert **12** L'Edel de Cleron **17** Fleur du Maquis

SEMI-SOFT AND MILD: **1** Monte Enebro **2** Noccetto (two cheeses) **3** Cabecou Feuille (three cheeses) **4** Ste. Maure **5** Pouligny St. Pierre **6** Roccaverano **7** Constant Bliss **24** Wabash Cannonball

FIRM AND SAVORY OR FULL-FLAVORED: **13** Gouda **14** Parmigiano-Reggiano **15** Roomano **16** Keens Cheddar **20** Zamorano

SOFT OR SEMI-SOFT AND STINKY: **10** La Sirena **11** Langres **18** Torta del Casar **19** Durrus **29** Forsterkase **30** Epoisses **31** Flada **32** Taleggio **33** Pave D'Auge **34** Alsatian Munster

BLUE: **21** Classic Blue Log **22** Gorgonzola Mountain **23** Bayley Hazen Blue **25** Rogue River Blue **26** Roquefort **27** Shropshire Blue **28** Stilton

SOME OF MY FAVORITE CHEESES

ASKING A CHEESE MONGER TO NAME HIS FAVORITE CHEESES is like asking a father to name his favorite children. I've never met a cheese I didn't like, but these are the ones that I never say "no" to. Some of them are more uncommon and hard-to-find than others, but they are all well worth your attention. Be adventurous and you'll find that a new cheese is always waiting to be discovered.

I've arranged the cheeses according to texture and flavor, as well as from mild to stronger (or strong to stronger) within each category. I've also included suggested wine pairings after each one. (Note: Variations from the basic category are in parentheses.)

SOFT AND MILD

NANCY'S HUDSON VALLEY CAMEMBERT Meltingly smooth and buttery, with the texture of a triple-crème, this upstate New York cheese, produced by Sally and Tom Clark of the Old Chatham Sheepherding Company, has a rich, mascarpone-like flavor that comes neatly packaged in a half-cow's-milk, half-sheep's-milk square. (Champagne)

PIERRE ROBERT Triple-crème cow's-milk cheese from the Île-de-France region of France. It's aged until the rind develops beige tones and the inside virtually collapses when cut. Rich, buttery, and superlative. Delicious with graham biscuits. (Champagne)

ROBIOLA INCAVOLATA Cow's and goat's milk come together in this treasure from the Piedmont region of northern Italy. It matures beautifully in the Savoy cabbage leaves in which it arrives. (Pinot Noir)

BIG HOLMES Made in Wisconsin, this sheep's-milk cheese is aged four to six weeks in a "coat" of rosemary, mint, and cedar. As it ages, those flavors permeate the cheese, making it a fine accompaniment to fresh fruit. (Sauvignon Blanc)

SEMI-SOFT AND MILD

HOJA SANTA (TANGY) The Mozzarella Cheese Company in Dallas, Texas, produces this cheese, wrapping each piece in a hoja santa leaf. Also known as "the root beer plant," hoja santa imparts a subtle sassafras flavor to the cheese. At Artisanal Premium Cheese, we mature it ourselves to produce a little mold on the rind. (Zinfandel)

POULIGNY SAINT PIERRE This Loire Valley goat's-milk cheese is instantly recognized by its four-sided conical shape, which has earned it the nickname "the pyramid" or "the Eiffel Tower." Bright and complex, with sweet, sour, and salty notes. (Vouvray Chenin Blanc)

CONSTANT BLISS A winning little raw Ayreshire cow's-milk cheese from Vermont that's made from fresh, uncooled evening milk. Chalky, silky, and milky with a strong rind, it has a very clean, creamy flavor punched up with hints of mushroom at the finish. (Champagne, Pinot Noir)

CABECOU SCHNAPPS (AKA CABECOU FEUILLE) Tiny round buttons of this raw goat's-milk cheese hail from the Midi-Pyrenées region of France, where they are marinated in prune brandy. This cheese is creamy, with a subtle, delicate taste of milk. (Sauvignon Blanc)

FIRM AND SAVORY OR FULL-FLAVORED

SPENWOOD A raw, hard ewe's-milk cheese named for the English village where it's made, Spencer's Wood. Matured for six months, it boasts a well-developed flavor, nutty with a hint of sweetness that may remind you of Manchego, though it's somewhat milder than that Spanish gem. (Sangiovese)

MONTE ENEBRO A rich, farmhouse goat cheese from Spain with unusual and wonderfully complex, fresh-tasting, mouth-puckering flavor. The kind of cheese only a dedicated and attentive artisan could produce. (Muscat)

ZAMORANO Produced in the Castile-Leon region of Spain exclusively from the milk of the Churra breed of sheep, Zamorano is richer and nuttier than its cousin Manchego. Sharp and moderately gamey with a milk-flavored bite that melts in your mouth. (Zinfandel)

GORWYDD CAERPHILLY A tomme-style cow's-milk cheese from Wales with a rustic flavor. When mature, the heart of the cheese is crumbly and slightly lemony while the outlying portion has an elastic, smooth texture with salty, complex flavor. (Viognier)

UPLANDS PLEASANT RIDGE RESERVE This exquisite American farmstead cow's-milk cheese from Wisconsin is made with milk from the artisan's own personal herd. Comparable to France's Beaufort, which inspired it, this cheese has a complexity that is all American. I consider it one of the best American cheeses. (Merlot)

TARENTAISE Based on a recipe for Alpine Gruyère and aged for at least six months, this cow's-milk cheese from cheesemaker John Putnam is made from beautiful Jersey milk and boasts a golden paste that's firm and chewy. The flavor is grassy, nutty, and buttery, all nods to the Alpine cheese, Abondance, that inspired it. More than 45 percent butterfat, it melts readily, making it a great cooking cheese. (Merlot)

SBRINZ The father of hard cheeses, Sbrinz lacks the transformative qualities of Parmigiano-Reggiano, but possesses a respectable nutty, granular texture and hearty character. Rich and fulfilling. (Pinot Noir)

MONTGOMERY CHEDDAR The undisputed king of cheddar, this clothbound cow's-milk cheese is produced on the Montgomerys' 500-year-old farm in the Somerset countryside of southwest England. Aged 13 months or more, it has a golden interior and satisfying bite that delivers perfect sharpness and a long, lingering finish. (Pinot Noir)

BEAUFORT ALPAGE This raw cow's-milk cheese from the Haute Savoie region of France, where it's produced in enormous 90-pound wheels, has a natural brushed rind and mild, sweet, fruity flavor. Hand-made rennet is responsible for its distinct flavor. (Champagne)

HOCH YBRIG Produced in a small canton in Switzerland every summer, this Appenzeller-family cheese is heavily washed in a white-wine brine. Its explosive, complex nuttiness makes it a fine fondue choice. (Riesling)

ROOMANO Skimmed cow's-milk gouda from Holland that's produced with long aging in mind (up to 6 years). Its texture is hard and crystalline; the flavor is defined by butterscotch tones that are a real crowd-pleaser. (Amarone)

PARMIGIANO-REGGIANO (Note: This cheese's place on the list will vary as it ages.) One of the world's great cheeses; pleasingly dry and salty and often grated and used in cooking. This cheese can be aged anywhere from 18 months to 8 years. My company sells one that's aged five years, during which time it becomes, surprisingly, less salty with a delicate, elegant flavor. If you can find one of these rare specimens, don't pass it up; it will impress even the already converted. (Proseco)

SOFT OR SEMI-SOFT AND STINKY

AZEITÃO A concentrated sheep's-milk cheese, made with cardoon thistle, Azeitão is named for the village where it was born in the foothills of the Serra de Arribida mountain range in Portugal. Molded in cloth, it has a rustic appearance that has helped establish its romantic aura. The texture ranges from soft and unctuous to semi-hard and chewy. Cut the top off a round and scoop it up with slabs of nutty bread. (Vouvray, Chenin Blanc)

VACHERON MONT D'OR A winter rarity, appropriately packaged in giftlike spruce bark box that keeps it from cracking, this cheese is so runny that at its peak it must be consumed with a spoon. As it ripens, it develops a unique aroma with hints of cedar. Surprisingly mild, it evokes the flavor of mushrooms and its light balsamic flavor embodies the aura of the pine forests of the Jura mountains. Only available overseas, I just had to mention it because if you ever have the chance to try it, you'll find it sublime. (Champagne)

QUESO DE LA SERENA One of Spain's most desirable cheeses; this sheep's-milk cheese is smooth and soft, blending fruity sharpness with an earthy, meaty, stewy flavor. (Blanc de Noirs)

TORTA DEL CASAR Rich, intense, and delightfully spreadable in the springtime batches, this sheep's-milk cheese from the Extremadura region of west central Spain is very similar in style to the French Vacherin Mont d'Or. As it ages, it becomes heavier and darkens to an ominous gray. Though not smoked, it has a lightly smoky flavor. Put your hands on a semi-soft "cake" (the cheese is named for the Spanish potato omelet called "tortilla"), cut a hole in the top and spoon the cheese right out of the rind and onto hunks of country bread. (Syrah, Châteauneuf du Pape)

TALEGGIO One of the world's best cow's-milk cheeses, Taleggio comes from the Lombardy region in northern Italy. A moist texture gives way to tangy notes and a pleasant, fruity finish that make it the most accepted stinky cheese. (Nebbiolo)

STANSER FLADÄ Vacherin-style cow's-milk cheese from one of Switzerland's most revered cheese-makers, Joseph Barmettler. Its soft, creamy texture releases a barnyard aroma. Pungent but appealingly so, and it comes in its own charming little box. (Also known as Chue Fladä.) (Vouvray, Chenin Blanc)

DURRUS Mild and creamy when young, with strong notes of butter, this semi-soft, washed-rind, cow's-milk St. Nectaire–style cheese develops into a headier, fruitier cheese as it ages. The rind, coral when young, develops gray, yellow, and pink molds as it matures. The paste is creamy yellow, comprising more than 55 percent butterfat. Sip a white sparkling wine to cut the richness, and discover a brilliant give-and-take of flavors. (Moulin-à-Vent, Fleurie)

REDHAWK This washed-rind, triple-cream version of Mount Tam is made from organic cow's milk and hails from Cowgirl Creamery in West Marin, California. It's aged for six weeks and washed with a brine that turns the rinds a stunning deep orange. One of the United States' finest cheeses. (Riesling)

BLUE

WESTFIELD FARM CLASSIC BLUE (SOFT) Some of the best, fresh goat's-milk cheese in the United States is produced in Massachusetts, home of this gem. Elegant and mild, this award-winning classic blue log is coated in blue glaucum mold and white inside; an inside-out blue cheese. (Zinfandel)

SHROPSHIRE BLUE Technically a cross between Stilton and Cheshire, this stunning firm cheese gets its orange color from the addition of annatto, a natural food coloring, though its blue veins persist. I think of it as Stilton's prettier sister. Creamier and less nutty than Stilton, but sometimes stronger as well. (Tawny port)

GREAT HILL BLUE Produced by Tim Stone of Great Hill Dairy, 50 miles south of Boston. Local cow's milk that's pasteurized but not homogenized produces a full-flavored, smooth yet sharp flavor and a sublime firm texture. Pair it with sweeter dessert wines such as Sauternes. (Madeira)

ROGUE RIVER BLUE This firm Oregon cow's-milk blue, with a rind washed in pear brandy, was the first U.S. cheese to beat out Stilton and Roquefort in international competition. It derives an earthy flavor from the grape leaves in which it is wrapped. So much in demand, customers often have to wait up to six months to get their hands on some. (Madeira)

STILTON Ample blue veining distinguishes this firm British cow's-milk blue. The best, creamiest Stilton is Colston-Bassett Stilton from Nottinghamshire, England; seek it out in December when wheels produced from rich August milk are released. (Tawny port)

ROQUEFORT The quintessential blue cheese, exclusively produced in the Aveyron district of south central France. Piquant, richly flavored, creamy, crumbly, salty sheep's milk cheese that melts in your mouth. Sublime with a glass of the sweet dessert wine Sauternes, and a valuable player in sauces, salads, and crumbled atop soups and pastas. (Sauternes)

EBORINATI DI PECORA This northeastern Italian sheep's-milk blue was inspired by the French Roquefort. Intense and explosive with a creamy but slightly grainy texture, it's very strong, even by blue standards. (Moscato d'Asti)

CABRALES One of Spain's more well-known cheeses, Cabrales is a semi-soft blue with a strong, spicy flavor. It's traditionally made with a combination of cow's, goat's, and sheep's milk, but is not always made that way. That said, my favorite is the three-milk version in which the sheep's milk smoothes out the texture and the goat's milk contributes a piquant flavor. (Pedro Ximenez Sherry)

SAMPLE CHEESE COURSES

HERE ARE SOME EXAMPLES OF CHEESE COURSES culled from "Some of My Favorite Cheeses" (pages 56 to 60).

ALL-AMERICAN PLATE
See how far the American artisanal cheese movement has come with this selection:

> Hoja Santa
> Constant Bliss
> Tarentaise
> Pleasant Ridge Reserve
> Rogue River Blue

CHAMPAGNE TRIO
Serving cheese as a welcome? Break out the bubbly and these three choices:

> Pierre Robert
> Beaufort
> Queso de la Serena

PINOT NOIR PLATE

A selection chosen for its affinity with the popular light-bodied red wine:

Azeitão
Robiola Incavolata
Zamorano
Taleggio
Montgomery Cheddar

SAUTERNES PLATE

Serve this after dinner with a glass of the famous dessert wine.

Red Hawk
Roquefort
Torta Del Casar

SAUVIGNON BLANC PLATE

A perfect light lunch with a glass of Sauvignon Blanc:

Pouligny St. Pierre
Big Holmes
Stanser Fladä

HORS D'OEUVRES

THE FRENCH TERM *hors d'oeuvres* translates literally to "outside the work," which makes sense because these little bites exist separately from the rest of the meal. They're passed during the cocktail hour, or set out on a coffee or buffet table.

Hors d'oeuvres should be easy on the cook, especially if they'll be followed by a two- or three-course meal. Many of the hors d'oeuvres in this chapter prove the value of a well-stocked pantry, and of following my philosophy of making every ingredient count. None of these recipes require that you spend too much time in the kitchen, but they make a big impression by calling on such inherently compelling components as artisanal cheeses and freshly baked bread, and on simple techniques for making crowd-pleasing favorites such as frittatas and fondues.

It's fitting that the restaurant equivalent of an hors d'oeuvre is a little bite sent out compliments of the chef, called an *amuse*. The name refers to its mission of "amusing," or stimulating, the palate. The hors d'oeuvres in this chapter do that and more, arousing the appetite as well as providing a pleasing surprise and a possible subject for conversation, such as an assortment of simple but stunning hors d'oeuvres served on teaspoons, and gourmet answers to such American touchstones as potato chips and grilled cheese sandwiches.

PICHOLINE'S MARINATED OLIVES

MAKES ABOUT 2 CUPS

Just as Artisanal restaurant's name has a meaning near and dear to my heart, so too does Picholine's. The restaurant takes its moniker from one variety of green olives, which are one of the most emblematic ingredients in all Mediterranean cuisine. Not only do they turn up in dish after dish in that region, but they also suggest the golden oil so closely associated with it.

When I first opened Picholine, I devised this house recipe for olives to be served at the dining tables. As the restaurant became more and more formal, they no longer seemed appropriate there, and we began serving them exclusively at the bar, a tradition we continue to this day.

These are wonderful with cocktails, or on their own for snacking. They can last for several weeks in the refrigerator, so I recommend keeping them on hand for unexpected or last-minute guests.

1½ CUPS OLIVES, PREFERABLY PICHOLINE OLIVES, STRAINED OF JUICE OR OIL

1 TABLESPOON FENNEL SEEDS

1 TABLESPOON CUMIN SEEDS

1 TABLESPOON CORIANDER SEEDS

1 CUP EXTRA VIRGIN OLIVE OIL

2 TABLESPOONS FINELY GRATED LEMON ZEST

¼ TEASPOON CRUSHED RED PEPPER FLAKES

1 TEASPOON THYME LEAVES

1 TEASPOON ROSEMARY LEAVES

2 BAY LEAVES

PUT the olives in a heatproof container and set aside.

PUT the fennel seeds, cumin seeds, and coriander seeds in an 8-inch sauté pan and toast over medium heat, shaking constantly, until fragrant, 2 to 3 minutes. Add them to the container with the olives. Add the oil, lemon zest, pepper flakes, thyme, rosemary, and bay leaves and toss well to incorporate. Cover and set aside at room temperature for at least 24 hours so the flavors can develop.

THE olives can be refrigerated for up to 1 month.

VARIATION Use different olives, or an assortment, if you prefer.

EMBELLISHMENT If you will be consuming the olives within 3 days, add 3 crushed garlic cloves along with the olives. (The garlic will take on an off flavor after 3 days.)

POTATO CHIPS WITH PARMESAN, PEPPER, AND LEMON

SERVES 4

One of the more fun aspects of contemporary American cuisine is how many chefs have elevated so-called "junk food" to a gourmet level. Here's my contribution: potato chips made with Yukon Gold potatoes, and coated with Parmesan, pepper, and lemon zest. These are so good that I almost bagged them for mass consumption, but there were so many brands on the market that I decided to stay out of the fray. For that reason, I'm especially glad to have this opportunity to share them with you.

1 TEASPOON FINELY GRATED LEMON ZEST

2 TABLESPOONS GRATED PARMIGIANO-REGGIANO

1/2 TABLESPOON SEA SALT

1/2 TEASPOON CRACKED BLACK PEPPER

1 POUND YUKON GOLD POTATOES, PEELED

3 QUARTS PEANUT OIL OR CANOLA OIL

PUT the lemon zest, Parmigiano-Reggiano, salt, and pepper in a small bowl. Stir together and set aside.

SLICE the potatoes into 1/16-inch-thick slices, ideally on a mandoline.

GATHER the slices in a large bowl. Release the starch by covering the potatoes with cold water, letting them soak for 5 minutes, gently agitating them, then draining. Repeat once.

POUR the oil into a wide, shallow pan and heat over medium heat to a temperature of 325°F.

MEANWHILE, dry the potatoes well in a salad spinner or pat them dry with paper towels.

CAREFULLY put one-third of the potatoes into the hot oil and cook until lightly golden but not dark, 6 to 7 minutes, using a slotted spoon to make sure none of them stick together. Remove from the oil with a slotted spoon, drain on paper towels, transfer to a clean, dry bowl, and toss while still warm with one-third of the cheese mixture.

REPEAT twice with the remaining potatoes and cheese mixture, letting the oil return to a temperature of 325°F between batches.

THESE potatoes are best freshly fried, but they can be kept in a plastic container at room temperature and eaten later on the day you make them.

THE REASON *The potatoes are fried until golden:* Over-frying ingredients can result in a bitter finish, so as a rule it's best to fry until crispy and golden, but not brown.

EMBELLISHMENTS Use Cumin Salt (page 20) or Garlic Salt (page 21) instead of sea salt to add another flavor. Or add herbs to the frying oil; rosemary is escpecially delicious.

SPOON HORS D'OEUVRES

THESE EYE-CATCHING HORS D'OEUVRES OFFER MORE than just an unusual presentation; they also allow you to pass foods that are traditionally plated. I first served them at Picholine, where they elicited gasps of pleasant surprise from our guests. At home, they will do the same, and cut down on the number of dishes you'll have to clean after dinner.

If time allows, I recommend making all of these recipes and serving an assortment, pleasing the eye and the palate. All three recipes can be doubled or tripled to serve larger groups.

CAULIFLOWER MOUSSELINE WITH CAVIAR
SERVES 4 (3 TEASPOONS PER PERSON)

4 CUPS WATER

½ POUND CAULIFLOWER FLORETS OF UNIFORM SIZE

KOSHER SALT

2 TABLESPOONS MASCARPONE CHEESE

WHITE PEPPER IN A MILL

1 OUNCE OSETRA OR SEVRUGA CAVIAR

POUR the water into a 2-quart saucepan. Add the cauliflower and 1 tablespoon salt. Bring to a boil over high heat, then lower the heat and simmer until the cauliflower is tender, 20 to 25 minutes. Drain the florets and return them to the pot. Cook the florets over low-medium heat, stirring gently, for 5 minutes to evaporate as much moisture as possible. Transfer them to a blender and puree until smooth, turning off the blender to scrape down the sides, several times if necessary, to ensure an even, creamy consistency. Blend in the mascarpone. Transfer the puree to a bowl and season with salt and 6 grinds of pepper, or to taste.

COVER the puree and refrigerate for at least 1 hour or overnight.

DIVIDE the cauliflower puree among 12 teaspoons, and top each serving with a dollop of caviar. Arrange the spoons in a circular pattern on a plate or platter with the handles facing outward, and serve cold.

VARIATIONS At home, I crush the cooked florets with butter and grated Parmigiano-Reggiano and serve it as a side dish. You can garnish the puree with chopped hard-boiled egg or grated Parmigiano-Reggiano cheese instead of caviar.

BEET TARTARE WITH GOAT CHEESE

SERVES 4 (3 TEASPOONS PER PERSON)

½ POUND LARGE BEETS WITH THE SKIN ON, SCRUBBED AND RINSED UNDER COLD RUNNING WATER

2 TABLESPOONS EXTRA VIRGIN OLIVE OIL

KOSHER SALT

1 TABLESPOON FRESHLY SQUEEZED LEMON JUICE

¾ TEASPOON DIJON MUSTARD

1 TABLESPOON FINELY DICED SHALLOTS

2 TEASPOONS THINLY SLICED CHIVES

PINCH CAYENNE

1½ TABLESPOONS CRUMBLED GOAT CHEESE (FROM 1 OUNCE CHEESE)

12 SPRIGS CHERVIL (OPTIONAL)

PREHEAT the oven to 400°F. Put the beets in a bowl, and toss with 1 tablespoon oil and salt. Wrap all the beets in a large piece of aluminum foil. Place the parcel in a small baking dish and bake in the oven until a thin-bladed knife easily pierces into the center of a beet, approximately 1 hour 30 minutes. Remove the beets from the oven and let cool. Peel the beets, finely dice them, and transfer to a mixing bowl.

ADD the lemon juice, mustard, shallots, chives, cayenne, goat cheese, and remaining tablespoon oil to the bowl with the diced beets. Stir to combine and season to taste with salt.

COVER the beet tartare and chill for at least 1 hour or overnight. Serve cold.

DIVIDE the tartare among 12 teaspoons, garnish each with a sprig of chervil, if using. Arrange the spoons in a circular pattern on a plate or platter with the handles facing outward, and serve.

EMBELLISHMENTS Top the tartare in each spoon with a scant teaspoon of caviar. Or toss some chopped tarragon leaves in along with the salt and pepper to add a nice complement to the beets.

SCALLOP CEVICHE WITH AVOCADO

SERVES 4 (3 TEASPOONS PER PERSON)

¼ POUND VERY FRESH, COLD SEA SCALLOPS (2 TO 3 SEA SCALLOPS), MUSCLE REMOVED, FINELY DICED

1 TABLESPOON FRESHLY SQUEEZED LIME JUICE

1 TEASPOON BALSAMIC VINEGAR

½ AVOCADO, PREFERABLY HAAS, PEELED AND FINELY DICED

1½ TEASPOONS SEEDED, MINCED JALAPEÑO PEPPER

1 TABLESPOON THINLY SLICED CHIVES

2 TEASPOONS THINLY SLICED CILANTRO LEAVES

½ TEASPOON KOSHER SALT

6 GRINDS BLACK PEPPER FROM A MILL

1 TABLESPOON EXTRA VIRGIN OLIVE OIL

PUT all ingredients in a medium mixing bowl and gently but thoroughly toss. Cover and let marinate in the refrigerator for 30 minutes.

DIVIDE the ceviche among 12 teaspoons, arrange the spoons in a circular pattern on a plate or platter with the handles facing outward, and serve.

TERMS AND TECHNIQUES Peruvian in origin, a *ceviche* is a dish in which the acid in a marinade (lime juice in this case) produces a chemical reaction that is said to "cook" fish or shellfish. This recipe produces a result somewhere between a tartare (which is raw) and a ceviche because the scallops are marinated for only 30 minutes, a relatively short time, in order to preserve their freshness and succulent texture.

Haas are the best, most dependable avocados. When shopping for them, select those that yield a bit to gentle pressure, which indicates ripeness.

VARIATIONS The ceviche is equally successful with sea bass or snapper. When they're in season, from November through March, make this dish with super-sweet Nantucket Bay scallops.

SHRIMP WITH SMOKED PAPRIKA

SERVES 6 (4 SHRIMP PER PERSON)

 **S**moked paprika is a priceless ingredient that imparts a great deal of flavor to anything it's served with. Here, it's made the basis of a simple oil that's tossed with cooked, cooled shrimp. This is a very easy recipe that will have everyone clamoring for more.

1½ TABLESPOONS SMOKED PAPRIKA (SEE SOURCES, PAGE 318)

¼ TEASPOON CAYENNE

2 TABLESPOONS FRESHLY SQUEEZED LIME JUICE

½ CUP EXTRA VIRGIN OLIVE OIL

12 CUPS WATER

KOSHER SALT

½ CUP DRY WHITE WINE

1 LEMON, THINLY SLICED

10 SPRIGS THYME

1 TABLESPOON BLACK PEPPERCORNS

2 BAY LEAVES

24 MEDIUM SHRIMP (1 TO 1¼ POUNDS TOTAL WEIGHT), IN THE SHELL

PUT the paprika, cayenne, lime juice, and oil in a medium bowl and mix together. Set aside.

POUR the water into a large, heavy-bottomed pot. Add 2 tablespoons salt, the wine, lemon slices, thyme, peppercorns, and bay leaves, and bring to a boil over high heat. Add the shrimp, remove the pot from the heat, cover, and let stand until the shrimp are firm and pink, approximately 3 minutes. Use a slotted spoon to remove the shrimp and set aside to cool. When cool, peel and devein the shrimp, add them to the bowl with the paprika-cayenne oil, and toss to coat them. Season to taste with salt.

COVER the shrimp and refrigerate for at least 2 hours or up to 24 hours. To serve, decoratively arrange the shrimp on a platter and pass with toothpicks alongside, or skewer them on cocktail forks and present the forks on a plate or platter.

VARIATION Use the vinaigrette to dress grilled octopus.

EMBELLISHMENTS For extra flavor, grill the shrimp rather than poaching them. Turn this into a plated first course by adding more shrimp, tossing the shrimp with spaghetti or angel hair pasta, pairing it with a simple white bean salad, or serving it over haricots verts.

PISSALADIÈRES
"PROVENÇAL PIZZAS"
SERVES 4 TO 6

T hese flat little tarts—think of them as Provençal pizzas—are endlessly adaptable. Here, they're made with the traditional topping of caramelized onions and my cheese of choice, Parmigiano-Reggiano, but you can substitute any number of alternatives (see Embellishments) or make an assortment and let everyone sample a variety.

2½ TABLESPOONS OLIVE OIL

I POUND ONION (ABOUT I LARGE ONION), VERY THINLY SLICED

2 TEASPOONS MINCED GARLIC

¼ CUP PITTED, ROUGHLY CHOPPED NIÇOISE OLIVES

I TABLESPOON (PREFERABLY SALT-PACKED), ROUGHLY CHOPPED ANCHOVY FILLETS (FROM ABOUT 4 FILLETS, SOAKED, DRAINED, AND PATTED DRY; SEE PAGE 11)

KOSHER SALT

BLACK PEPPER IN A MILL

STORE-BOUGHT PUFF PASTRY, CUT INTO 4 ROUNDS, 5-INCHES IN DIAMETER EACH (FROM ABOUT 6 OUNCES PASTRY)

¼ CUP GRATED PARMIGIANO-REGGIANO (FROM ABOUT I OUNCE CHEESE)

PREHEAT the oven to 350°F. Heat the oil in a 10-inch sauté pan over medium-low heat. Add the onion and sauté, stirring frequently, until caramelized to a dark amber, 20 to 25 minutes. Add the garlic, olives, and anchovies and cook for 2 minutes. Mix well and season with salt and about 4 grinds of pepper, or to taste.

DOCK the surface of each puff pastry round. Arrange on a nonstick baking sheet without crowding and bake in the oven for 10 minutes. Remove from oven. Let cool.

DIVIDE the onion mixture evenly among the pastry rounds and sprinkle with Parmigiano-Reggiano. Press down gently to ensure even baking. Return to the oven and bake until the cheese is slightly browned and the dough is crispy, approximately 6 minutes. Remove from oven, cut each pissaladiere into 6 pieces, arrange on plates or a large platter, and serve.

TERMS AND TECHNIQUES *Docking:* Docking means to poke holes all over the surface of pastry or dough with the tines of a fork to keep it from raising too much.

VARIATION Rather than slicing each pissaladière, you can leave them whole and serve 1 to each person as an appetizer or light lunch.

EMBELLISHMENTS For a wonderful brunch dish, top each pissaladière with a fried egg: Heat a 10-inch sauté pan over medium heat. Pour in ½ teaspoon olive oil. Crack 2 eggs into the pan and cook sunny side up, approximately 2 minutes. Season with salt and pepper. Use a spatula to set each egg atop a pissaladière and repeat with another ½ teaspoon oil and 2 more eggs.

Top the pissaladière with thinly sliced, sushi-grade tuna, some Aïoli (page 30), and grilled or roasted Niçoise vegetables such as zucchini, tomato, fennel, and/or eggplant.

BASQUE-STYLE FRITTATA

SERVES 8 TO 10

The two distinguishing differences between the Italian omelet called *frittata* and the American version, which is based on the French one, is that a frittata is cooked "open faced," rather than being folded over, and it's often finished in the oven or under the broiler where the eggs firm up to the point that the frittata can be sliced like a pie. The Spanish make omelets similarly to the Italians. Here I use "frittata" to refer to my Basque-style version of the Spanish potato omelet called a *tortilla*, not to be confused with the flour tortillas that are so familiar to Americans.

Frittatas' firm quality makes it easy to serve them as hors d'oeuvres, cutting them into bite-size squares that can be picked up with toothpicks. This recipe is a useful model for countless other frittatas that can be whipped up on a moment's notice (see Variations).

PINCH CAYENNE

10 LARGE EGGS, BEATEN

1/4 POUND FINGERLING POTATOES (ABOUT 4 POTATOES)

4 CUPS COLD WATER

KOSHER SALT

2 TABLESPOONS OLIVE OIL

1/3 CUP ONION, VERY THINLY SLICED

1/3 CUP RED PEPPER, JULIENNE

1 TABLESPOON MINCED GARLIC

1/4 POUND CURED (DRY) CHORIZO, CUT INTO 1/4-INCH COINS

ABOUT 5 GRINDS WHITE PEPPER FROM A MILL

EXTRA VIRGIN OLIVE OIL

STIR the cayenne into the eggs and set aside.

PUT the potatoes and water into a heavy-bottomed, 2-quart pot. Add 1 tablespoon salt and bring to a boil over high heat. Lower the heat and cook the potatoes at a simmer until a fork pierces easily to the center of a potato, approximately 20 minutes. Drain in a colander and when cool enough to handle, cut crosswise into 1/4-inch-thick slices. Set aside.

PREHEAT the oven to 325°F. Put the olive oil in a 10-inch nonstick sauté pan and heat it over medium-low heat. Add the onion, red pepper, and garlic and cook until the vegetables begin to soften, 4 to 5 minutes. Add the chorizo and potatoes and gently stir. Add the eggs, stirring and scrambling them. Cook until they begin to set up, approximately 4 minutes, then transfer the pan to the oven and bake until the eggs turn nicely golden, approximately 7 minutes. Invert onto a large plate.

SEASON with salt and white pepper and drizzle with extra virgin olive oil. (If planning to refrigerate the frittata, see the next paragraph; don't season until just before serving.)

LET the frittata cool, then cut it into 1-inch squares. Serve warm or at room temperature with toothpicks or cocktail forks. The frittata can also be covered snugly with plastic wrap, refrigerated for up to 24 hours, and served cold.

VARIATIONS This would also be delicious with diced tomato and zucchini in the summer and sautéed wild mushrooms in the fall. You can also leave out the sausage or replace it with diced bacon.

Frittatas are also a good way to use leftovers in your refrigerator; chop them and add them to the egg mix.

EMBELLISHMENTS This is delicious with Aïoli (page 30) and/or Tapenade (page 33). It can also be topped with any type of cheese. For a finishing touch, drizzle the frittata with Parsley Pistou (page 248).

CROUSTADES

IN A CLASSIC *croustade* (the name comes from the Provençal *croustado*), bread or pastry is shaped or hollowed out to serve as a container for the dish's central ingredient(s). Like many contemporary chefs, I don't hollow out the slices of bread, which means that I'm essentially using the word croustade as a fancy way of saying "crouton." Here are three of my favorite croustades.

CROUSTADES WITH FENNEL-BASIL TAPENADE

SERVES 4 (3 CROUSTADES PER PERSON)

4 CUPS WATER

KOSHER SALT

2 SMALL FENNEL BULBS (ABOUT 1 POUND EACH), CLEANED AND CUT INTO ¼-INCH DICE (ABOUT 1 CUP DICE)

3 TABLESPOONS TAPENADE, PREFERABLY HOMEMADE (PAGE 33)

2 TABLESPOONS THINLY SLICED BASIL

12 DIAGONAL SLICES FRENCH BAGUETTE, ¼ INCH THICK

2 TABLESPOONS OLIVE OIL

PREHEAT the oven to 325°F. Pour the water into a 2-quart pot. Add 1 teaspoon salt and bring to a boil over high heat. Add the fennel and boil until tender, 3 to 4 minutes.

DRAIN the fennel and pat it dry with paper towels or a clean kitchen towel. Transfer to a bowl. Add the tapenade, basil, and ¼ teaspoon salt or to taste, and stir to combine.

THE fennel-basil tapenade can be covered and refrigerated for up to 2 days. If refrigerated, serve cold or let come to room temperature.

ARRANGE the bread in a single layer on a baking sheet without crowding. Drizzle both sides of the slices with the olive oil. Toast in the oven until lightly golden-brown, cooked through, and crunchy, approximately 5 minutes per side. Remove the sheet from the oven and let the croustades cool.

DIVIDE the tapenade mixture among the croustades, spreading it out into an even layer. Arrange the croustades on a platter or plate and serve within 15 to 20 minutes.

EMBELLISHMENTS Top each croustade with chopped Oven-Dried Tomatoes (page 31). You can also add chopped fennel fronds.

CROUSTADES with TOMATO CONFIT

SERVES 4 (3 CROUSTADES PER PERSON)

2 CUPS PLUS 2 TABLESPOONS OLIVE OIL,
PLUS MORE IF STORING TOMATO CONFIT

1 HEAD GARLIC, SPLIT HORIZONTALLY, EXCESS
PAPERY SKIN REMOVED

10 SPRIGS THYME

2 BAY LEAVES

1 TEASPOON KOSHER SALT

¼ TEASPOON FRESHLY GROUND BLACK
PEPPER

6 ROMA TOMATOES (ABOUT 1¼ POUNDS TOTAL
WEIGHT), PEELED (IF NECESSARY; SEE
TERMS AND TECHNIQUES, PAGE 95), HALVED,
AND SEEDED

12 DIAGONAL SLICES FRENCH BAGUETTE,
¼ INCH THICK

PREHEAT the oven to 225°F. Put the 2 cups oil, the garlic, thyme, bay leaves, salt, and pepper in a baking dish and stir to combine. Submerge the tomatoes in the mixture, cover with aluminum foil, and bake for 2 hours and 20 minutes. Remove the dish from the oven and let cool.

IF not using immediately, transfer the contents of the baking dish to a jar and cover with oil. Refrigerate for up to 1 week.

WHEN ready to proceed, preheat the oven to 325°F. Remove the tomatoes from the mixture and coarsely chop them.

ARRANGE the bread in a single layer on a baking sheet without crowding. Drizzle the slices with the remaining 2 tablespoons oil. Toast in the oven until lightly golden-brown, cooked through, and crunchy, approximately 5 minutes per side. Remove the sheet from the oven and let the croustades cool.

DIVIDE the tomato confit among the croustades, spreading it out into an even layer. Arrange the croustades on a platter or plate and serve within 15 to 20 minutes.

EMBELLISHMENTS Top these with crumbled goat cheese and/or thinly sliced basil leaves or olives. The confit itself is something I love to have on hand to toss with pasta or serve as a quick sauce or condiment.

CROUSTADES WITH ROQUEFORT SPREAD

SERVES 4 (3 CROUSTADES PER PERSON)

¼ POUND BLUE CHEESE, PREFERABLY ROQUEFORT, CRUMBLED (ABOUT ¾ CUP CRUMBLED), AT ROOM TEMPERATURE

1 TEASPOON HONEY

1 TABLESPOON SAUTERNES (OPTIONAL)

12 DIAGONAL SLICES FRENCH BAGUETTE, ¼ INCH THICK

2 TABLESPOONS OLIVE OIL

1½ TABLESPOONS CHOPPED TOASTED WALNUTS

PUT the cheese, honey, and Sauternes, if using, in the bowl of a standing mixer fitted with the paddle attachment. Paddle until all ingredients are incorporated and the cheese is soft. Remove the bowl from the mixer and set aside.

THE Roquefort spread can be covered and kept in the refrigerator for up to 3 days, during which time the flavors will develop.

PREHEAT the oven to 325°F. Arrange the bread in a single layer on a baking sheet without crowding. Drizzle the slices on both sides with the oil. Toast in the oven until lightly golden-brown, cooked through, and crunchy, approximately 5 minutes per side. Remove the sheet from the oven and let the croustades cool.

DIVIDE the Roquefort mixture among the croustades, spreading it out into an even layer. Top the Roquefort on each croustade with walnuts. Arrange the croustades on a platter or plate and serve within 15 to 20 minutes.

THE REASON The croustades should be served within 15 to 20 minutes of being assembled because you want the topping to flavor and slightly soften the toasted bread, but not to turn it soggy.

GOUGÈRES
FRENCH CHEESE PUFFS
MAKES 55 GOUGÈRES

G*ougères* is the classic French name for the hors d'oeuvre known to most Americans as cheese puffs. I prefer the traditional name *gougères* because it hints at the elegance they exude when properly made. These are the most popular hors d'oeuvre at Artisanal restaurant, and it's not at all unusual to see little paper-lined baskets full of these bite-size delicacies on more than half the tables in the dining room at any given time. One of the most appealing things about them in a home kitchen is convenience; they can be made ahead of time and reheated in the oven in a matter of minutes.

Gougères are the perfect choice for virtually any occasion. In addition to being just as appropriate to a summer afternoon cookout as they are to a black-tie New Year's Eve gala, they are a natural match for Champagne or sparkling wine and the savory of choice for wine tastings in Burgundy. In a home setting, they are a moveable piece in the menu-planning puzzle; call on them for a passed hors d'oeuvre, or serve them with soups or salads at the table.

---

4 TABLESPOONS (½ STICK) UNSALTED BUTTER

¼ CUP PLUS 2 TABLESPOONS MILK

½ CUP WATER

1¼ TEASPOONS COARSE SEA SALT

2 PINCHES CAYENNE

¾ CUP ALL-PURPOSE FLOUR SIFTED WITH ⅛ TEASPOON BAKING POWDER

1 CUP PLUS 2 TABLESPOONS COARSELY GRATED GRUYÈRE CHEESE

3 EGGS, AT ROOM TEMPERATURE

PREHEAT the oven to 400°F. Put the butter, ¼ cup milk, water, ¼ teaspoon sea salt, and the cayenne in a 2-quart saucepot and set over medium heat. Bring to a boil, then add the sifted flour and baking powder. Remove from heat. Stir well with a wooden spoon and return to the heat. Cook, stirring constantly, until the dough pulls away from the side of the pot, approximately 4 minutes. Remove the pot from the heat and transfer the dough to the bowl of an electric mixer fitted with the paddle attachment. Add 1 cup of the cheese and paddle on low (setting number 3) until just warm, approximately 2 minutes.

ADD the eggs to the mixer, 1 at a time, and paddle until the mixture comes together in a ball. Continue to mix for a total time of 10 minutes. The mixture should be cool.

LINE 2 large baking sheets with parchment paper. Place the dough into a pastry bag fitted with a #6 tip.

USE the pastry bag to pipe the gougères into small mounds on the baking sheets, approximately 1 inch in diameter and ½ inch high. Make sure that the gougères are evenly spaced, leaving ¼ inch between them. Place about 28 gougères on each baking sheet.

BRUSH the tops of the gougères with the remaining 2 tablespoons milk and sprinkle with the remaining cheese and sea salt.

PLACE the baking sheets in the oven and bake for 5 minutes. Turn the trays around and continue to bake until the gougères take on a deep, golden-brown color, approximately 7 more minutes. Serve hot from the oven or keep the gougères, loosely covered, at room temperature for up to 2 hours, then reheat in a 400°F oven for 2½ minutes.

THE REASON *The batter features baking powder and is paddled for a long time:* In order to produce a light and airy result, this recipe adds baking powder to the batter and calls for more paddling than most gougères recipes.

EMBELLISHMENTS Adapt *gougères* to include your favorite cheese, such as Roquefort or Parmigiano-Reggiano, in place of the Gruyère. No matter what the cheese, you can also add 1 to 2 tablespoons of minced herbs or chives to the batter, or add 3 tablespoons finely diced, browned, and cooled bacon to the batter just before transferring it to the pastry bag.

For a rich and elegant hors d'oeuvre, halve each *gougère* horizontally, place a generous teaspoon of Roquefort Spread (page 80) on the bottom half, and replace the top.

MINIATURE GRILLED CHEESE SANDWICHES

THE POWER OF GREAT RAW INGREDIENTS is never more apparent than when they're used to elevate a taken-for-granted staple. Here are two grilled cheese sandwiches that may change the way you think about the category. The first is a sly adaptation of a *croque monsieur*, the ultimate ham and cheese sandwich, which is traditionally made with ham and gruyère, coated with egg batter, and grilled to perfection. It was inspired by a popular combination, cream cheese and smoked salmon. The second brings a balance of sweet, tart apple and smoky, crunchy bacon to the deceptively humble confines of a cheddar cheese sandwich. In both cases, high-quality bread takes the sandwich to a new level.

SMOKED SALMON "CROQUE MONSIEUR"

SERVES 4

¼ POUND THINLY SLICED SMOKED SALMON

4 SLICES ARTISANAL COUNTRY BREAD, ½ INCH THICK, FROM A MEDIUM TO LARGE LOAF

1 CUP (LIGHTLY PACKED) GRATED GRUYÈRE (FROM ABOUT 4½ OUNCES CHEESE) AT ROOM TEMPERATURE

2 TABLESPOONS UNSALTED BUTTER, SOFTENED AT ROOM TEMPERATURE

DIVIDE the salmon slices between 2 slices of bread. Top each salmon portion with ½ cup grated Gruyère, then with 2 more slices of salmon. Cover each sandwich with a slice of bread. Spread the outside of each sandwich with ½ tablespoon butter per side.

HEAT a 12-inch, nonstick, ovenproof sauté pan over medium heat. Add the sandwiches and cook until golden-brown and the cheese has melted, 3 to 4 minutes per side, pressing down with a spatula to flatten the sandwich and integrate the ingredients. (If the bread looks golden and done but the cheese hasn't completely melted, arrange the pieces in a single layer on a cookie sheet and finish the sandwiches in an oven preheated to 350°F.)

TRANSFER the sandwiches to a cutting board and cut them into bite-size pieces, about 8 per sandwich. Arrange the pieces on a plate or platter and serve.

VARIATION Needless to say, you can also serve these without the salmon, as grilled cheese sandwiches in their own right.

CHEDDAR, APPLE, AND BACON SANDWICH

SERVES 4

8 SLICES APPLE-SMOKED BACON (ABOUT 6 OUNCES TOTAL WEIGHT)

6 OUNCES FARMSTEAD CHEDDAR, SUCH AS SHELBURNE FARMS, GRATED (ABOUT 1 CUP GRATED) AT ROOM TEMPERATURE

4 SLICES COUNTRY BREAD, ½ INCH THICK, FROM A MEDIUM TO LARGE LOAF

1 QUARTER GRANNY SMITH APPLE, PEELED, SEEDS REMOVED, SLICED 1/16-INCH THICK, IDEALLY ON A MANDOLINE

2 TABLESPOONS UNSALTED BUTTER, AT ROOM TEMPERATURE

PREHEAT the oven to 325°F. Arrange the bacon in a single layer on a baking sheet and bake in the oven, turning once after 10 minutes, until crispy, approximately 20 minutes, depending on the thickness of the slices. Remove the sheet from the oven and drain the bacon on paper towels.

DIVIDE half of the cheese between 2 slices of bread. Divide the apple slices between the open-faced sandwiches. Put 4 slices of cooked bacon on top of each sandwich. Top with the remaining cheese. Cover the sandwiches with the remaining slices of bread. Spread the outside of each sandwich with ½ tablespoon butter per side (1 tablespoon per sandwich total). Heat a 12-inch, nonstick, ovenproof sauté pan over medium heat. Add the sandwiches and cook until golden-brown and the cheese has melted, 3 to 4 minutes per side, pressing down with a spatula to flatten the sandwiches and integrate the ingredients. (If the bread looks golden and done but the cheese hasn't completely melted, arrange the pieces in a single layer on a cookie sheet and finish the sandwiches in an oven preheated to 350°F.)

TRANSFER the sandwiches to a cutting board and cut them into eighths. Arrange the pieces on a plate or platter and serve.

FONDUES

J UST ABOUT ALL OF MY FAVORITE THINGS about food come together in fondues. These little cauldrons of melted cheese are steeped in tradition, simple to prepare, fun to eat, and endlessly flexible. A ceramic fondue pot is the classic way to make it, an aesthetically appealing choice to be sure. But fondue made in a stainless steel pot can taste just as sublime. If not using a fondue pot, you will need to briefly return the fondue to the stovetop after about 5 minutes to keep it melted and warm. You can also keep the fondue's pot warm on a hot plate at the table.

To me, fondue is the ultimate selection "après ski" or as a winter's day lunch, accompanied by a green salad and a glass of wine. Everyone knows about dipping bread cubes in fondue, but other accompaniments such as sliced raw vegetables, smoked and cured meats, and even pickled vegetables are just as traditional and satisfying.

ARTISANAL BLEND FONDUE

SERVES 6

KOSHER SALT

I CLOVE GARLIC, PEELED AND CUT

3 CUPS GRATED HOCH YBRIG, EMMENTHALER, AND/OR BEAUFORT (IDEALLY I CUP EACH, FROM ABOUT 4 OUNCES EACH), AT ROOM TEMPERATURE

I TABLESPOON PLUS 2 TEASPOONS CORNSTARCH

I CUP DRY WHITE WINE

I TEASPOON FRESHLY SQUEEZED LEMON JUICE

PINCH NUTMEG

BLACK PEPPER IN A MILL

PUT 1 teaspoon salt in a fondue pot or a heavy-bottomed, 2-quart, stainless steel saucepan. Vigorously rub the exposed end of the garlic over the surface of the pot, starting in the salt and coating the entire surface. Discard the garlic.

IN a medium bowl, combine the grated cheese and cornstarch, mixing well to distribute the cornstarch evenly. Set aside.

POUR the wine and lemon juice into the prepared fondue pot and bring to a boil over medium-high heat.

ONCE the liquid has come to a boil, slowly add the cheese and cornstarch mixture, whisking continuously.

ONCE all of the cheese has been added, cook over medium heat for 1 minute. Season with the nutmeg, salt, and 4 grinds of pepper, or to taste.

REMOVE the pot from the heat and serve.

THE REASON *The garlic is cut:* Cutting the garlic exposes its juices to the fondue pot, which is essential to coating the pot.

Cornstarch and lemon juice are added to the cheese: Cornstarch thickens the cheese in fondue and the lemon juice helps keep it smooth rather than stringy when melted. (The acid in the wine helps achieve this effect as well, but I add lemon juice to ensure it.)

EMBELLISHMENTS Serve with cubed bread. Day-old bread is best, but any crusty bread will work well. Artisanal Blend Fondue may also be served with boiled fingerling potatoes, sautéed beef tips, pickled vegetables, air-dried beef, Kielbasa, and/or sausage.

STILTON AND PORT FONDUE
SERVES 6

I CUP PORT

¼ CUP CORNSTARCH

2 TABLESPOONS CREAM CHEESE, AT ROOM TEMPERATURE

12 OUNCES STILTON, CRUMBLED (ABOUT 1²⁄₃ CUPS CRUMBLED), AT ROOM TEMPERATURE

KOSHER SALT

IN a medium bowl, combine the port and cornstarch, mixing well to dissolve the cornstarch. Pour the mixture into a fondue pot or heavy-bottomed, 2-quart, stainless steel saucepan, and bring to a boil over medium-high heat.

ONCE the liquid has come to a boil slowly, add the cream cheese, whisking continuously. Make sure each addition is completely melted and incorporated before the next addition. Then add the Stilton. Once all of the cheese has been added, cook over medium heat for 1 more minute.

SEASON with salt to taste. Remove from heat and serve.

THE REASON *Cream cheese is added to the Stilton:* Stilton is a very fatty cheese, which means it separates more easily than other cheeses. The cream cheese helps stabilize the Stilton, preventing separation.

EMBELLISHMENTS Serve with cubed bread. Walnut bread is best, but any crusty bread will work well. Stilton Fondue may also be served with boiled fingerling potatoes, sautéed beef tips, pickled vegetables, air-dried beef, or cubed pears.

FONTINA AND ROSEMARY FONDUE

SERVES 6

KOSHER SALT

1 CLOVE GARLIC, PEELED AND CUT

3 CUPS SHREDDED FONTINA (FROM 12 OUNCES CHEESE), AT ROOM TEMPERATURE

2 TABLESPOONS PLUS 2 TEASPOONS CORNSTARCH

1 CUP DRY WHITE WINE

1 TEASPOON FRESHLY SQUEEZED LEMON JUICE

BLACK PEPPER IN A MILL

2 TEASPOONS CHOPPED ROSEMARY LEAVES

1 TABLESPOON WHITE TRUFFLE OIL (OPTIONAL)

PUT 1 teaspoon salt in a fondue pot or a heavy-bottomed, 2-quart, stainless steel saucepan. Vigorously rub the exposed end of the garlic over the surface of the pot, starting in the salt and coating the entire surface. Discard the garlic.

IN a medium bowl, combine the shredded cheese and cornstarch, mixing well to distribute the cornstarch evenly. Set aside.

ADD the wine and lemon juice to the prepared fondue pot and bring to a boil over medium-high heat.

ONCE the liquid has come to a boil, slowly add the cheese and cornstarch mixture, whisking continuously.

ONCE all of the cheese has melted, continue to cook over medium heat for 1 minute. Season with salt and 4 grinds of pepper, or to taste. Stir in the rosemary and truffle oil, if using, and mix well.

REMOVE the pot from the heat and serve.

EMBELLISHMENTS Serve with cubed bread. Day-old bread is best, but any crusty bread will work well. The Fontina Fondue may also be served with roasted fingerling potatoes, sautéed beef tips, pickled vegetables, or air-dried beef.

CLASSIC SWISS FONDUE

SERVES 6

KOSHER SALT

1 CLOVE GARLIC, PEELED AND CUT

12 OUNCES (6 OUNCES EACH) GRUYÈRE AND
EMMENTHALER, COARSELY GRATED (ABOUT
3 CUPS GRATED), AT ROOM TEMPERATURE

2 TABLESPOONS PLUS 2 TEASPOONS
CORNSTARCH

1 CUP DRY WHITE WINE

2 TEASPOONS FRESHLY SQUEEZED LEMON
JUICE

BLACK PEPPER IN A MILL

PINCH NUTMEG

3 TABLESPOONS KIRSCH

PUT 1 teaspoon salt in a fondue pot or a heavy-bottomed, 2-quart, stainless steel saucepan. Vigorously rub the exposed end of the garlic over the surface of the pot, starting in the salt and coating the entire surface. Discard the garlic.

IN a medium bowl, combine the grated cheese and cornstarch, mixing well to distribute the cornstarch evenly. Set aside.

ADD the wine and lemon juice to the prepared fondue pot and bring to a boil over medium-high heat.

ONCE the liquid has come to a boil, slowly add the cheese and cornstarch mixture, whisking continuously.

ONCE all of the cheese has melted, continue to cook over medium heat for 1 minute. Season with salt, 4 grinds of pepper, and a pinch of nutmeg, or to taste, then stir in the Kirsch.

REMOVE from heat and serve.

EMBELLISHMENTS Serve with cubed bread. Day-old bread is best, but any crusty bread will work well. Classic Swiss Fondue may also be served with boiled fingerling potatoes, sautéed beef tips, pickled vegetables, or air-dried beef.

If you like, enjoy this with a glass of chilled Kirsch like they do in Switzerland.

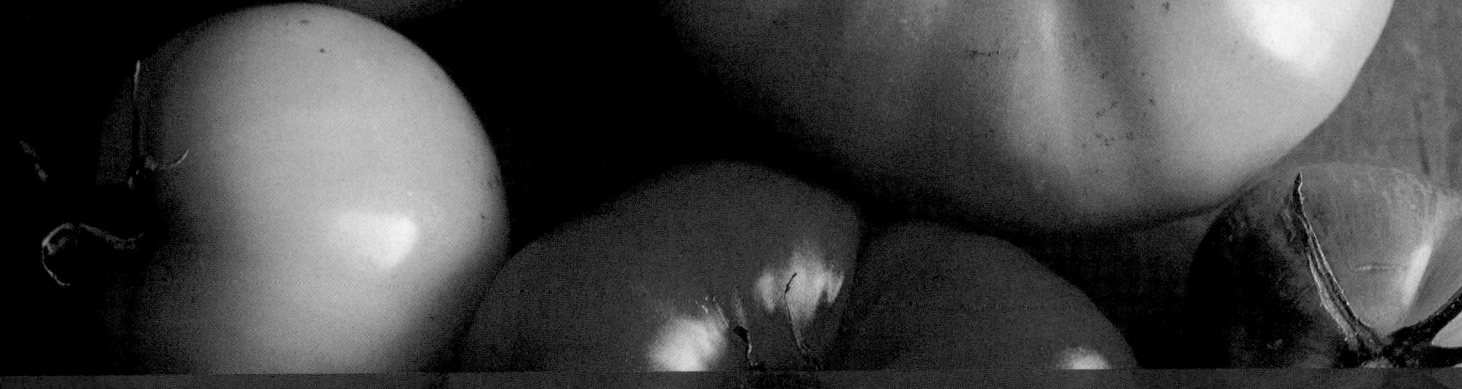

SALADS AND FIRST COURSES

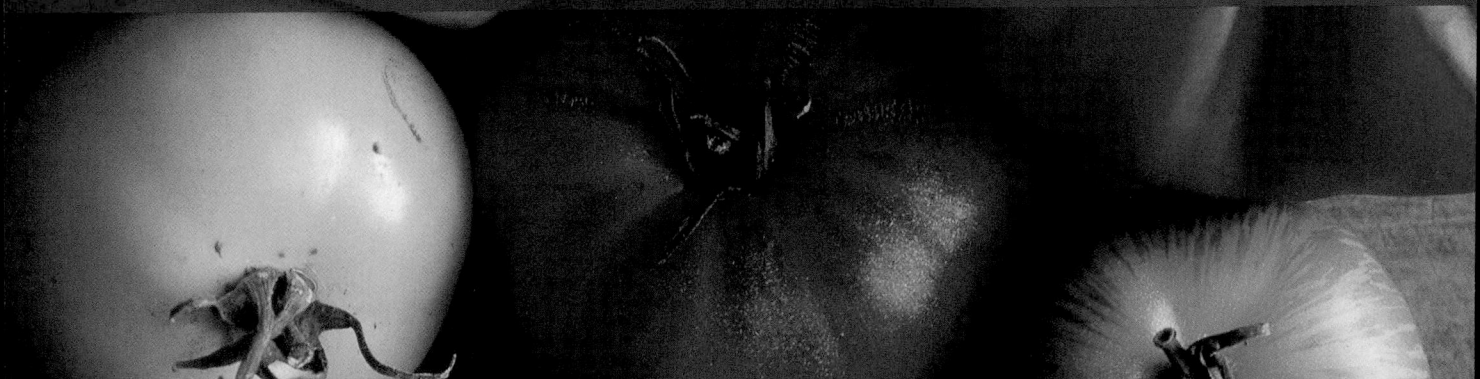

WHEN I THINK BACK ON THE TIME I SPENT WORKING IN FRANCE, some of the most indelible memories are of exquisitely simple lunches enjoyed in a Parisian bistro, at an open-air countryside café, or during weekends with friends, preparing meals spontaneously from ingredients purchased at neighborhood markets. Like the dishes that I enjoyed in the meals, the ones in this chapter are very flexible: The salads can be first or main courses, and many of the cooked dishes can be a meal in themselves, especially at lunch, when relatively modest portions prevail.

I'm a devoutly seasonal chef. The different ingredients that each time of year brings stimulate my appetite and creativity. Most of the dishes in this chapter are seasonally inspired, especially those featuring spring and summer fruits and vegetables with relatively short annual availability.

Not all of these dishes are created equal. Some, such as the Beet Salad with Goat Cheese Mousse and Walnut Vinaigrette (page 107) and Râclette with Fingerling Potatoes (page 122), are more appropriate as a small lunch or for an informal gathering. A few, such as Lobster with Vanilla–Brown Butter Vinaigrette (page 131) and Duck Pastrami with Pomegranate Vinaigrette (page 117), are admittedly ambitious, more suitable for a dinner party or a day when you simply feel like losing yourself in a recipe and perhaps learning a new kitchen technique.

Many of the recipes in this chapter feature at least one component that's presented separately. This is to facilitate making vinaigrettes and garnishes in advance. It's also to make it easier for you to call on elements like Anchovy Toasts (page 96) and Parmesan Tuilles (page 100) in your own day-to-day cooking, when they can be used to add an uncommon flourish that will perk up even the most ordinary of salads.

HEIRLOOM TOMATO SALAD WITH ANCHOVY TOAST

SERVES 4

At Picholine restaurant, the menu page that lists nightly specials also names a daily tomato preparation in July, August, and September, when we fête this fruit in a different way every day. Tomatoes are one of my favorite seasonal foods and this is one of several recipes celebrating them that you'll find throughout this book, most of them adapted from Picholine dishes.

In supermarkets, tomatoes seem to know no season; they are always plentiful, piled high in bins in the produce section. But those largely bland fruits, even the hothouse ones marketed as "vine-ripened," don't stack up at all next to in-season, locally grown tomatoes. When tomatoes are not in season I simply don't use them anywhere on the menu. I'm happy to adhere to this policy because the anticipation it creates for late-summer tomatoes makes their annual arrival truly exciting. That said, at home you can, in a pinch, use Oven-Dried Tomatoes (page 31).

The most dramatic-looking and flavorful tomatoes are categorized as heirloom, grown from ancient seed varieties that almost became extinct a few decades ago. (According to *Taylor's Guide to Heirloom Vegetables,* to qualify as "heirloom," a variety of tomato must have been in existence for more than fifty years, be "true to type" from seeds saved from each fruit, and have a history or folklore of its own.) Heirloom tomatoes come in imperfect shapes and a staggering array of colors, including deep purple, bright orange, and crimson red; one especially beguiling one, Garden Peach, has a peachlike fuzz covering its surface. These tomatoes are almost exclusively available at farmers' markets, roadside stands, and upscale supermarkets. Sometimes they're so ripe that they are kept under glass like museum pieces and need to be handled gingerly. They can also be unattractive to the eye, looking as though they fell off the truck on the way to the market. Don't be put off by appearances; these details actually signal that the tomatoes are ripe and at their absolute peak of flavor.

Whatever their stage of freshness, tomatoes should never be refrigerated, because refrigeration compromises their flavor; keep them at room temperature right up until you plan to serve or cook them.

3 TABLESPOONS RED-WINE VINEGAR

½ CUP EXTRA VIRGIN OLIVE OIL

3 CLOVES GARLIC CONFIT (PAGE 36), OR
1 CLOVE MINCED FRESH GARLIC

1 TEASPOON KOSHER SALT

2 POUNDS HEIRLOOM TOMATOES, PEELED (SEE
TERMS AND TECHNIQUES), CORED, AND CUT
INTO BITE-SIZED PIECES OF VARYING
SHAPES, BASED ON THE NATURAL SHAPE
OF THE INDIVIDUAL TOMATOES

BLACK PEPPER IN A MILL

2 BUNCHES ARUGULA (ABOUT 2 OUNCES
EACH), TOUGH STEMS REMOVED, WELL
WASHED IN SEVERAL CHANGES OF COLD
WATER AND SPUN DRY

ANCHOVY TOASTS (RECIPE FOLLOWS)

MAKE the vinaigrette by whisking together the vinegar, oil, garlic confit, and salt in a mixing bowl.

PUT the tomatoes in a bowl, add half the vinaigrette, and gently toss. Cover and let marinate for at least 30 minutes, or up to 3 hours, at room temperature.

WHEN ready to serve, season the tomatoes generously with about 10 turns of the pepper mill. Add the arugula to the bowl holding the remaining vinaigrette and toss well. Divide the salad and tomatoes among 4 salad plates and lean an anchovy toast against the salad on each plate. Serve.

TERMS AND TECHNIQUES *Peeling tomatoes:* At home I rarely peel tomatoes, but if tomatoes have a firm skin, peeling them helps them integrate more seamlessly into a dish. Some types of tomatoes do not need to be peeled, but when peeling is necessary, here is how to do it:

Bring 4 quarts of water to a boil in a pot set over high heat. Fill a large bowl halfway with ice water. Remove the core from the top of the tomatoes (where the stem meets the flesh) with a paring knife, and score the bottom of each tomato with shallow X. Submerge the tomatoes in boiling water and blanch until the peel begins to pull away from the flesh, 10 to 15 seconds. Use tongs or a slotted spoon to transfer the tomatoes to the ice water to keep them from cooking further. Remove the skins by pulling them off by hand, or with the aid of a paring knife.

THE REASON *The tomatoes are preseasoned with vinaigrette:* Letting tomatoes marinate in vinaigrette or even just preseasoning them with salt and pepper is, generally speaking, a good idea in raw preparations. The seasonings extract some of the tomato's juices and deepen the overall flavor of the dish. Those juices, by the way, are called "tomato water," and can be poured into demitasse cups and served alongside this and other tomato dishes.

EMBELLISHMENTS Tomatoes pair well with a wide variety of flavors: Add a scattering of basil chiffonade, or a drizzle of basil pesto or Parsley Pistou (page 248) to this salad. Crumbled blue cheese, goat cheese, or a dollop of ricotta cheese are also fine additions, as is sliced mozzarella tossed with the tomatoes.

ANCHOVY TOASTS MAKES 4 TOASTS

Pair this decidedly Provençal flourish with salads and soups featuring the defining flavors of that region such as lemons, olives, and roasted red peppers.

- 4 CROSSWISE SLICES COUNTRY BREAD (BOULE), APPROXIMATELY 6 INCHES HIGH AND ½ INCH THICK

- 2 TABLESPOONS (PACKED) FINELY CHOPPED ANCHOVY FILLETS (FROM ABOUT 8 FILLETS, SOAKED, DRAINED, AND PATTED DRY; SEE PAGE 11)

- 3 CLOVES GARLIC CONFIT (PAGE 36), OR 1 CLOVE MINCED FRESH GARLIC

- 2 TABLESPOONS EXTRA VIRGIN OLIVE OIL

- 2 TABLESPOONS FINELY GRATED PARMIGIANO-REGGIANO

- 2 TABLESPOONS FINELY SNIPPED FLAT-LEAF PARSLEY

PREHEAT the broiler. Arrange the bread slices in a single layer on a cookie sheet and broil until crisp and lightly golden, approximately 1 minute. Turn the slices over and broil until crisp and lightly golden on the other side; the bread should be crusty on the outside, but still chewy. Remove the sheet from the oven and set aside to cool.

MEANWHILE, put the anchovies and garlic confit into the bowl of a mortar and pestle and mash into a paste. Add the oil and Parmigiano-Reggiano and continue to mash into a coarse but spreadable mixture. Spread the paste on the toasts, then cut the toasts in half.

THESE toasts can be kept at room temperature, loosely covered with plastic wrap, for up to 1 hour. When ready to serve, pass under the broiler for 30 seconds, then finish with the parsley.

THE REASON *Garlic confit is added to the anchovy mixture:* In addition to adding a depth of flavor, the confit causes the mixture to emulsify.

EMBELLISHMENT Brush or drizzle tomato water (see The Reason, page 95) over the croutons before adding the anchovy mixture.

SPRING VEGETABLE SALAD WITH PARMESAN TUILLE AND HERB VINAIGRETTE

SERVES 4

A fragrant tribute to the bounty of spring, this salad features a variety of blanched seasonal vegetables dressed with a complex, herbaceous vinaigrette. The salad should be light in every regard: the vegetables blanched and cooled so they retain their garden freshness, the greens spun dry to the point of seeming weightlessness and lightly dressed, and the Parmesan shards and tuille adding just a hint of salt and crunch.

---

8 CUPS WATER

KOSHER SALT

1 CUP FAVA BEANS, FROM ABOUT 2 POUNDS FAVAS IN THE POD

12 OUNCES MEDIUM ASPARAGUS, TRIMMED AND CUT INTO 3-INCH PIECES STARTING FROM THE TOP OF THE TIP

½ CUP FRESH, SWEET ENGLISH PEAS (ABOUT 2 OUNCES)

1 POUND BABY ARTICHOKES (ABOUT 5 ARTICHOKES), STEM AND OUTER LEAVES REMOVED, QUARTERED AND KEPT IN COLD WATER ACIDULATED WITH 1 TABLESPOON LEMON JUICE (SEE TERMS AND TECHNIQUES) (OPTIONAL)

1 TABLESPOON OLIVE OIL

½ CUP WATER OR WHITE CHICKEN STOCK (PAGE 45)

¼ CUP PLUS 2 TABLESPOONS SHERRY VINAIGRETTE (RECIPE FOLLOWS)

2 TABLESPOONS FINELY SLICED CHERVIL

1 TABLESPOON FINELY SLICED CHIVES

1 TEASPOON FINELY SLICED TARRAGON LEAVES

1 TEASPOON FINELY SLICED DILL

2 TABLESPOONS FINELY SLICED BASIL LEAVES

1½ CUPS (ABOUT 2 OUNCES) LOOSELY PACKED PEA LEAVES, BIBB LETTUCE LEAVES, OR FIELD GREENS

¼ CUP PARMIGIANO-REGGIANO SHARDS, SHAVED WITH A VEGETABLE PEELER (FROM ABOUT 1 OUNCE CHEESE)

PARMESAN TUILLE (RECIPE FOLLOWS)

POUR the water into a large pot, add 2 tablespoons salt, and bring to a boil over high heat. Fill a large bowl halfway with ice water. Add the fava beans to the boiling water and blanch for 1 minute. Remove them with a strainer or slotted spoon and immediately transfer them to the ice water to stop the cooking and preserve their color. Remove them with the strainer or spoon, drain them, remove the outer skin from the beans, and set the beans aside in a clean, dry bowl.

WHEN the water returns to the boil, add the asparagus pieces and blanch for 1½ minutes. Remove them with a strainer or slotted spoon and immediately transfer them to the ice water. Remove them with the strainer or spoon and transfer them to the bowl with the favas.

WHEN the water returns to the boil, add the peas and blanch them for 1 minute. Use the strainer or spoon to transfer them to the ice water, then use the strainer or spoon to transfer them to the bowl with the other vegetables.

PAT all of the vegetables dry with paper towels.

DRAIN the artichokes if using and spin them dry in a salad spinner, or pat them dry with paper towels. Heat the olive oil in a heavy-bottomed sauté pan set over medium-high heat. Add the artichokes and cook, stirring or shaking the pan frequently, until crisp but still firm and holding their shape, approximately 3 minutes. Add the ½ cup water or chicken stock, and continue cooking until the liquid evaporates, 3 to 4 more minutes. Let the artichokes cool to room temperature, then add them to the bowl with the other vegetables.

PUT ¼ cup of the vinaigrette in the bowl with the vegetables. Add the chervil, chives, tarragon, dill, and basil, season with salt, and gently toss to coat the vegetables.

DIVIDE the vegetables evenly among 4 chilled salad plates. Put the pea leaves and 2 tablespoons of the vinaigrette in another mixing bowl and toss gently. Divide the Parmigiano-Reggiano shards among the salads, scattering them over the top. Top each with a tuille and serve.

TERMS AND TECHNIQUES *Trimming an artichoke:* Pull off the tough outer leaves. Use a large chef's knife to remove the stem, if any. Cut the choke just above the heart, about 1½ inches from the stem end. Use a paring knife to trim away the green leaves until you get down to the yellow part (the heart). Cut the artichoke in half lengthwise and scoop out the hairy choke. Cut the halves lengthwise to make quarters. Keep in water acidulated with lemon juice to prevent discoloration.

THE REASON *The vegetables are patted dry:* This keeps any excess water from diluting the vinaigrette when they're dressed.

SHERRY VINAIGRETTE MAKES ABOUT 1½ CUPS

This is a useful vinaigrette to have in your repertoire, appropriate to most salads, and a good "house dressing" for everyday cooking.

1 TABLESPOON DIJON MUSTARD

¼ CUP SHERRY VINEGAR

½ TEASPOON KOSHER SALT

½ TEASPOON FRESHLY GROUND WHITE PEPPER

1 CUP EXTRA VIRGIN OLIVE OIL

1 TO 2 TABLESPOONS WATER, IF NEEDED

PUT the mustard, vinegar, salt, and pepper in a blender. With the motor running, slowly add the oil in a thin stream to form an emulsified vinaigrette. (You can also whisk the vinaigrette by hand in a mixing bowl.) If the vinaigrette seems too thick, blend in 1 to 2 tablespoons water.

THE vinaigrette can be covered and refrigerated for up to 3 weeks. Let it warm slightly before serving.

VARIATION This dressing is also very good with Banyuls vinegar in place of the sherry vinegar.

EMBELLISHMENT Add diced shallots to the dressing after blending. If you do this, only refrigerate it for up to 1 week.

PARMESAN TUILLE MAKES 4 TUILLES

This impressive-looking tuille is a perfect garnish for many salads. Formed into smaller disks rather than oval tuilles, they can be served as an hors d'oeuvre on their own. You will need a coffee can, canister, or rolling pin, to shape the tuilles.

¼ CUP PLUS 2 TABLESPOONS FINELY GRATED PARMIGIANO-REGGIANO (FROM ABOUT 1½ OUNCES CHEESE)

PREHEAT the oven to 325°F. Form 4 tuilles on a nonstick cookie sheet by putting the cheese on the sheet in 2-tablespoon portions, shaping each one so it's 2 inches wide and 6 inches long. (It's all right, even desirable, for the tuilles to look a bit airy; this will keep them from becoming too thick and chewy.) Repeat to form 4 tuilles.

PUT the cookie sheet in the oven and bake until the tuilles are lightly golden, 4 to 5 minutes, turning the pan 180 degrees after 2½ minutes. Turn the coffee can on its side. Remove the sheet from the oven, let cool for 1 minute, and use an offset spatula to carefully remove the tuilles, one at a time, and set them over the can, canister, or rolling pin; as they cool, they will achieve the desired concave shape and turn hard and crispy. The tuilles are very fragile, so handle them carefully.

THE tuilles can be made in advance and kept, covered, at room temperature for up to 6 hours.

SUMMER MEDITERRANEAN SALAD WITH BAGÑA CAUDA SAUCE

SERVES 4

T here's no time of year that puts me more in mind of Provence than summer, and this salad puts the region right there on the plate with red peppers, fennel, zucchini, and eggplant. *Bagña cauda* (the name means "hot bath") sauce originated in Piedmont, Italy, where it's made with anchovies, garlic, and olive oil, but I've turned it into a Provençal condiment with the addition of olives, capers, basil, and lemon zest.

BAGÑA CAUDA SAUCE

¾ CUP EXTRA VIRGIN OLIVE OIL

6 (PREFERABLY SALT-PACKED) ANCHOVY FILLETS (SOAKED, DRAINED, AND PATTED DRY; SEE PAGE 11)

24 NIÇOISE OLIVES, PITTED

1½ TEASPOONS BRINE-PACKED CAPERS, RINSED AND DRAINED

1 CLOVE GARLIC, PEELED

¼ CUP FINELY SLICED BASIL LEAVES PLUS 12 LEAVES BASIL FOR GARNISH

1 TEASPOON FINELY GRATED LEMON ZEST

6 CUPS WATER

½ POUND BABY FENNEL, CLEANED, OR 1 MEDIUM BULB, CLEANED AND CUT INTO 8 LENGTHWISE PIECES

½ POUND ZUCCHINI, CUT DIAGONALLY INTO ¼-INCH-THICK ROUNDS

½ POUND JAPANESE EGGPLANT OR REGULAR EGGPLANT, CUT DIAGONALLY INTO ¼-INCH-THICK SLICES

¾ POUND RED BELL PEPPERS (ABOUT 2 PEPPERS)

1½ POUNDS TOMATOES, PEELED (SEE PAGE 95), CORED, HALVED, AND CUT INTO ¼-INCH SLICES

MAKE the bagña cauda sauce: Pour ½ cup of the extra virgin olive oil into a saucepan over medium heat and heat until the oil is warm, 2 to 3 minutes. Meanwhile, put the anchovies, olives, capers, garlic, sliced basil, and lemon zest in a mortar and pestle and pulverize to a paste. (This can also be done in the bowl of a food processor fitted with the steel blade.) Transfer the paste to a bowl and pour the hot oil over it; cover and let steep for 2 hours. Once cool, the sauce can be covered and refrigerated for up to 3 days.

POUR the 6 cups of water into a 2-quart, heavy-bottomed pot and bring it to a boil over high heat. Fill a large bowl halfway with ice water. Add the fennel to the boiling water and cook until tender, approximately 6 minutes. Use tongs to transfer the fennel to the ice water to shock it and stop the cooking. Drain, halve lengthwise, and set aside.

PREHEAT the broiler. Rub the zucchini and eggplant slices with some of the remaining oil to coat them, arrange in a single layer on a cookie sheet, and broil until just barely cooked, 1 minute per side, but no longer; this is a summer dish, so you want each vegetable to retain its flavor and crunch and not turn too soft. Transfer them to a bowl and set aside.

PREHEAT the oven to 375°F. Rub the peppers with the remaining olive oil. Arrange them on a cookie sheet in a single layer and roast until the skin blisters, approximately 14 minutes. Transfer them to a bowl and cover the bowl with plastic wrap. Let the peppers steam in their own heat for 10 minutes to loosen their skins, then use a paring knife to remove the peppers' skin. Seed the peppers. Cut each pepper lengthwise into 6 slices and add to the bowl with the zucchini and eggplant. Add the fennel halves and tomato slices to the bowl.

DRIZZLE ½ cup of the bagña cauda over the vegetables and toss gently to coat the vegetables with the sauce. (You may not use all of the sauce.) Divide the salad decoratively among 4 chilled salad plates. Top each salad with 3 basil leaves. Drizzle any extra sauce around the salad. Serve.

VARIATION The bagña cauda sauce also goes well with grilled steaks, lamb, poultry, and fish. For a main dish, top each salad with 2 grilled lamb chops (see cover photo).

EMBELLISHMENT Grill the vegetables to add another dimension of flavor to this salad.

ARTICHOKE SALAD WITH LEMON VINAIGRETTE

SERVES 4

Artichokes and lemon are a match made in culinary heaven, and this is even more true of roasted artichokes because the lemon cuts both the natural mineral richness of the vegetable and the lightly charred flavor produced in the oven. Add cool, whipped ricotta cheese and you're guaranteed an enticing combination in each and every bite.

---

24 BABY ARTICHOKES (ABOUT 6 POUNDS TOTAL WEIGHT)

⅓ CUP OLIVE OIL

2 CLOVES GARLIC, LIGHTLY CRUSHED IN THEIR SKINS

1 TABLESPOON THYME LEAVES

KOSHER SALT

BLACK PEPPER IN MILL

¼ CUP RICOTTA CHEESE, PLUS 4 DOLLOPS FOR SERVING

½ CUP TOMATO CONFIT (PAGE 79), OR DICED, SEEDED, FRESH TOMATO

2 BUNCHES ARUGULA (ABOUT 4 OUNCES TOTAL WEIGHT), TOUGH STEMS DISCARDED, WELL WASHED IN SEVERAL CHANGES OF COLD WATER AND SPUN DRY

LEMON VINAIGRETTE (RECIPE FOLLOWS)

2 TABLESPOONS CRUMBLED RICOTTA SALATA, OR 2 TABLESPOONS GRATED PARMIGIANO-REGGIANO OR PECORINO ROMANO

PREHEAT the oven to 375°F. Clean and peel the artichokes down to the heart. (See page 99 for instructions on trimming an artichoke.) Cut each one in half and remove the choke.

SPREAD the artichokes out on a rimmed cookie sheet. Drizzle with the olive oil and add the garlic and thyme. Season with salt and pepper, turning the artichokes to coat them evenly with oil and seasoning. Roast, shaking the pan from time to time, until the artichokes are nicely browned around the edges, 15 to 18 minutes. Let cool.

MEANWHILE, put the ricotta in a small mixing bowl. Season with salt and about 4 grinds of pepper, or to taste, and whip with a whisk or rubber spatula until creamy.

PUT the artichokes, tomato confit, and arugula in a stainless-steel mixing bowl and drizzle with the lemon vinaigrette. Toss to dress the salad with the vinaigrette. Divide the salad among 4 salad plates, being sure to include a good mix of ingredients in each serving. Top each salad with a dollop of ricotta cheese, and sprinkle with crumbled ricotta salata. Serve.

EMBELLISHMENT Garnish each serving with thinly sliced raw baby artichokes dressed with lemon juice and extra virgin olive oil. Or add sliced vegetables such as fennel and zucchini, arranging them artfully around the plate.

LEMON VINAIGRETTE MAKES ABOUT ⅔ CUP

This vinaigrette is delicious with spring vegetables, or drizzled over fish or poultry.

3 TABLESPOONS GARLIC CONFIT (PAGE 36), OR 1 CLOVE FRESH GARLIC, MINCED

3 TABLESPOONS FRESHLY SQUEEZED LEMON JUICE

1 TABLESPOON BALSAMIC VINEGAR

¾ TEASPOON KOSHER SALT

½ TEASPOON FRESHLY GROUND BLACK PEPPER

½ CUP EXTRA-VIRGIN OLIVE OIL

PUT the garlic confit, lemon juice, balsamic vinegar, salt, and pepper in a standing blender. With the motor running, slowly add the oil in a thin stream to make an emulsified vinaigrette. Transfer to a bowl.

THIS vinaigrette can be covered and refrigerated for up to 1 week. Let come to room temperature before serving.

BEET SALAD with GOAT CHEESE MOUSSE and WALNUT VINAIGRETTE

SERVES 4

One of the most enduring pairings to grace a salad plate is the classic bistro duo of creamy, fresh goat cheese and cooled, roasted beets. I could go on and on about what makes this combination so compelling. First and most important, a great many people simply love both of these ingredients. Second, when gathered together, they add up to more than the sum of their already delicious parts: The sweet beets perfectly complement the tang of the cheese. Like Bogart and Bacall, beets and goat cheese have chemistry; they belong together.

Another remarkable thing about this combination is that it's complete—beets and goat cheese are all you need for a salad—yet it invites embellishment. Here, the flavors are enhanced with chopped, toasted walnuts, the clean crunch of Belgian endive, peppery arugula, and walnut vinaigrette.

1½ POUNDS BEETS (ABOUT 6 BEETS) WITH THE SKIN ON, RINSED AND SCRUBBED UNDER COLD RUNNING WATER

1 TABLESPOON EXTRA VIRGIN OLIVE OIL

¼ CUP COARSELY CHOPPED WALNUTS

1 CUP (ABOUT 4 OUNCES) FRESH GOAT CHEESE, SOFTENED AT ROOM TEMPERATURE

1 TEASPOON WALNUT OIL

KOSHER SALT

BLACK PEPPER IN A MILL

¾ POUND BELGIAN ENDIVE (ABOUT 2 ENDIVES), SPLIT AND CUT CROSSWISE INTO ¾-INCH PIECES

2 OUNCES ARUGULA, TOUGH STEMS DISCARDED, WELL WASHED IN SEVERAL CHANGES OF COLD WATER AND SPUN DRY (3½ CUPS LIGHTLY PACKED)

½ CUP WALNUT VINAIGRETTE (RECIPE FOLLOWS)

PREHEAT the oven to 325°F. Put the beets on a large piece of aluminum foil, rub each beet with olive oil, and wrap up the sides of the foil to create a bundle. Place on a cookie sheet and roast until a thin-bladed knife pierces easily into the center of a beet, 1½ to 2 hours, depending on the size of the beets.

MEANWHILE, put the walnuts in an 8-inch sauté pan and toast over medium heat, shaking constantly, until they are fragrant, 2 to 3 minutes. Transfer the nuts to a small bowl and set aside.

PUT the goat cheese and walnut oil in a bowl. Use a wooden spoon to stir vigorously until the cheese is whipped to a mousselike consistency. Season with salt and about 4 grinds of pepper, or to taste, and set aside.

WHEN the beets are done, remove the cookie sheet from the oven. Set the beets aside to cool. When the beets are completely cooled, remove the skins (they will come right off with the aid of a paring knife) and cut them into ¾-inch dice.

PUT the diced beets in a bowl. Add the diced endive, arugula, and walnuts. Drizzle with the walnut vinaigrette and toss gently to coat the ingredients.

DIVIDE the salad evenly among 4 salad plates or bowls, being sure to include a good mix of ingredients in each serving. Put a tablespoon of whipped goat cheese on top of each salad, and serve.

VARIATIONS In the fall, replace the goat cheese with richer blue cheese. Or add ¾-inch cubes of crisp apples. In the spring, use young baby beets, roasting them for about 25 minutes and quartering them after they've cooled.

EMBELLISHMENTS Whip fresh herbs such as tarragon and parsley into the goat cheese along with the walnut oil. Top each salad with a tablespoon or so of grated, hard, aged goat cheese to add an extra flavor punch.

WALNUT VINAIGRETTE MAKES ABOUT 1 CUP

In the fall, dress salads, especially those featuring nuts, with this vinaigrette. A few notes about walnut and other nut oils: Be sure to purchase a high-quality one and use it within three to six months, even if the expiration date indicates a longer shelf life; they turn rancid relatively quickly. Store them away from sunlight and taste them before using to ensure freshness.

Unlike many of the vinaigrettes in the book, this one is nonemulsified (referred to as "broken"), meaning that oil and vinegar will show separately on the plate.

2 TABLESPOONS SHERRY VINEGAR OR RED-WINE VINEGAR

1 TABLESPOON FINELY DICED SHALLOTS

⅓ CUP WALNUT OIL

ABOUT 1 TEASPOON KOSHER SALT

BLACK PEPPER IN A MILL

PUT the vinegar and shallots in a mixing bowl. Slowly whisk in the oil, then whisk in the salt and about 6 grinds of pepper and taste. Add more salt, if necessary.

THIS vinaigrette can be covered and refrigerated for up to 3 days, or up to 1 month if you omit the shallots.

WATERMELON AND ARUGULA SALAD WITH FETA AND TAPENADE

SERVES 4

Various versions of this salad, currently one of my personal favorites, have been turning up on New York City restaurant menus over the past several years, enticing diners with the once-unexpected juxtaposition of salty cheese and sweet, crunchy watermelon. This version calls for less common goat cheese feta and derives extra texture and salinity from the olive tapenade. If you love watermelon in the summertime, this is a surprising way to serve it at the table. It's especially appropriate for outdoor lunch and dinner parties.

VINAIGRETTE

3 TABLESPOONS FRESHLY SQUEEZED LIME JUICE

I TABLESPOON LIGHT CORN SYRUP

¼ CUP PLUS 2 TABLESPOONS EXTRA VIRGIN OLIVE OIL

KOSHER SALT

BLACK PEPPER IN A MILL

¼ CUP TAPENADE (PAGE 33)

ABOUT 3 POUNDS SEEDLESS WATERMELON, RIND REMOVED, CUT INTO I-INCH CUBES

4 CUPS LOOSELY PACKED ARUGULA (ABOUT 2 OUNCES ARUGULA), TOUGH STEMS REMOVED, WELL WASHED IN SEVERAL CHANGES OF COLD WATER AND SPUN DRY

½ CUP CRUMBLED GOAT CHEESE FETA (FROM ABOUT 3 OUNCES CHEESE) (SEE SOURCES, PAGE 318)

MAKE the vinaigrette: Put the lime juice, corn syrup, and oil in a mixing bowl and whisk them together. Season with ½ teaspoon salt and about 6 grinds black pepper. Add the tapenade to the bowl and stir it into the vinaigrette.

DIVIDE the watermelon cubes among 4 chilled salad plates. Dress the arugula with the vinaigrette and divide among the plates, piling it atop the watermelon. Scatter some crumbled cheese over each salad. Serve.

VARIATION Use sheep's-milk or "regular" feta in place of the goat cheese feta.

CARPACCIO OF TUNA WITH CITRUS-SOY VINAIGRETTE

SERVES 4

First served in Venice as a dish featuring paper-thin slices of raw beef dressed with mayonnaise, carpaccio has become a vehicle for everything from seafood to vegetables. My version of choice, a mainstay on the menu at Picholine since we opened in 1993, dresses lightly pounded slices of tuna with citrus-soy vinaigrette, rounding out the flavors with the distinct heat of three ingredients—jalapeño, radish, and ginger.

Be sure to purchase sushi-grade tuna, and don't add the dressing until the last second to keep the acid in the vinaigrette from "cooking" the fish.

This dish would be especially delicious with toro (the fatty belly of a tuna), which is fattier and richer and offers a more pronounced contrast to the crunch of the sea salt. For a change of pace, try hamachi, a sublime albeit tough-to-find alternative to tuna.

I TABLESPOON WHITE SESAME SEEDS

12 OUNCES SUSHI-GRADE TUNA (IF POSSIBLE, HAVE YOUR FISHMONGER CUT 4 CIRCULAR SLICES, OR FOUR 3-OUNCE RECTANGULAR PIECES, 1½ INCHES BY 2 INCHES EACH)

MALDEN SEA SALT OR KOSHER SALT

½ CUP CITRUS-SOY VINAIGRETTE (RECIPE FOLLOWS)

24 VERY THIN CROSSWISE SLICES JALAPEÑO PEPPER WITH THE SEEDS INTACT (FROM 2 PEPPERS)

½ CUP LOOSELY PACKED RADISH SPROUTS OR DAIKON SPROUTS (ABOUT ½ OUNCE) (OPTIONAL)

3 RED RADISHES, VERY THINLY SLICED, PREFERABLY WITH A MANDOLINE

PUT the sesame seeds in an 8-inch sauté pan and toast over medium heat, shaking constantly, until fragrant, approximately 2 minutes. Remove the pan from the heat and let the seeds cool to room temperature.

MEANWHILE, one by one, put the tuna pieces between 2 pieces of plastic wrap and use a mallet or the smooth side of a meat tenderizer to pound them to a thickness of $\frac{1}{16}$ inch.

REMOVE the plastic from one side of a piece of pounded tuna. Center the unwrapped side on a chilled salad plate and peel off the other piece of plastic. Repeat with the remaining portions and 3 more chilled plates.

SPRINKLE the carpaccio evenly with salt and drizzle about 2 tablespoons of vinaigrette over each serving. Arrange 6 jalapeño slices over each serving. Divide the sprouts, if using, evenly over the carpaccio and evenly divide the radish slices among the servings, arranging them on top of the sprouts. Scatter the sesame seeds over the tuna and serve.

THE REASON *The tuna is pounded between sheets of plastic:* Pounding the tuna in this way helps give it a uniform thickness, keeps it from breaking, and makes handling easier.

CITRUS-SOY VINAIGRETTE MAKES ABOUT ½ CUP

I've always loved the way the sweetness of citrus fruits complements the saltiness of soy sauce. Use this vinaigrette to bring that combination to Asian-themed salads, especially those featuring fish and poultry.

1½ CUPS ORANGE JUICE, PREFERABLY FRESHLY SQUEEZED FROM 5 TO 6 ORANGES, STRAINED

1½ TABLESPOONS FRESHLY SQUEEZED LEMON JUICE

½ TABLESPOON HIGH-QUALITY OR ORGANIC SOY SAUCE

1 TEASPOON MINCED, PEELED FRESH GINGER

1 TABLESPOON RED-WINE VINEGAR

¼ CUP GRAPESEED OIL OR CANOLA OIL

KOSHER SALT TO TASTE, IF NECESSARY

POUR the orange juice and lemon juice into a heavy-bottomed saucepan and bring to a boil over high heat. Lower the heat and let simmer until the mixture reduces to ½ cup, approximately 10 to 12 minutes. Remove the pan from the heat, and stir in the soy sauce, ginger, and vinegar. Let the mixture cool completely. Slowly whisk in the oil. Taste and season with salt, if necessary.

THIS vinaigrette can be covered and refrigerated for up to 1 week. Let come to room temperature before using.

THE REASON *The salt is added to the vinaigrette at the end of its preparation:* Because of the salty character of soy sauce, recipes featuring it often don't require any salt, so always taste recipes containing soy before seasoning at all, unless otherwise instructed.

QUAIL SALAD WITH TABBOULEH AND HARISSA DRESSING

SERVES 4

This Middle Eastern–inspired dish calls on two of the most popular dishes of that region: tabbouleh, the parsley, lemon, and cracked wheat salad; and harissa, the red-hot pepper and garlic puree that's used as a condiment for roasted meats and poultry.

2 TABLESPOONS OLIVE OIL

4 BONELESS QUAILS, 4 TO 6 OUNCES EACH

KOSHER SALT

BLACK PEPPER IN A MILL

TABBOULEH (RECIPE FOLLOWS)

HARISSA DRESSING (RECIPE FOLLOWS)

HEAT the oil in a 10-inch sauté pan over medium heat. Season the quails with salt and about 10 grinds pepper. Add the quails to the pan, breast-side down, without crowding, and cook for 2 to 2½ minutes on each side. The inside of the breast should be pink, indicating medium doneness. Transfer the quails to a clean, dry surface and cover loosely with foil to keep them warm.

DIVIDE the tabbouleh evenly among 4 salad plates. Set 1 quail in the center of each mound. Drizzle some harissa vinaigrette over and around the quail on each plate and serve.

THE REASON *The oil is heated before the food is added to the pan:* This keeps food from sticking to the surface of the pan when searing.

TABBOULEH MAKES 2 ½ CUPS

Full of fresh flavors perked up with lemon juice and extra virgin olive oil, tabbouleh is a perfect picnic dish or salad in its own right. It's also a fine accompaniment to fish and poultry.

½ CUP BULGUR (CRACKED WHEAT)

ABOUT 1 CUP COLD WATER

¾ TEASPOON KOSHER SALT

¼ CUP EXTRA VIRGIN OLIVE OIL

1½ TABLESPOONS SEEDED, PEELED, FINELY DICED CUCUMBER

1 TABLESPOON FINELY DICED RED ONION

1½ TABLESPOONS FINELY DICED RED BELL PEPPER

¼ CUP COARSELY SNIPPED FLAT-LEAF PARSLEY LEAVES (LOOSELY PACKED)

¼ CUP FINELY SLICED CHIVES

1½ TABLESPOONS FRESHLY SQUEEZED LEMON JUICE

¼ CUP SLICED MINT LEAVES

½ TEASPOON CAYENNE

PUT the bulgur in a bowl. Add 1 cup cold water, or enough to cover, and let soak for 30 minutes. Strain the bulgur in a fine-mesh strainer and refresh under cold, running water. Shake the strainer to drain well.

TRANSFER the drained bulgur to a bowl. Add the salt, oil, cucumber, onion, red pepper, parsley, chives, lemon juice, mint, and cayenne, and toss well.

THE tabbouleh can be covered and refrigerated for up to 2 days. Serve cold or at room temperature.

HARISSA DRESSING MAKES ABOUT ½ CUP

In addition to dressing the quail salad, serve this dressing with seafood, chicken, or lamb.

I RED BELL PEPPER, HALVED LENGTHWISE, SEEDS AND STEM REMOVED

I JALAPEÑO PEPPER, HALVED LENGTHWISE, SEEDS REMOVED

¼ CUP WHITE ONION, LARGE DICE

2 PLUM TOMATOES (12 TO 14 OUNCES TOTAL WEIGHT), CORED

½ CUP EXTRA VIRGIN OLIVE OIL

I TEASPOON CORIANDER SEED (OPTIONAL)

2 CLOVES GARLIC, CRUSHED AND PEELED

KOSHER SALT

2 TEASPOONS FRESHLY SQUEEZED LEMON JUICE

I TEASPOON CAYENNE

PREHEAT the oven to 375°F. Put the red pepper, jalapeño pepper, onion, and tomatoes in a bowl and toss with 2 tablespoons of the extra virgin olive oil. Spread the vegetables out in a single layer on a large, rimmed cookie sheet and roast until the pepper skins blister, 20 to 25 minutes.

MEANWHILE, if using the coriander, put the seeds in an 8-inch sauté pan and toast over medium heat, shaking constantly, until fragrant, 2 to 3 minutes. Transfer the seeds to a spice grinder and grind. Set aside.

PUT the peppers in a bowl, cover with plastic wrap, and let them steam in their own heat for 15 minutes to loosen their skins.

MEANWHILE, peel the tomatoes (Terms and Techniques, page 95) and discard the skins. Put the tomatoes in the bowl of a standing blender. Add the onion, coriander, and garlic.

WHEN the peppers have steamed for 15 minutes, use a paring knife to peel off their skins. Discard the skins and add the peppers to the blender. Season with salt and add the remaining 6 tablespoons extra virgin olive oil, the lemon juice, and cayenne. Puree until smooth.

THE vinaigrette can be covered, transferred to a bowl or airtight container, and refrigerated for up to 3 days. Let come to room temperature before serving.

DUCK PASTRAMI WITH POMEGRANATE VINAIGRETTE

SERVES 4

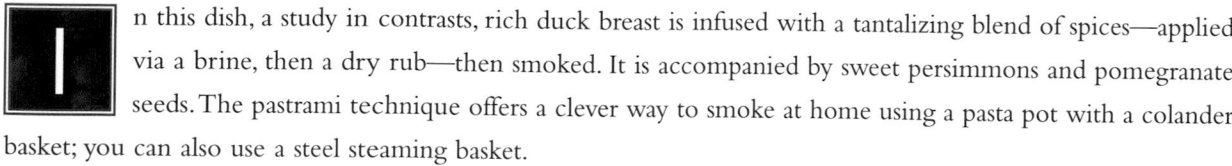

In this dish, a study in contrasts, rich duck breast is infused with a tantalizing blend of spices—applied via a brine, then a dry rub—then smoked. It is accompanied by sweet persimmons and pomegranate seeds. The pastrami technique offers a clever way to smoke at home using a pasta pot with a colander basket; you can also use a steel steaming basket.

Rather than smoking the duck, you can brine it, then sauté it, or skip the brining step and smoke it from its natural state.

Incidentally, brining is a technique you should keep in mind for pork and poultry; it helps meats that tend to turn dry stay moist and juicy.

Note: Smoking the duck may set off your smoke detector, so ventilate your kitchen as well as possible, turning on any available fans and opening windows.

---

4 CUPS WATER

KOSHER SALT

¼ CUP BLACK PEPPERCORNS

½ CUP DARK BROWN SUGAR

¼ CUP PLUS I TABLESPOON CORIANDER SEED

4 BAY LEAVES

2 CINNAMON STICKS

I HEAD GARLIC, HALVED HORIZONTALLY, EXCESS PAPERY SKIN REMOVED

3 STAR ANISE

2 SKINLESS MALLARD DUCK BREASTS, APPROXIMATELY I½ POUNDS TOTAL WEIGHT

2 TABLESPOONS ALLSPICE

3 TABLESPOONS FENNEL SEED

2 TEASPOONS JUNIPER BERRIES

I CUP HICKORY WOOD CHIPS

2 RIPE FUJI PERSIMMONS, PEELED, SLICED INTO SIX ¼-INCH-THICK ROUNDS PER PERSIMMON

3 HEADS FRISÉE, YELLOW AND WHITE PART, CORE REMOVED, WASHED, AND DRIED

2 BELGIAN ENDIVE, CUT CROSSWISE INTO ½-INCH PIECES

POMEGRANATE VINAIGRETTE (RECIPE FOLLOWS)

I POMEGRANATE, SPLIT, SEEDS REMOVED

POUR the water into a 2-quart pot. Add ½ cup salt, 1 tablespoon black peppercorns, the brown sugar, 2 tablespoons of the coriander, the bay leaves, cinnamon, garlic, and anise, and bring to a boil over high heat. Remove the pot from the heat and let the liquid steep as it cools. Once the brine is cool to the touch, chill it in the refrigerator. Add the duck breasts, cover, and refrigerate for 12 to 24 hours.

WHEN ready to proceed, preheat the oven to 325°F. Put the remaining 3 tablespoons coriander, the allspice, fennel seed, the remaining 3 tablespoons black peppercorns, and the juniper berries in an 8-inch sauté pan and toast over medium heat, shaking constantly, until fragrant, 2 to 3 minutes. Let cool, then transfer to a spice or coffee grinder. Add ½ teaspoon salt to the grinder. Grind finely to make a dry rub. Transfer the rub to a small bowl.

REMOVE the breasts from the brine and pat them dry with paper towels. Rub with the dry rub to coat well.

SMOKE the duck (remember to ventilate the kitchen): Put a large, heavy-bottomed pasta pot over low heat and add the wood chips. When the chips start to smoke, put the breasts in the colander in a single layer, put the colander over the chips, and cover with a lid or foil. Let smoke gently, removing the cover partially if necessary to control the level, for 10 minutes. (If your pot darkens, clean it by boiling water in it for 5 minutes, then scrubbing it.)

TRANSFER the duck breasts to a cookie sheet in a single layer and cook in the oven for 5 minutes or until an instant-read thermometer inserted to the center of a breast reads 125°F. Remove from the oven and let rest. The pastrami can be cooled, wrapped in plastic, and refrigerated for up to 3 days.

WHEN ready to serve, thinly slice the duck breasts.

PUT the persimmons, frisée, and endive in a mixing bowl. Drizzle the vinaigrette over the salad and toss. Divide the salad among 4 salad plates, mounding it in the center of the plate. Drape slices of duck over the salad on each plate. Scatter the pomegranate seeds around the plate. Serve.

VARIATION The salad makes a fine accompaniment to other delicacies such as foie gras, sautéed duck breast, or other meats.

POMEGRANATE VINAIGRETTE MAKES 1¼ CUPS

- 1¼ CUPS POMEGRANATE JUICE (AVAILABLE BOTTLED IN GOURMET STORES AND SOME SUPERMARKETS; SEE TERMS AND TECHNIQUES)

- 3 TABLESPOONS SUGAR

- ¼ CUP BANYULS VINEGAR OR RED-WINE VINEGAR

- KOSHER SALT

- ½ TABLESPOON FRESHLY SQUEEZED LEMON JUICE

- 3 TABLESPOONS CANOLA OIL

PUT the juice and sugar in a 2-quart pot and bring to a boil over high heat. Continue to boil until reduced by 25 percent, approximately 5 minutes. Add the vinegar, and season with salt. Remove the pot from the heat and let cool. Pour the mixture into a standing blender and blend on low speed. With the motor running, add the lemon juice, then add the oil in a thin stream to form an emulsified vinaigrette.

TERMS AND TECHNIQUES *Juicing a pomegranate:* To make pomegranate juice, roll a pomegranate firmly on a cutting board to loosen the seeds. Quarter the pomegranate, remove the seeds, then press the seeds in a food mill. Be careful not to spill or splash the juice; it stains.

CHEESE SOUFFLÉ

SERVES 6

Most home cooks are afraid of soufflés, but in reality, they're not that difficult to make. Serve this dish as a first course and your guests will be doubly impressed, not just because you've made a soufflé, but also because most people don't expect to be served one until the end of a meal. (Just think of how you have to order soufflés for dessert shortly after you sit down in a restaurant.) Cheese soufflé is also a more elegant way of serving cheese at the beginning of a meal than the more communal fondue.

You can make this with just one of the cheeses, or select another one altogether, preferably a firm mountain cheese such as Appenzeller or Emmenthaler.

---

6 TABLESPOONS UNSALTED BUTTER AT ROOM TEMPERATURE

¼ CUP PLUS 1 TABLESPOON ALL-PURPOSE FLOUR

PINCH NUTMEG

1½ TEASPOONS KOSHER SALT

1¼ CUPS MILK

1 TEASPOON MINCED GARLIC

⅔ CUP FINELY GRATED COMTÉ CHEESE (FROM 3 OUNCES CHEESE)

⅔ CUP FINELY GRATED HOCH YBRIG CHEESE (FROM 3 OUNCES CHEESE)

⅔ CUP FINELY GRATED GRUYÈRE CHEESE (FROM 3 OUNCES CHEESE)

3 EGGS, SEPARATED, AT ROOM TEMPERATURE

¼ CUP FINELY GRATED PARMIGIANO-REGGIANO (FROM ABOUT 1 OUNCE CHEESE)

PINCH CREAM OF TARTAR, OR SALT

PREHEAT the oven to 325°F. Melt 4 tablespoons of the butter in a 2-quart, heavy-bottomed saucepan over low heat. Whisk in the flour, nutmeg, and salt, and continue whisking for 5 minutes, without browning. Whisk in the milk and garlic until the mixture is uniformly thick. Continue to simmer over low heat, whisking occasionally, until the mixture takes on the consistency of a pudding and forms ribbons when the whisk is lifted from the pan, approximately 10 minutes.

STIR in the Comté, Hoch Ybrig, and Gruyère. Cook, stirring, until the cheese melts. Remove the pot from the heat, stir in the egg yolks one at a time, and transfer the mixture to a mixing bowl. Let cool to room temperature.

USING a pastry brush, butter the insides of six 6-ounce crocks, ramekins, or soufflé dishes with the remaining 2 tablespoons butter. Use 2 tablespoons of the Parmigiano-Reggiano to dust the inside of the crocks by putting some cheese into each crock, turning the crock on its side, rotating it in your hand until the cheese adheres to the butter on all sides, then inverting the crock to pour out any cheese that hasn't adhered.

PUT the egg whites in the bowl of a standing mixer fitted with the whisk attachment, add the cream of tartar, and whisk the whites until peaks have formed, stiffened, and hold their shape. (This can also be done with a whisk by hand.) If the whites appear wet or watery, they are overwhipped and will not cook properly, and you should begin this step again with 3 new whites.

MIX one-quarter of the whipped whites into the cheese mixture, then fold in the remaining whites gently with a rubber spatula. Divide the mixture among the crocks, filling them three-quarters of the way up the sides. Sprinkle the tops of the crocks with the remaining 2 tablespoons of Parmigiano. Lightly shake the bottom of each crock to settle and even out the mixture.

PUT the crocks on a sturdy cookie sheet or baking sheet. Bake on the middle rack of the oven until the tops are puffed and golden and a toothpick inserted to the center of a soufflé comes out clean, approximately 20 minutes. Remove the soufflés from the oven and serve immediately.

THE REASON *Cream of tartar is added to the whites:* Cream of tartar (or a pinch of salt or some lemon juice) added to whipped egg whites acts as a stabilizer, helping them maintain their shape.

EMBELLISHMENT Serve the soufflés with a well-dressed salad for a light lunch or dinner.

RÂCLETTE with FINGERLING POTATOES

A râclette is the name given to both a family of creamy, raw-cow's-milk cheeses and dishes that feature it melted and served with accompaniments like potatoes and bread. In France and Switzerland, râclette is such a beloved tradition that there are ovens designed just to melt these cheeses and, in ski chalets, the cheese is often cooked right in the fireplace. Here, an ovenproof dish does the trick.

---

8 CUPS COLD WATER

I POUND FINGERLING POTATOES (ABOUT 12 POTATOES)

KOSHER SALT

8 OUNCES RÂCLETTE (HARD MOUNTAIN CHEESES LIKE EMMENTHALER AND GRUYÈRE CAN BE SUBSTITUTED), SLICED AS THINLY AS POSSIBLE, IDEALLY WITH A CHEESE SLICER

BLACK PEPPER IN A MILL

POUR the cold water into a 3-quart, heavy-bottomed pot. Add the potatoes and 1 tablespoon salt, and bring to a boil over high heat. Lower the heat and let simmer until the potatoes are tender when pierced with a fork, approximately 25 minutes. Drain the potatoes, and set them aside to cool.

MEANWHILE, preheat the broiler. When cool enough to handle, cut the potatoes in half lengthwise. Divide the warm potatoes, cut-side down, evenly among 4 ovenproof plates, arranging them in a pinwheel pattern. Arrange one quarter of the cheese slices in a single layer over each portion of potatoes, taking care to completely cover all potatoes.

PUT the plates in the oven and bake until the cheese melts, 1½ to 2 minutes. Remove the plates from the oven, season each serving with salt and 1 or 2 grinds of pepper, or to taste, and serve hot.

VARIATION For a change of pace, add some butter and Parmesan cheese. Crush the potatoes while still warm, grate the cheese, and stir it into the potatoes. Serve as an accompaniment to grilled and roasted poultry and meats.

EMBELLISHMENTS Serve this with accompaniments like Pickled Vegetables (page 37), cornichon, and pickled onion; pair it with a simple green salad for a light lunch; and/or top the servings with a shaving of black or white truffles for a very indulgent treat.

POTATO AND CHEESE TART WITH BACON

SERVES 4

These deceptively easy-to-make tarts use phyllo dough—blind baking it in a mold, then adding a mixture of potatoes, cream, and cheese. You can make miniature versions as an hors d'oeuvre by using mini-muffin tins. This is another one of those appetizers that would be a fine lunch accompanied by a simple salad. The tarts also lend themselves to free adaptation: You can replace the Beaufort with Cheddar and/or leave out the bacon and they will still be delicious.

- 4 SHEETS PHYLLO DOUGH, 12 INCHES BY 17 INCHES EACH (IF FROZEN, LET THAW TO REFRIGERATOR TEMPERATURE)

- 2 TABLESPOONS UNSALTED BUTTER, MELTED, PLUS 1 TABLESPOON UNSALTED BUTTER AT ROOM TEMPERATURE

- ¾ POUND FINGERLING POTATOES OR YUKON GOLD POTATOES (ABOUT 6 POTATOES)

- 8 CUPS COLD WATER

- KOSHER SALT

- 8 SLICES (5 OUNCES) APPLEWOOD-SMOKED BACON, ⅛-INCH THICK (OR THINNER, IF POSSIBLE)

- ½ CUP FINELY DICED ONION

- ¾ CUP CRÈME FRAÎCHE OR SOUR CREAM

- ⅔ CUP FINELY GRATED BEAUFORT OR OTHER HARD MOUNTAIN CHEESE SUCH AS GRUYÈRE OR COMTÉ (FROM ABOUT 3½ OUNCES CHEESE)

- 2 TABLESPOONS FINELY GRATED PARMIGIANO-REGGIANO

- BLACK PEPPER IN A MILL

PREHEAT the oven to 325°F. Put 1 layer of phyllo onto a flat surface. Use a pastry brush to brush the dough sparingly with melted butter, making sure to lightly coat the corners. Top with another sheet of phyllo and brush with butter. Repeat with the remaining sheets of phyllo, making a single stack, but do not apply butter to the top of last phyllo layer. Cut four 4¾-inch circles out of the dough.

SHAPE the dough circles into 3¼-inch wide by ¾-inch deep metal molds. Fill each mold with pie weights or beans and blind bake until the phyllo is golden-brown, 6 to 7 minutes. Remove the weights; set aside.

PUT the fingerling potatoes in a large, heavy-bottomed pot and cover with the water. Add 1 tablespoon salt and bring to a boil over high heat. Lower the heat and simmer until the potatoes are tender to the tines of a fork, approximately 25 minutes. Drain the potatoes.

For a rustic effect, leave the peels on the potatoes; for a more formal dish, peel them when they are cool enough to handle. Set aside.

WHILE the potatoes are cooking, cook the bacon and onion: Put the bacon slices on a rimmed cookie sheet and cook in the oven until the bacon is crispy, approximately 20 minutes. If you like your bacon extra-crispy, use tongs to turn the slices over once about halfway through the cooking time. Transfer the bacon to a paper-towel-lined plate to drain. (Do not turn off the oven.) Set aside.

PUT the 1 tablespoon of room-temperature butter in a small, heavy-bottomed saucepan and melt it over low heat. Add the onion and a pinch of salt and cook over medium heat until softened but not browned, approximately 8 minutes.

DRAIN the potatoes and return them to the pot. Mash them with a potato masher or fork. Stir in the onion crème fraîche, Beaufort, Parmigiano-Reggiano, 1 teaspoon salt, and about 6 grinds of pepper, or to taste. Cook, stirring, for 2 minutes over medium heat just until the cheese melts; the potatoes should still be chunky.

IMMEDIATELY fill the phyllo crusts with the mixture and top each tart with 2 slices of bacon. Rewarm in the oven for 1 minute, then remove from the oven, unmold onto individual plates, and serve.

THE REASON *The potatoes are added to the cold water before it boils:* When boiling potatoes and root vegetables, you should always put the vegetables and cold water on the heat at the same time rather than adding the vegetables after the water has come to a boil; this ensures that the vegetable cooks evenly from the outside in. (If you were to add potatoes to already boiling water, the outermost portion would be overcooked by the time the center was done.)

EMBELLISHMENT Top each tart with thinly sliced scallions or chives.

SHEEP'S-MILK RICOTTA GNOCCHI WITH MORELS AND ASPARAGUS

**A** longtime favorite at Picholine, this starter is centered around feather-light gnocchi (little dumplings) made with sheep's-milk ricotta cheese in place of the traditional semolina flour or potato. The flavor of the gnocchi is the perfect complement to the springtime duo of morel mushrooms and asparagus. As with classic potato gnocchi, the key to success here is not to overwork the dough.

This recipe can be doubled for the main course.

---

1 CUP SHEEP'S-MILK RICOTTA OR REGULAR RICOTTA

2 TABLESPOONS FINELY GRATED PARMIGIANO-REGGIANO

ABOUT ¼ CUP PLUS 3 TABLESPOONS ALL-PURPOSE FLOUR, PLUS MORE FOR DUSTING A WORK SURFACE

1 EGG YOLK

KOSHER SALT

PINCH GROUND NUTMEG

PINCH CAYENNE

8 QUARTS WATER

¼ POUND MEDIUM ASPARAGUS, BOTTOM STEMS TRIMMED, PEELED FROM 1 INCH BELOW THE TIP, AND CUT DIAGONALLY INTO 1½-INCH PIECES

1½ TABLESPOONS OLIVE OIL (IF MAKING THE GNOCCHI IN ADVANCE; SEE RECIPE)

MOREL SAUCE (RECIPE FOLLOWS)

PUT the ricotta in a cheesecloth-lined colander and use a rubber spatula to push as much liquid as possible out of the cheese. Then gather up the ends of the cloth and turn them over and over again (as though wringing a towel), tightening its hold on the cheese and squeezing any lingering liquid out of it.

PUT the ricotta, Parmigiano-Reggiano, flour, egg yolk, ½ teaspoon salt, nutmeg, and cayenne in the bowl of a food processor fitted with the steel blade. Process until the mixture comes together into a smooth ball of dough, taking care not to overmix. If the dough feels sticky, work in some more flour. Put the dough in a bowl, cover with plastic wrap, and refrigerate for 30 minutes.

DUST a rimmed baking sheet or cookie sheet lightly with flour. Lightly flour a work surface and turn the dough out onto it. Divide the dough into 4 equal portions. Roll 1 portion at a time into a ropelike cylinder, ¾ inch in diameter, and cut the cylinder into 1-inch pieces. Gently make an indentation with your thumb in 1 side of each piece and gather the pieces in a single layer on the baking sheet. Repeat with the remaining cylinders, adding more flour to the surface as needed.

COVER the gnocchi with plastic wrap and refrigerate for 1 hour; this will firm them up and help them hold their shape when cooked.

POUR 2 quarts of water into a 3-quart stockpot, add 2 tablespoons of salt, and bring to a boil over high heat. Fill a large bowl halfway with ice water. Add the asparagus to the boiling water and cook until al dente, approximately 3 minutes. Drain and transfer the asparagus to the ice water to stop the cooking and preserve the color. Once chilled, drain again.

POUR 6 quarts of water into an 8-quart, heavy-bottomed stockpot, add 1 tablespoon salt, and bring to a boil over high heat. Fill a large bowl halfway with ice water. Add the gnocchi to the boiling water and cook until they float to the surface, 2 to 3 minutes. Use a slotted spoon to transfer the gnocchi to the ice water, then to a clean, dry bowl. If not serving the gnocchi immediately, toss with the olive oil, cover, and set aside for up to 1 hour, or refrigerate for up to 24 hours. When ready to serve, reheat in boiling water until they rise to the surface.

HEAT the morel sauce in a sauté pan over medium heat. Add the gnocchi and asparagus and toss to heat and combine the components of the dish. Divide among 4 dinner plates or bowls and serve.

EMBELLISHMENTS Shave some black truffle and/or toss some blanched fava beans or pea tendrils into each serving.

MOREL SAUCE MAKES ABOUT 1¼ CUPS

This sauce really brings out the natural flavor of morels. It works beautifully with gnocchi and is especially delicious with chicken and veal.

- 1 CUP FRESH MORELS (2 TO 2½ OUNCES), LARGER ONES CUT IN HALF
- 4 CUPS WARM WATER
- 1 TABLESPOON UNSALTED BUTTER
- 2 TABLESPOONS FINELY DICED SHALLOTS
- KOSHER SALT
- ½ CUP WHITE CHICKEN STOCK (PAGE 45) OR LOW-SODIUM, STORE-BOUGHT CHICKEN BROTH
- 1¼ CUPS HEAVY CREAM

PUT the morels in a bowl and cover with the warm water. Soak, agitating the mushrooms in the water to release any dirt or grit. Use your hands to lift the mushrooms out of the water, then discard the water. Do this 2 or 3 times, or more if necessary.

MELT the butter in a heavy-bottomed saucepan set over medium heat. Add the shallots and a pinch of salt, and cook until softened but not browned, approximately 2 minutes. Add the morels and cook, stirring, approximately 5 minutes.

POUR in the stock, bring to a boil over high heat, and cook until reduced by three-quarters, approximately 3 minutes. Lower the heat, stir in the cream, and let simmer until reduced by half, approximately 12 minutes. The mixture should have reduced to about 1¼ cups and be thick enough to coat the back of a wooden spoon. Season with salt.

THE sauce can be kept covered and warm at room temperature for up to 1 hour.

TERMS AND TECHNIQUES *Cleaning mushrooms:* Because moisture causes them to deteriorate, mushrooms should only be cleaned just before cooking. More delicate mushrooms like porcini should be gently wiped with a damp towel.

THE REASON *The mushrooms are lifted out of the soaking liquid:* By lifting the mushrooms out of their soaking liquid you ensure that they remain clean. Draining them in a colander can leave some grit behind as the dirty water is essentially poured back over the mushrooms. (For more on cleaning mushrooms, see Terms and Techniques.)

EMBELLISHMENT For a more pronounced morel flavor, add some dried morels to a little extra warm chicken stock and let infuse for 30 minutes. Drain, filter out any grit, then add to stock to be reduced.

SHRIMP AND AVOCADO WITH COCKTAIL SAUCE GRANITÉ

SERVES 4

The centerpiece of this extremely refreshing plated version of shrimp cocktail is a granité, or shaved ice, made with the essential ingredients of a cocktail sauce.

Be sure to allow two hours for the granité to freeze; if you don't feel like waiting, stir the granité ingredients together, leaving out the water, to make a quick cocktail sauce.

¼ CUP KETCHUP

1 TABLESPOON (LIGHTLY PACKED) FRESHLY GRATED HORSERADISH, OR ½ TABLESPOON PREPARED HORSERADISH

½ TEASPOON WORCESTERSHIRE SAUCE

6 DROPS TABASCO SAUCE

¼ TEASPOON MINCED GARLIC

3 TABLESPOONS FRESHLY SQUEEZED LEMON JUICE

½ TEASPOON SUGAR

KOSHER SALT

14½ CUPS WATER

12 COLOSSAL SHRIMP, OR 20 JUMBO SHRIMP (1 TO 1¼ POUND TOTAL WEIGHT), IN THE SHELL

2 HAAS AVOCADOS (SEE NOTE, PAGE 71)

BLACK PEPPER IN A MILL

MUSTARD DRESSING (RECIPE FOLLOWS)

MAKE the granité: Put the ketchup, horseradish, Worcestershire, Tabasco, minced garlic, 2 tablespoons of the lemon juice, the sugar, 1 teaspoon salt, and ½ cup water in a mixing bowl and stir together. Pour the mixture into an 8-inch by 8-inch Pyrex dish. Put in the freezer. Freeze for at least 2 hours, scraping the mixture with a fork every half-hour or so, to break it into ice crystals. The granité can be frozen for up to 1 week.

POUR 12 cups of water into a large, heavy-bottomed pot. Add 3 tablespoons salt and bring to a boil over high heat. Add the shrimp, remove the pot from the heat, cover, and let stand until the shrimp are firm and pink and cooked through, approximately 3 minutes. Use a slotted spoon to remove the shrimp and set aside to cool. When cool, peel and devein the shrimp, then cover and refrigerate until chilled, at least 1 hour.

CUT the avocados in half lengthwise and twist the halves apart. Remove the pit by embedding the heel of a large knife into it and pulling it out. Gently work a tablespoon in between the flesh and skin of one avocado half. Work it around the edge of the avocado and gradually toward the bottom, carefully loosening the flesh until you can remove it in one unbroken, unblemished piece. Cut a bit from the center of the curved, skinned side of each half so the halves can stay upright on their backs without wobbling.

PUT the remaining tablespoon of lemon juice in a bowl with 2 cups of water and dip the avocado halves into the acidulated water to prevent them from browning, letting any excess water run off. Season the avocado pieces with salt and about 2 grinds of pepper each, or to taste.

PUT the shrimp and half the mustard sauce in a mixing bowl and toss gently to coat the shrimp. Put half an avocado in the center of each of 4 chilled salad plates. Arrange 3 or 5 shrimp, depending on which size you are using, around each avocado half. Put an ice-cream scoop of granité inside the cavity of each avocado half. Drizzle 1 tablespoon of the remaining sauce around the perimeter of each plate and serve.

EMBELLISHMENT For a smoother texture, prepare the granité in a blender before freezing it, or freeze it in an ice-cream machine according to the manufacturer's instructions.

MUSTARD DRESSING MAKES ABOUT ½ CUP

This sauce uses equal parts Dijon and grain mustard for a smooth, balanced flavor with more complexity than either variety provides on its own. It's an ideal dressing for shellfish, poultry, and beef.

2 TABLESPOONS DIJON MUSTARD

2 TABLESPOONS GRAIN MUSTARD

2 TABLESPOONS WHITE-WINE VINEGAR

½ TEASPOON KOSHER SALT

½ TEASPOON FRESHLY GROUND BLACK PEPPER

½ CUP PLUS 2 TABLESPOONS CANOLA OIL

PUT the Dijon mustard, grain mustard, vinegar, salt, and pepper in a mixing bowl and whisk together. Slowly add the oil in a thin stream, whisking to form an emulsified vinaigrette.

THIS vinaigrette can be covered and refrigerated for up to 1 month. Let come to room temperature before serving.

LOBSTER WITH VANILLA–BROWN BUTTER VINAIGRETTE

SERVES 4

 **A** few well-chosen ingredients can produce surprisingly complex results, as in this first course of lobster enlivened with a bittersweet combination of lightly caramelized endive and brown butter sauce that's kissed with the flavor of vanilla. The ingredient list is short, but the flavors and textures make a big impact.

---

2 MAINE LOBSTERS, 1½ POUNDS EACH

8 CUPS WATER

KOSHER SALT

½ CUP (1 STICK) PLUS 1 TABLESPOON UNSALTED BUTTER, CUT INTO PIECES

½ VANILLA BEAN, SPLIT LENGTHWISE AND SCRAPED, BEAN DISCARDED

1 TABLESPOON AGED BALSAMIC VINEGAR

2 TABLESPOONS CANOLA OIL

2 CUPS CHOPPED ENDIVE (FROM ABOUT 3 ENDIVE)

KILL the lobsters by driving a heavy knife right between their eyes and pulling the handle down like a lever; this will kill them instantly. Remove the tails and claws from their bodies.

POUR the water into a large, heavy-bottomed pot; add 1 tablespoon salt. Bring to a boil over high heat. Add the lobster claws and simmer for 5 minutes. Use tongs to remove the claws and set them aside, covered and warm. Raise the heat to high and bring the water back to a boil. Add the lobster tails and immediately remove the pot from the heat. Let the tails steep for 7½ to 8 minutes. Use tongs to remove the tails from the water and set aside to cool. When cool enough to handle, split the tails in half lengthwise. Remove the meat from the tails in 2 pieces by running your finger underneath it. Crack the claws with the back of a heavy kitchen knife and remove the meat from the claws in 1 piece.

MAKE the vinaigrette: Put ½ cup of the butter in a heavy-bottomed nonstick saucepan. Set over medium–high heat and brown to a dark, amber color, swirling the pan as the butter starts to bubble, approximately 3½ minutes. Remove the pot from the heat and let cool slightly for 5 minutes. Stir in the vanilla seeds and vinegar. (Note: The vinaigrette will not emulsify; it is a "broken" vinaigrette.) Set aside, covered to keep it warm.

PREPARE the endive: Put the oil and 1 tablespoon butter into a heavy-bottomed sauté pan and set over medium–high heat. The butter will sizzle and foam. When the foam begins to subside, lower the heat to medium, add the endive, and cook, stirring every minute, until caramelized, approximately 5 minutes. Season with salt and set aside, covered to keep it warm.

DIVIDE the endive among 4 salad plates. Put half a lobster tail and 1 claw on top of the endive on each plate. Whisk the brown butter vinaigrette and spoon it over and around the lobster. Serve.

MOROCCAN-SPICED LAMB WITH TAHINI DRESSING

SERVES 4

The signature flavors of Moroccan food are increasingly popular in restaurants and home kitchens all over the United States. This recipe seasons one of the most popular meats of the region, lamb, with a ground spice blend of cumin, coriander, and cinnamon, searing it onto the meat. The lamb is then sliced and drizzled with a tahini dressing that perks up the flavors, adding cool relief to the spices, an appealing contrast.

I TABLESPOON CUMIN SEED

I TABLESPOON CORIANDER SEED

½ TEASPOON BLACK PEPPERCORNS

KOSHER SALT

½ TEASPOON GROUND CINNAMON

¼ TEASPOON CAYENNE

4 PIECES BONELESS LAMB LOIN, 3 OUNCES EACH

2 TABLESPOONS OLIVE OIL

I CUP LOOSELY PACKED DANDELION GREENS OR MESCLUN GREENS (ABOUT ½ OUNCE)

¾ CUP SHAVED FENNEL (OPTIONAL)

TAHINI DRESSING (RECIPE FOLLOWS)

¼ CUP THINLY SLICED RED ONION

PREHEAT the oven to 350°F. Put the cumin, coriander, and peppercorns in an 8-inch sauté pan and toast over medium heat, shaking constantly, until fragrant, 2 to 3 minutes. Remove the pan from the heat and let cool, then transfer the spices to a spice or coffee grinder.

ADD 1 teaspoon salt, the cinnamon, and the cayenne to the grinder and grind together. Transfer the spice mixture to a mixing bowl large enough to hold a piece of the lamb loin.

ONE by one, put the lamb loins in the bowl and coat them with a thin layer of the mixture, patting down on the spices to make sure they adhere to the meat.

HEAT a heavy-bottomed, 10-inch sauté pan over medium-high heat. Add the oil and heat it. Add the loins without crowding, and cook for 2 minutes on each side, then transfer the pan to the oven. Roast until an instant-read thermometer inserted in the thickest part of a loin reads 120°F to 125°F, 3 to 4 minutes, then remove from the oven, transfer to a plate, and let rest for 5 minutes.

THE lamb can be served warm, at room temperature, or cold. Or, it can be cooled and refrigerated in an airtight plastic container for up to 24 hours.

THINLY slice the lamb. Lay the slices of 1 loin on each of 4 salad plates. Sprinkle each loin with a pinch of salt. In a mixing bowl, toss the greens and fennel, if using, with 2 tablespoons of the tahini dressing. Drizzle the remaining dressing over and around the lamb. Top the lamb on each plate with some dressed greens, fennel, and onion slices. Serve.

EMBELLISHMENT Just before serving, season the lamb with Lemon Salt (page 21) or Cumin Salt (page 20) to further enhance the Moroccan-themed flavorings.

TAHINI DRESSING MAKES 1 ½ CUPS

Find new complexity in a tomato and field greens salad by tossing it with this dressing.

½ CUP TAHINI PASTE (SEE SOURCES, PAGE 318)

¼ CUP FRESHLY SQUEEZED LEMON JUICE

1 TABLESPOON WHITE-WINE VINEGAR

1 CLOVE GARLIC, MINCED

1 TEASPOON SPANISH PAPRIKA (SEE SOURCES, PAGE 318)

PINCH CAYENNE PEPPER

KOSHER SALT

1 CUP EXTRA VIRGIN OLIVE OIL

PUT the tahini, lemon juice, vinegar, garlic, paprika, and cayenne in the bowl of a food processor fitted with the steel blade, and season with salt. With the motor running, slowly add the oil in a thin stream to form an emulsified dressing. Transfer to a bowl, scraping down the sides.

THIS dressing can be covered and refrigerated for up to 5 days. Let come to room temperature before serving.

TERMS AND TECHNIQUES *Tahini:* Tahini is a sesame paste popular in Middle Eastern cuisine.

EMBELLISHMENT Whip some Lemon Marmalade (page 41) or crumbled feta cheese into the dressing.

SWEETBREADS WITH PICKLED VEGETABLES AND RAISIN-MUSTARD EMULSION

SERVES 4

Some people unfamiliar with sweetbreads find the idea of their being the thymus gland of calves off-putting, but I urge you to try this dish and see if you share my affection for this delicacy. A lot of chefs love sweetbreads. Maybe it's because we were trained to cook them correctly, which is to say we learned early how to avoid the common pitfall of overcooking them. By first soaking them overnight and then poaching them gently in an aromatic court bouillon, the chef can maintain their tender texture and rich flavor.

A crucial aspect of any successful sweetbread dish is adding elements that cut the slightly gamy flavor of the sweetbreads, accomplished here with the raisin-mustard emulsion and pickled vegetables; in fact, the pickling liquid in the recipe on page 37 was actually designed to complement the flavors in this dish.

1½ POUNDS SWEETBREADS

12 CUPS WATER, PLUS MORE FOR SOAKING

KOSHER SALT

2 HEADS GARLIC, SPLIT HORIZONTALLY, EXCESS PAPERY SKIN REMOVED

1 CUP WHITE ONION, MEDIUM DICE

1 CUP PEELED CARROTS, MEDIUM DICE

1 CUP DRY WHITE WINE

5 SPRIGS THYME

4 BAY LEAVES

2 TABLESPOONS GOLDEN RAISINS

2 TABLESPOONS GRAIN MUSTARD

3 TABLESPOONS BANYULS VINEGAR OR SHERRY VINEGAR

1¾ TEASPOONS CAPERS, RINSED AND DRAINED

½ CUP PLUS 3 TABLESPOONS CANOLA OIL

1 CUP WONDRA FLOUR, OR ALL-PURPOSE FLOUR

3 TO 4 CUPS ASSORTED PICKLED VEGETABLES SUCH AS CAULIFLOWER, CARROTS, BEETS, AND MUSHROOMS, PREFERABLY HOMEMADE (PAGE 37)

CHIVES, FOR GARNISH

PUT the sweetbreads in a bowl and cover by 4 inches with cold water. Soak in the refrigerator overnight, changing the water three or four times. Drain.

MAKE a court bouillon: Pour the 12 cups water into a large, heavy-bottomed pot. Add ¼ cup salt, the garlic, onion, carrots, wine, thyme, and bay leaves and bring to a boil over high heat. Remove the pot from the heat and let it cool completely.

WHILE the liquid is cooling, put the raisins in a small bowl, cover with warm water, and let soak for 10 minutes. Drain.

ADD the sweetbreads to the cooled court bouillon, return the pot to the stove, and bring to a simmer over medium heat. Let simmer until the sweetbreads are just beginning to firm up, 12 to 15 minutes, and an instant-read thermometer inserted to thickest part of a sweetbread reads 130°F. (Lift a sweetbread out of the water with a slotted spoon before inserting the thermometer.)

MEANWHILE, make the raisin-mustard emulsion: Put the mustard, vinegar, raisins, capers, and ¾ teaspoon salt in a blender and blend on medium-high speed. With the motor running, slowly add ½ cup of the canola oil in a thin stream to make an emulsion. Transfer the emulsion to a bowl, scraping down the sides. Set aside.

WHEN the sweetbreads are done, use a slotted spoon to remove the sweetbreads and set aside to cool, then chill them in the refrigerator until cold. Once cooled, trim the fat and excess membrane. Slice the sweetbreads on an angle into a total of twelve ½-inch-thick slices.

PUT the flour and 1 tablespoon salt in a baking dish and stir together. Dredge each sweetbread slice in the seasoned flour and shake off any excess flour.

STRAIN the pickled vegetables and gather them in a bowl. Set aside.

POUR the remaining 3 tablespoons of oil into a heavy-bottomed, 12-inch sauté pan and heat it over high heat until it shimmers. Add the sweetbreads and cook until golden-brown on both sides, approximately 3 minutes per side.

SPOON 1 tablespoon mustard emulsion into the center of each of 4 salad plates. Top with 3 slices of sweetbreads. Divide the vegetables evenly among the plates. Garnish by snipping the chives into 4-inch pieces over each dish. Serve.

TERMS AND TECHNIQUES *Court bouillon:* A court bouillon is a highly seasoned broth in which fish or meats are cooked. They are often tailored to coax a flavor suited to a particular dish, but generally include an acid of some kind (wine in this recipe) and a selection of aromatics.

The word *sweetbreads* also refers to the pancreas of calves, lambs, and pigs. The pancreas is not used much in contemporary cooking, but when faced with a choice between the thymus gland (from the throat) and the pancreas, select the former, also known as the kernel. It should look bright and pinkish; avoid any that appear brown or dull.

THE REASON *The sweetbread cooking liquid is cooled:* The sweetbread cooking liquid is cooled before the sweetbreads are added because gently cooking them from a cold state draws out any lingering impurities and helps them cook gently and evenly.

The sweetbreads are soaked overnight: Soaking the sweetbreads draws out blood and other impurities.

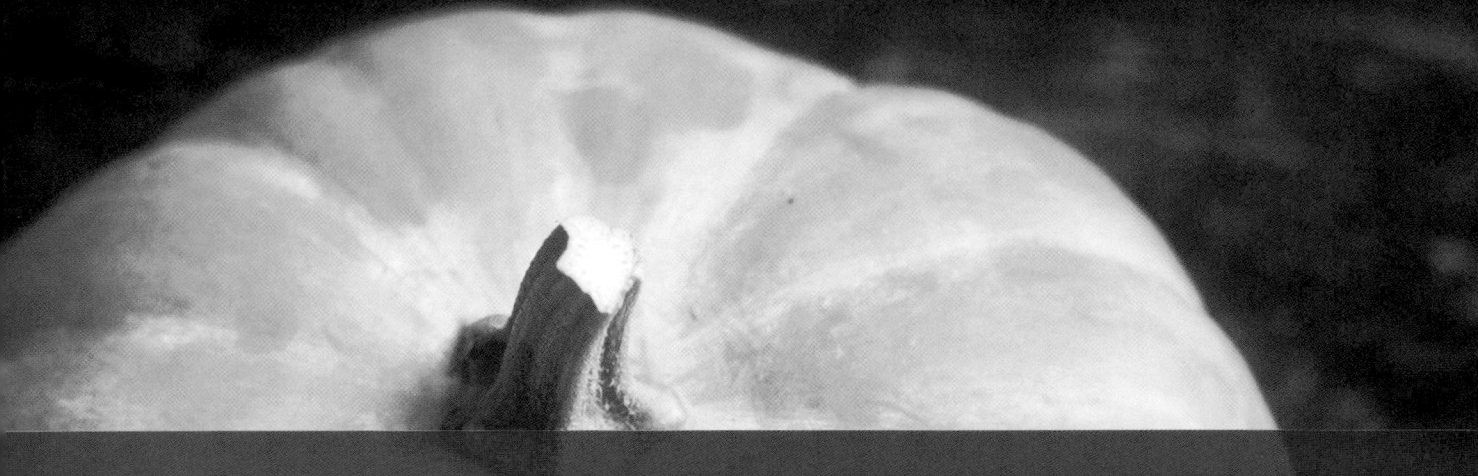

SOUPS

FOR A SEASONAL-FOODS DEVOTEE LIKE ME, soups are the purest way to celebrate favorite ingredients. In soups, as in no other type of dish, one seasonal ingredient can dominate the bowl, offering the ultimate expression of a vegetable's or fruit's charms.

I often turn to pureed soups because they essentially make the main ingredient into the soup, rather than a mere player floating in a broth. Examples of this abound in the following pages: Chilled Pea Soup with Mint Chutney (page 166), White Bean and Escarole Soup with Shrimp (page 144), and Roasted Butternut Squash Soup with Blue Cheese and Walnuts (page 150).

Most of these soups feature at least one component—a compote, granité, ceviche, and so on—that can be omitted. They add important flavors and textures to the bowl, but if you leave them out, you will still be left with valuable additions to your soup repertoire. You can, for example, make the White Gazpacho without the Red Gazpacho Granité (page 159), the Chestnut-Fennel Soup without the Apple-Walnut Chutney (page 153), and the Cauliflower Soup without the Cheddar Cheese Croutons (page 156).

Note: When blending or processing hot liquid, be especially careful during the transfer of the liquid from the pot to the blender. Use a ladle and don't fill the blender more than halfway. Be sure to leave the center piece of the blender lid or the top of the processor's feeding tube out so that steam and heat can escape, and cover the open top loosely with a towel to keep liquid from escaping. You can maximize the volume of each batch by adding more liquid after the initial portion has been blended.

CHEESE BOUILLON WITH PARMESAN FLAN

SERVES 4

Parmigiano-Reggiano and prosciutto di Parma, both produced in Italy's rightfully renowned Parma region, are sublime examples of the natural affinity products from the same region often have for one another. Usually encountered together in pasta dishes or as part of an antipasto platter, the earthy, salty meat and cheese seem made for each other.

A common piece of kitchen wisdom suggests saving the rinds of Parmigiano-Reggiano to use as a flavoring agent in soups and other dishes after the Italian tradition of extracting as much utility as possible from each and every ingredient. This soup uses a pound of rinds as the primary source of flavor. (If you don't save rinds, ask your local cheese merchant to save some for you.) Like the rind, the prosciutto itself is strained out, but its flavor infuses the soup.

If you and your guests are true cheese lovers, serve a basket of Gougères (page 81) alongside this soup.

¼ CUP EXTRA-VIRGIN OLIVE OIL

½ CUP MEDIUM-CHOPPED LEEKS, WHITE AND LIGHT GREEN PARTS ONLY, WELL RINSED

⅔ CUP MEDIUM-CHOPPED WHITE ONION

1 HEAD GARLIC, OUTER SKIN REMOVED, HALVED

KOSHER SALT

1 POUND PARMIGIANO-REGGIANO RINDS, SCRUBBED CLEAN UNDER COLD RUNNING WATER

2 OUNCES THINLY SLICED PROSCIUTTO DI PARMA

1 CUP DRY WHITE WINE

4 BAY LEAVES

6 CUPS HOMEMADE WHITE CHICKEN STOCK (PAGE 145) OR LOW-SODIUM, STORE-BOUGHT CHICKEN BROTH

4 SPRIGS THYME

BLACK PEPPER IN A MILL

PARMESAN FLAN (RECIPE FOLLOWS)

2 TABLESPOONS FINELY SLICED CHIVES

POUR the oil into a large, heavy-bottomed stockpot and warm it over medium heat. Add the leeks, onion, garlic, and a pinch of salt, and cook, stirring, until softened but not browned, approximately 5 minutes.

ADD the cheese rind(s) and prosciutto and continue to cook gently for 5 minutes. Add the wine and bay leaves. Bring to a boil, then lower the heat and simmer until reduced by half, approximately 3 minutes. Use a spoon to scrape up any flavorful bits cooked onto the bottom of the pot. Pour in the stock and bring to a boil over high heat. Lower the heat and simmer, stirring occasionally to keep the rinds from burning at the bottom of the pot, for 30 minutes. Add the thyme, remove the pot from the heat, and let the soup steep, covered, at room temperature for 1 hour. Spoon off any oil that has risen to the surface, or use a basting bulb to remove it.

STRAIN the soup through a fine-mesh strainer set over a clean pot. Discard the solids. If any additional oil rises to the surface, suction it off with a basting bulb or pat it with a paper towel. Season the soup with salt and 4 grinds of pepper, or to taste. The soup can be cooled, covered, and refrigerated for up to 3 days or frozen for up to 1 month. Reheat the bouillon over medium heat.

UNMOLD 1 flan in the center of each of 4 shallow bowls. Ladle hot bouillon around the flan. Garnish with chives and serve.

VARIATION You can make the soup with the rinds of other types of hard-rind cheeses such as Gouda.

EMBELLISHMENT If you like, reserve the prosciutto that's been strained out of the soup, chop it, and scatter it over the surface of the soup as a garnish. Garnish with blanched leeks.

PARMESAN FLAN MAKES 4 FLANS

These flans are a delicious centerpiece to the cheese bouillon and other brothy soups, such as minestrone, as well as to vegetable salads. They can be garnished with sautéed mushrooms and served as an appetizer, or served alongside roasted poultry and meats. They are also a nice addition to the Mediterranean Salad with Bagña Cauda Sauce (page 101).

½ CUP HEAVY CREAM

2 TABLESPOONS MILK

2 TABLESPOONS FINELY GRATED PARMIGIANO-REGGIANO

1 TABLESPOON GARLIC CONFIT (PAGE 36), OR ⅛ TEASPOON MINCED FRESH GARLIC

APPROXIMATELY 1 TABLESPOON UNSALTED BUTTER FOR GREASING MOLDS, AT ROOM TEMPERATURE

1 LARGE EGG PLUS 1 LARGE EGG YOLK, BEATEN TOGETHER

⅛ TEASPOON KOSHER SALT

PINCH CAYENNE

PUT the cream, milk, cheese, and garlic confit into a heavy-bottomed saucepan and bring to a boil over medium-high heat. Remove the pot from the heat and let sit for 30 minutes.

PREHEAT the oven to 225°F. Lightly butter four 2-ounce, stainless steel timbale molds or ramekins.

GRADUALLY whisk the beaten eggs into the cream-milk mixture. Strain the mixture through a fine-mesh strainer set over a bowl. Season the custard with the salt and cayenne.

DIVIDE the custard equally among the molds. Put the molds into a shallow baking pan and pour hot water into the pan and halfway up the sides of the molds. Cover the pan snugly with foil, poke some holes in the foil (to prevent condensation), and bake until the custards are set (a toothpick inserted into the center of one mold will come out clean), 45 to 50 minutes.

THE flans can be made up to 24 hours ahead of time. Cover them with plastic wrap and refrigerate. When ready to serve, set the molds in a baking pan, fill the pan with warm water halfway up the sides of the molds, and bake in an oven preheated to 300°F just to warm the flans, 12 to 15 minutes.

RUN a small butter knife along the perimeter of each custard to loosen it. Unmold the custards by inverting them onto a plate or into the center of a bowl, and serve.

ARTISANAL'S FRENCH ONION SOUP

SERVES 4

 dapted from Artisanal restaurant, where we serve our version of a number of bistro classics, this onion soup achieves its distinction with four members of the onion family (Spanish onion, red onion, shallots, and leeks), and four different cheeses. This is one of the few times when it's truly essential to use your own stock; homemade beef stock is the only way to make the soup sufficiently rich.

As complex as the soup is, you can also make it with just one of the specified cheeses and top it with Parmigiano-Reggiano and it will still be delicious.

I like to be deliberately sloppy when preparing this soup, arranging the cheese so that it really piles up on top of the bowl and spills over the edge when it melts. When it cools, you can break off the hardened cheese (the French call it *croûte*) and eat it.

---

8 SLICES FRENCH BAGUETTE, ¼ INCH THICK

I CLOVE GARLIC, END CUT OFF AND DISCARDED

¼ CUP CANOLA OIL

2 CUPS THINLY SLICED SPANISH ONIONS (FROM ABOUT 2 MEDIUM ONIONS, THINLY SLICED)

I ½ CUPS THINLY SLICED RED ONIONS (FROM ABOUT 3 MEDIUM ONIONS)

½ CUP THINLY SLICED SHALLOTS

½ CUP LEEKS, WHITE AND LIGHT GREEN PARTS ONLY, WELL RINSED, MEDIUM DICE

2 CUPS DRY WHITE WINE

¼ CUP SHERRY

4 CUPS WHITE BEEF STOCK (PAGE 47)

HERB SACHET: 4 SPRIGS THYME, 3 BAY LEAVES, I TEASPOON CRUSHED BLACK PEPPERCORNS, AND 3 CRUSHED GARLIC CLOVES TIED IN A CHEESECLOTH BUNDLE

I TABLESPOON SHERRY VINEGAR

KOSHER SALT AND BLACK PEPPER IN A MILL

¼ CUP PLUS 2 TABLESPOONS GRATED GRUYÈRE (FROM ABOUT 2 ½ OUNCES CHEESE)

¼ CUP PLUS 2 TABLESPOONS GRATED BEAUFORT (FROM ABOUT 2 ½ OUNCES CHEESE)

¼ CUP PLUS 2 TABLESPOONS GRATED EMMENTHALER (FROM ABOUT 2 ½ OUNCES CHEESE)

¼ CUP PLUS 2 TABLESPOONS GRATED PARMIGIANO-REGGIANO (FROM ABOUT 2 ½ OUNCES CHEESE)

PREHEAT the oven to 325°F. Put the baguette slices in a single layer on a cookie sheet and bake in the oven until crisp-hard and dark golden-brown, approximately 5 minutes. Rub both sides of the bread slices with the exposed tip of the garlic clove. Set aside.

POUR the canola oil into a large, heavy-bottomed stockpot and warm it over medium heat. Add the Spanish onions, red onions, shallots, and leeks and cook, stirring every few minutes, until deeply caramelized to a dark amber brown, 25 to 30 minutes. Pour in the wine and sherry and stir to scrape up any crusty bits cooked onto the bottom of the pot. Cook until the wine is reduced by two-thirds, 8 to 10 minutes.

POUR in the stock and add the herb sachet. Bring the stock to a boil over high heat, then lower the heat and let simmer until the onions loose their texture, 35 to 40 minutes. Discard the herb sachet, squeezing any liquid back into the pot, stir in the sherry vinegar, and season to taste with salt and pepper. The soup can be made to this point, covered, and refrigerated for up to 3 days. Reheat before proceeding, bringing the soup to a boil.

IF continuing or when soup is reheated, in a bowl, stir together the Gruyère, Beaufort, and Emmenthaler.

POSITION a rack 4 inches from the heating element of the broiler and preheat the broiler. Put four 8-ounce ovenproof soup crocks on a sturdy cookie sheet or baking pan. Divide the hot soup among the crocks, filling them just high enough to allow the croutons to be flush with the top of the crock. Float 2 croutons on the surface of the soup in each bowl. Divide the grated cheese mixture among the 4 crocks and sprinkle the Parmigiano-Reggiano over them.

PUT the sheet under the broiler and cook until the cheese is bubbly and golden, approximately 5 minutes. Carefully remove the sheet from the oven and serve.

VARIATION In the summer we make a lighter version of this soup, replacing half of the beef stock with White Chicken Stock (page 45).

WHITE BEAN AND ESCAROLE SOUP WITH SHRIMP

SERVES 4

One of the most defining ingredients in this soup is the rosemary that infuses it with a rustic, woodsy character as it cooks. It's substantial and restorative, a perfect cold-weather soup, that's also satisfying without the shrimp. You can skip the step of pureeing the soup and it will still be delicious, although it will have a decidedly lighter mouthfeel.

- ½ POUND (I CUP PLUS 2 TABLESPOONS) DRIED CANNELLINI BEANS OR OTHER DRIED WHITE BEANS
- ¼ CUP PLUS 2 TABLESPOONS EXTRA VIRGIN OLIVE OIL
- ¼ CUP FINELY DICED FENNEL
- ½ CUP FINELY DICED SPANISH ONION
- ¼ CUP FINELY DICED CARROT
- 2 TABLESPOONS FINELY DICED CELERY
- I TABLESPOON PLUS I TEASPOON FINELY CHOPPED GARLIC
- KOSHER SALT

- 4 SPRIGS ROSEMARY, TIED IN A CHEESE-CLOTH BUNDLE
- 5 CUPS WHITE CHICKEN STOCK (PAGE 45) OR LOW-SODIUM, STORE-BOUGHT CHICKEN BROTH
- ½ LEMON, ZESTED AND JUICED
- ¼ POUND ESCAROLE, TOUGH OUTER LEAVES REMOVED, CORED, AND CHOPPED INTO I-INCH-SQUARE PIECES (FROM ABOUT I-POUND HEAD ESCAROLE)
- BLACK PEPPER IN A MILL
- 4 CUPS WATER
- 12 JUMBO SHRIMP (ABOUT ½ POUND), WITH THE SHELL ON

PUT the beans in a bowl and cover by 4 inches with room-temperature water. Cover and let soak overnight at room temperature. Drain.

POUR ¼ cup of the oil into a large, heavy-bottomed pot and heat it over medium heat. Add the fennel, onion, carrot, celery, 1 tablespoon of the garlic, and a pinch of salt and cook until softened but not browned, approximately 5 minutes. Add the beans and rosemary, pour in the stock, raise the heat to high, and bring to a boil. Lower the heat and simmer, covered, until the beans are tender, 1 hour and 15 to 1 hour and 20 minutes. Use tongs or a slotted spoon to fish out and discard the rosemary sprigs. Add the lemon juice, zest, and 2 teaspoons salt, or more to taste.

MEANWHILE, about 10 minutes before the soup is done cooking, heat the remaining 2 tablespoons oil in a heavy-bottomed sauté pan. Add the remaining 1 teaspoon garlic and sauté for 30 seconds, being careful to not brown it. Add the escarole and sauté until wilted, 6 to 8 minutes. Season with salt and 4 grinds of pepper, or to taste. Remove the pan from the heat and set aside, covered to keep warm.

USE an immersion blender to puree about half the soup in the pot, or transfer about half the soup to a standing blender, puree, and return to the pot. (See safety note, page 137.)

POUR the 4 cups water into a large, heavy-bottomed pot. Add 1 tablespoon salt and bring to a boil over high heat. Add the shrimp, remove the pot from the heat, and poach the shrimp until firm and pink, approximately 3 minutes. Drain and set aside to cool, then peel and devein.

STIR the escarole into the soup and divide the soup among 4 bowls. Add 3 shrimp to each bowl and serve.

EMBELLISHMENTS Sprinkle grated Parmigiano-Reggiano or Pecorino Romano cheese over each serving, drizzle the surface of each bowl of soup with some Provençal Oil (page 28) or extra virgin olive oil, and/or crumble Parmesan Tuilles (page 100) over the surface.

PUMPKIN BISQUE WITH WILD MUSHROOMS

**A**ny dish featuring both pumpkin and cranberries, not to mention wild mushrooms, is perfect for the Thanksgiving table, or any fall feast. This recipe calls for cheese pumpkin because its low water content helps produce a concentrated flavor. Though named a bisque, this soup doesn't feature any cream; it gets its smooth richness from the mascarpone cheese.

I must put in a word for my favorite mushrooms, porcini, which have a distinctly earthy flavor and voluptuous texture. Other mushrooms such as chanterelles would also be good here, but if you can obtain fresh porcini, make a point of using them.

---

4 POUNDS CHEESE PUMPKIN, SEEDED, PEELED, AND QUARTERED,

8 TABLESPOONS (1 STICK) UNSALTED BUTTER, SOFTENED AT ROOM TEMPERATURE

KOSHER SALT

WHITE PEPPER IN A MILL

¼ CUP SPANISH ONION, MEDIUM DICE

2 TABLESPOONS CELERY, MEDIUM DICE

4 CUPS HOMEMADE VEGETABLE STOCK (PAGE 49) OR LOW-SODIUM, STORE-BOUGHT VEGETABLE BROTH OR WATER

2 TABLESPOONS MASCARPONE CHEESE, OR ¼ CUP HEAVY CREAM

½ CUP CANNED PUMPKIN PUREE

2 TABLESPOONS FINELY DICED SHALLOTS

1 CUP PORCINI MUSHROOMS, STEMS AND CAPS SEPARATED, STEMS PEELED AND SLICED INTO ¼-INCH SLICES, CAPS SLICED ¼ INCH THICK, OR CHANTERELLES, HALVED OR QUARTERED BASED ON SIZE

FEW TABLESPOONS WHITE CHICKEN STOCK (PAGE 45), IF NEEDED (OPTIONAL)

PINCH GROUND NUTMEG

1 TEASPOON FINELY GRATED ORANGE ZEST

CRANBERRY COMPOTE (OPTIONAL; RECIPE FOLLOWS)

PREHEAT the oven to 325°F. Put the pumpkin quarters in a bowl. Add 3 tablespoons of the softened butter, season with salt and pepper, and toss to coat the pumpkin. Spread the quarters out on a rimmed cookie sheet or baking sheet. Roast until tender to a fork-tip, 50 minutes to 1 hour. Remove from the oven and, when cool enough to handle, scoop out the flesh. You should have approximately 3 cups of roasted pumpkin.

PUT 3 tablespoons butter into a large, heavy-bottomed pot and warm it over low heat. Add the onion, celery, and a pinch of salt, and cook, stirring occasionally, until the vegetables are softened but not browned, approximately 20 minutes. Pour in the stock and add the roasted pumpkin. Bring to boil over high heat. Lower the heat and simmer for 20 minutes. Whisk in the mascarpone and pumpkin puree.

PUT 2 tablespoons butter into a medium, heavy-bottomed sauté pan and warm it over medium-low heat. Add the shallots and, if using porcini, mushroom stems and sauté for 1 minute, then add the caps and sauté for another 2 minutes or, if using chanterelles, add the pieces along with the shallots and sauté for approximately 3 minutes. If the mushrooms look dry, add a tablespoon or two of water or stock. Season with salt and 3 grinds of pepper, or to taste. Set the mushrooms aside, covered, to keep them warm.

DO the following in batches: Put the soup in a blender and puree until velvety smooth. (See safety note, page 137.) Season to taste with salt. Continue to blend until smooth. Strain the soup through a fine-mesh strainer set over a bowl. Add the nutmeg, orange zest, and 3 grinds of white pepper to the soup.

DIVIDE the soup among 6 wide, shallow bowls. Garnish each serving with 1 heaping tablespoon cranberry compote, if desired. Divide the mushrooms equally among the bowls, scattering them over the surface of the soup, and serve.

EMBELLISHMENT Melt 2 tablespoons butter in a saucepan over medium-high heat and let cook until the butter turns brown. Add it to the soup while blending one batch.

CRANBERRY COMPOTE MAKES 1 CUP

This compote is also a delicious accompaniment to game and poultry.

2 TABLESPOONS UNSALTED BUTTER

1½ CUPS FRESH CRANBERRIES

½ CUP PLUS 2 TABLESPOONS GRANULATED SUGAR

2 TEASPOONS GRATED ORANGE ZEST

2 TABLESPOONS GRAND MARNIER (OPTIONAL)

PINCH CINNAMON

1 TEASPOON GRATED FRESH GINGER

MELT the butter in a heavy-bottomed sauté pan set over low heat. Stir in the cranberries, sugar, orange zest, Grand Marnier, cinnamon, and ginger.

COOK, stirring occasionally, until the cranberries begin to burst, approximately 6 minutes. The mixture will be bubbling and foamy. Continue to cook for another 3 minutes.

REMOVE the pan from the heat and let cool. The compote can be cooled, covered, and refrigerated for up to 1 week.

ROASTED BUTTERNUT SQUASH SOUP
WITH BLUE CHEESE AND WALNUTS

SERVES 6

This is one of the first dishes I introduced to the menu at Anabelle's, on New York City's Upper East Side, the restaurant where I became head chef for the first time. I don't recall why I thought to scatter blue cheese and walnuts over a squash soup, except that all of these flavors are closely associated with fall cooking. You can make this with other squash such as acorn, pumpkin, or Delicata.

---

3 POUNDS BUTTERNUT SQUASH (1 LARGE SQUASH)

¼ CUP CANOLA OIL

3 TEASPOONS PLUS A PINCH KOSHER SALT

WHITE PEPPER IN A MILL

¼ CUP PLUS 1 TABLESPOON CRUSHED WALNUTS (FROM ABOUT 12 WALNUT HALVES)

½ CUP SPANISH ONION, MEDIUM DICE

½ CUP CORED, PEELED PEAR, ANY VARIETY, MEDIUM DICE

½ CUP RIESLING OR OTHER FULL-BODIED WHITE WINE

5 ½ CUPS VEGETABLE STOCK (PAGE 49) OR LOW-SODIUM, STORE-BOUGHT VEGETABLE BROTH OR WATER

2 TEASPOONS HONEY

½ CUP CRUMBLED ROQUEFORT OR OTHER BLUE CHEESE (FROM ABOUT 2 OUNCES CHEESE), AT ROOM TEMPERATURE

PREHEAT the oven to 350°F. Cut off the ends of the squash. Cut the squash in half lengthwise and remove the seeds and strings, using a tablespoon or small scoop. Rub the cut sides lightly with 2 tablespoons of the oil, season with a total of 1 teaspoon salt and 4 grinds of pepper, and place cut-side down on a cookie sheet. Roast until tender to a knife-tip, approximately 1 hour. Remove from the oven and, when cool enough to handle, scoop out the flesh. You should have 3 cups of roasted squash.

MEANWHILE, put the nuts in an 8-inch sauté pan and toast over medium heat, shaking constantly, until fragrant, 2 to 3 minutes. Remove from the heat and set aside.

POUR the remaining 2 tablespoons oil into a large, heavy-bottomed pot and heat over medium heat. Add the onion, pear, and a pinch of salt and cook without browning for 20 minutes. Pour in the Riesling and cook, scraping up any bits stuck to the bottom of the pot, until all of the wine has reduced by two-thirds, approximately 5 minutes. Pour in the stock and bring to a boil over high heat. Add the roasted butternut squash. Lower the heat and simmer for 30 minutes.

WHEN the soup is done, pour it into a blender in batches and blend until smooth. (See safety note, page 137.) Season with the salt and add the honey. Strain the soup through a fine-mesh strainer; if it seems too thick, add a few tablespoons of water to thin it slightly. (It should just coat the back of a wooden spoon.)

DIVIDE the soup among 4 warm soup bowls. Garnish each bowl with 1 tablespoon crumbled cheese and one-fourth of the crushed nuts. Serve.

VARIATION In the early fall, replace the pears with apples.

EMBELLISHMENTS Melt 2 tablespoons butter in a saucepan over medium-high heat and let cook until the butter turns brown. Add it to the soup while blending one batch.

Add sautéed wild mushrooms to the bowl and spoon the soup over them, or pile them in the center of the bowl and carefully ladle the soup around them.

CHESTNUT-FENNEL SOUP WITH APPLE-WALNUT CHUTNEY

SERVES 6

**T**his is my personal favorite fall soup, a sentiment echoed by *Gourmet* magazine editor in-chief Ruth Reichl, who—when she was the restaurant critic for the *New York Times*—called it "the best winter dish I ever ate." It is one of the remove-it-at-my-own-risk selections on the Picholine menu, where our guests have come to expect it year after year; as soon as the mercury begins to drop, they request it.

One of the wonders of this recipe is that it produces a creamy, velvety texture with no cream or excessive butter; the pureed chestnuts are all that's required for this effect. You could make it without the chutney, but the way the apples and walnuts play off the earthy soup takes this to a level that shouldn't be missed.

Try to buy your chestnuts from a store that keeps them in a refrigerator or refrigerated section, rather than out in the common area in large bins. It's difficult to tell a fresh chestnut from one that's past its prime, so this is your best bet of securing good ones.

¼ CUP PLUS 2 TABLESPOONS CANOLA OIL

½ CUP ROUGHLY CHOPPED WHITE ONION

1½ CUPS ROUGHLY CHOPPED FENNEL (FROM ABOUT 2 FENNEL BULBS)

½ CUP ROUGHLY CHOPPED CELERY

FRESH CHESTNUTS, PEELED AND ROASTED (PAGE 154), OR 3½ CUPS DEFROSTED FROZEN PEELED CHESTNUTS (SEE TERMS AND TECHNIQUES)

½ CUP PEELED, ROUGHLY CHOPPED, FIRM, TART APPLE SUCH AS GRANNY SMITH

1 TABLESPOON PLUS ¼ TEASPOON PLUS A PINCH KOSHER SALT

½ CUP PLUS 2 TABLESPOONS PERNOD OR OTHER ANISE-FLAVORED LIQUEUR LIKE ANISETTE (OPTIONAL)

1 CUP ORANGE JUICE, PREFERABLY FRESH-SQUEEZED (FROM ABOUT 3½ ORANGES)

6 CUPS WHITE CHICKEN STOCK (PAGE 45) OR LOW-SODIUM, STORE-BOUGHT CHICKEN BROTH

¼ TEASPOON FRESHLY GROUND WHITE PEPPER

APPLE-WALNUT CHUTNEY (RECIPE FOLLOWS)

HEAT the oil in a large, heavy-bottomed stockpot set over medium-low heat. Add the onion, fennel, celery, chestnuts, apple, and a pinch of salt, and cook, stirring, until softened but not browned, approximately 20 minutes.

POUR in ¼ cup of the Pernod, if using, and the orange juice and stir, scraping up any bits of food cooked onto the bottom of the pot. Continue to cook until the liquid comes to a boil and is reduced by two-thirds, approximately 7 minutes. Pour in the stock and bring it to a boil over high heat. Lower the heat and simmer until the vegetables and chestnuts are tender, approximately 25 minutes.

YOU may need to do the following in batches: Puree the soup in a blender or the bowl of a food processor fitted with the steel blade. (It should just coat the back of a spoon.) While the blender is still running, slowly add the remaining 2 tablespoons Pernod, if using, to the final batch.

POUR the soup through a fine-mesh strainer set over a bowl, pressing down on the solids to extract as much flavorful liquid as possible. Season with salt and pepper. The soup can be made to this point, cooled, covered, and refrigerated for up to 3 days. Reheat gently before proceeding.

DIVIDE the soup among 6 warm, shallow soup bowls. Mound some chutney in the center of each bowl and serve.

EMBELLISHMENTS Sautéed, diced game sausage, mounded atop the chutney, adds yet another level of complexity. Or you can omit the chutney in favor of sausage for an extraordinarily hearty soup. Or add sautéed wild mushrooms.

Drizzle each serving with walnut oil.

TERMS AND TECHNIQUES *Peeling chestnuts:* Cut a small, shallow "X" on the flat side and roast in an oven preheated to 400° F for 20 minutes until they crack open. Let cool, then peel.

APPLE-WALNUT CHUTNEY MAKES ½ CUP

In addition to this soup, this chutney is a fine accompaniment to chicken and game dishes, and blue cheese.

- 2 TABLESPOONS CHESTNUT HONEY OR REGULAR HONEY
- 2 TABLESPOONS SHERRY VINEGAR
- 2 TABLESPOONS FINELY DICED ONION
- ¼ TEASPOON KOSHER SALT
- ½ CUP PEELED, FINELY DICED APPLE
- ¼ CUP WALNUTS, TOASTED, CRUSHED (FROM ABOUT 25 WALNUTS)

PUT the honey, vinegar, and onion in a 2-quart, heavy-bottomed saucepan and bring to a boil over low heat. Cook slowly until the onion is softened but not browned, approximately 5 minutes. Add the apples and walnuts and cook until the liquid evaporates and the mixture begins to look like a unified mass, approximately 15 minutes. Season with the salt.

THE chutney can be cooled, covered, and refrigerated for up to 1 week. Let come to room temperature before using.

CAULIFLOWER SOUP WITH CHEDDAR CROUTONS

SERVES 6

 I have always thought that cauliflower is one of the most undervalued vegetables. It has a delicate flavor that, if properly handled, can be understated and elegant. To ensure that its flavor isn't overwhelmed, this soup is made with water rather than stock. When shopping for cauliflower, seek out one that is firm and unblemished and seems heavy for its size.

¼ CUP CANOLA OIL

¼ CUP SPANISH ONION, MEDIUM DICE

¼ CUP CELERY, MEDIUM-DICE

KOSHER SALT

3 POUNDS CAULIFLOWER, CLEANED AND CUT INTO FLORETS (APPROXIMATELY 2¼ POUNDS FLORETS)

4 CUPS WATER, PLUS MORE IF NEEDED

¼ CUP GRATED CHEDDAR CHEESE (FROM ABOUT 1 OUNCE CHEESE), AT ROOM TEMPERATURE

WHITE PEPPER IN A MILL

18 PIECES CHERVIL (OPTIONAL)

CHEDDAR CROUTONS (RECIPE FOLLOWS)

POUR the oil into a large, heavy-bottomed stockpot and warm it over low heat. Add the onions, celery, and a pinch of salt and cook until softened but not browned, approximately 4 minutes. Add the cauliflower and cook without browning for another 3 minutes. Pour in the water and bring to a boil over high heat, then lower the heat and simmer until the cauliflower is tender, approximately 30 minutes. Stir in the cheddar cheese.

DO the following in batches: Put the soup in a blender and puree until smooth. (See safety note, page 137.) If necessary, add some water to achieve a smooth consistency. (The soup should coat the back of a wooden spoon.) Season with salt and 4 grinds of pepper, or to taste. Divide the soup among 6 hot bowls. Garnish each bowl with croutons and 3 pieces chervil, if using. Serve.

VARIATION This soup can also be made with broccoli.

CHEDDAR CROUTONS SERVES 6 AS A GARNISH

2 CUPS ¾ INCH CUBES COUNTRY BREAD OR BAGUETTE WITH THE CRUST ON

1 TABLESPOON EXTRA VIRGIN OLIVE OIL

1 TABLESPOON UNSALTED BUTTER

¼ CUP PLUS 1 TABLESPOON FINELY GRATED CHEDDAR CHEESE AT ROOM TEMPERATURE

¼ TEASPOON KOSHER SALT

PREHEAT the oven to 325°F. Put the bread cubes into a mixing bowl and set them aside.

WARM the olive oil and melt the butter in a heavy-bottomed saucepan set over low heat. Pour over the bread cubes and stir to coat the cubes evenly. Sprinkle the cheese and salt over the cubes and toss gently to coat the cubes evenly.

POUR the croutons onto a cookie sheet or baking sheet, spread them out in a single layer, and bake them in the oven until golden-brown and crisp on the outside but still chewy inside, 5 to 6 minutes. Remove the baking sheet from the oven and serve the croutons warm or let cool. The croutons can be made in advance and kept at room temperature for up to 3 hours.

THE REASON *The croutons are hard on the outside, but soft on the inside:* Rock-hard croutons can disrupt the experience of eating most dishes. I prefer croutons that are just hard enough to not become soggy when dressed, but are pleasingly chewy inside.

WHITE GAZPACHO WITH RED GAZPACHO GRANITÉ

SERVES 6

t Picholine, we make an unconventional and very refreshing white gazpacho of grapes, cucumbers, garlic, almonds, and vinegar that has become one of the seasonal classics that our guests look forward to every summer. It's creamy white and rich thanks to the almonds and oil, but as you'll see, there's no actual cream whatsoever.

---

2 CUPS PLUS 3 TABLESPOONS PEELED, THINLY SLICED ALMONDS

1 CUP SEEDLESS GREEN GRAPES

¾ CUP CUCUMBER JUICE, EXTRACTED FROM PEELED CUCUMBERS IN A JUICER OR PURCHASED FROM A JUICE BAR

2 TABLESPOONS PLUS 2 TEASPOONS SHERRY VINEGAR

¼ CUP VERJUS, OR 2 TABLESPOONS SHERRY VINEGAR

¼ CUP PLUS 2 TABLESPOONS FRUITY EXTRA VIRGIN OLIVE OIL

2 SMALL CLOVES GARLIC, OR MORE TO TASTE, PEELED

3 CUPS WATER

1 CUP SMALL, CRUSTLESS WHITE BREAD CUBES (FROM 1½ OUNCES, OR 2 TO 3 SLICES BREAD)

1 TABLESPOON KOSHER SALT

½ TEASPOON CAYENNE

1 TABLESPOON FINELY DICED RED BELL PEPPER (OPTIONAL)

1 TABLESPOON FINELY DICED, PEELED, SEEDLESS CUCUMBER (OPTIONAL)

1 TABLESPOON FINELY DICED RED ONION (OPTIONAL)

1 TABLESPOON FINELY DICED CELERY (OPTIONAL)

RED GAZPACHO GRANITÉ (RECIPE FOLLOWS)

30 CILANTRO LEAVES

DO the following in batches: Put 2 cups of the almonds, the grapes, cucumber juice, verjus, oil, vinegar, and garlic into a blender. Pour in the water and blend until uniformly smooth, approximately 4 minutes. Add the bread and process for 1 more minute. Taste, season with the salt and cayenne, taste again, and add more salt if necessary. Strain through a fine mesh strainer set over a bowl, pressing down on the solids to extract as much flavorful liquid as possible. Cover, and refrigerate for at least 3 hours or up to 24 hours. If it appears too thick after refrigeration, whisk in some cold water to thin the soup.

WHEN ready to serve, put the remaining 3 tablespoons almonds in an 8-inch sauté pan and toast over medium heat, shaking constantly, until fragrant, 1 to 2 minutes. Transfer to a small bowl and let cool to room temperature.

IF using some or all of the vegetables, put the red pepper, cucumber, red onion, and celery in a small bowl and stir gently but thoroughly. This is your garnish.

DIVIDE the white gazpacho among 6 shallow soup bowls. Put a ¼-cup scoop of red gazpacho granité in the center of each bowl, scatter some reserved almonds and vegetables, if using, over each serving, and arrange 5 cilantro leaves decoratively on top.

TERMS AND TECHNIQUES *Verjus:* Verjus is a fermented grape juice that is sometimes employed as an alternative source of acidic flavor. It is available in gourmet markets and by mail order. (See Sources, page 318.)

THE REASON *The soup is served in shallow bowls:* A shallow bowl shows off the red gazpacho better than a deeper, narrower one would. Keep this in mind for any soups that are finished or augmented with attractive elements.

EMBELLISHMENT Garnish the soup with chilled, poached shellfish such as bay scallops, shrimp, or lobster. Top the granité with some Shrimp with Smoked Paprika (page 73), or lean the shrimp against the granité in each bowl.

RED GAZPACHO GRANITÉ MAKES ABOUT 1 CUP

In addition to being a contrast in taste and color to the white gazpacho, this refreshing savory ice can be served as an *amuse* (a small taste to stimulate the appetite and begin a meal), or between courses as an *intermezzo*, a unique take on palate-cleansing sorbet.

1 POUND FRESH BEEFSTEAK TOMATOES, CORED AND PASSED THROUGH A FOOD MILL (ABOUT 1½ CUPS MILLED TOMATOES)

2 TABLESPOONS CUCUMBER JUICE, EXTRACTED FROM PEELED CUCUMBERS IN A JUICER OR PURCHASED FROM A JUICE BAR

1 TABLESPOON RED-PEPPER JUICE, EXTRACTED IN A JUICER OR PURCHASED FROM A JUICE BAR

2 TEASPOONS CELERY JUICE, EXTRACTED IN A JUICER OR PURCHASED FROM A JUICE BAR

1 TABLESPOON SHERRY VINEGAR

1 TEASPOON FINELY CHOPPED GARLIC

KOSHER SALT

PINCH CAYENNE PEPPER, OR MORE TO TASTE

PUT all ingredients except the salt and cayenne in a mixing bowl and stir together. Season with salt and a pinch of cayenne, or more for a spicier granité. Pour the mixture into a 9-inch by 9-inch Pyrex dish and put in the freezer. Freeze for at least 2 hours, or until frozen, scraping the mixture with a fork every half-hour to break it into ice crystals.

THE granité can be covered and frozen for up to 1 week. When ready to serve, scoop out portions with an ice-cream scoop.

RAW TOMATO SOUP WITH BASIL GUACAMOLE AND MARINATED SCALLOPS

SERVES 6

ooking seasonal fruits and vegetables, while often necessary, can't help but put some distance between the diner and purely fresh food. This is especially true with tomatoes, which I feel are all too often overhandled by cooks. Because I use tomatoes only when they are at the peak of season, I prefer to eat them raw whenever possible, even in a soup.

In this dish, tomato juice is enriched with extra virgin olive oil and balsamic vinegar, then paired with two highly complementary components: a guacamole of avocado and basil, and marinated scallops.

---

4 POUNDS HEIRLOOM TOMATOES (ABOUT 5 LARGE TOMATOES), PEELED (SEE TERMS AND TECHNIQUES, PAGE 95), CORED, AND ROUGHLY CHOPPED

1½ TABLESPOONS SHERRY VINEGAR

½ TEASPOON MINCED GARLIC

½ CUP EXTRA VIRGIN OLIVE OIL

1 TEASPOON CELERY SALT (OPTIONAL) (PAGE 19)

KOSHER SALT

BLACK PEPPER IN A MILL

2 RIPE HAAS AVOCADOS (ABOUT 8 OUNCES EACH)

1 TEASPOON FINELY DICED JALAPEÑO PEPPER

1 TEASPOON FINELY DICED RED ONION

8 MEDIUM BASIL LEAVES, SLICED INTO BITE-SIZE PIECES

2 TEASPOONS FRESHLY SQUEEZED LIME JUICE

MARINATED SCALLOPS (RECIPE FOLLOWS)

PUT the tomatoes, vinegar, garlic, and ¼ cup plus 2 tablespoons of the oil in a standing blender and process until smooth. Strain through a fine mesh strainer into a bowl, pressing down on the solids to extract as much flavorful liquid as possible. Season with the celery salt (or 1 teaspoon kosher salt if not using celery salt) and 3 or 4 grinds of pepper, or to taste, Cover the bowl and refrigerate for at least 1 hour and up to 24 hours.

MAKE the Basil Guacamole: Cut the avocados in half lengthwise and twist the halves apart. Remove the pit by embedding the heel of a large knife into it and pulling it out. Score the avocado flesh with a knife. Gently work a tablespoon in between the flesh and skin of one avocado half. Work it around the edge of the avocado and gradually toward the bottom, carefully loosening the flesh until you can remove it; it should fall out in dice. Repeat with the remaining avocado halves. Put the avocado flesh into a mixing bowl. Mash it with a fork until coarse. Fold in the jalapeño, red onion, basil, and lime juice. Season to taste with approximately 1 teaspoon salt. This guacamole can be made up to 1 hour ahead of time, covered, and refrigerated.

IF using, mound some of the marinated scallops in the center of each of 6 chilled, shallow soup bowls. Top each serving with a rounded tablespoon of guacamole. Carefully pour the soup around the scallops in each bowl. Finish by drizzling the surface of the soup with the remaining 2 tablespoons extra virgin olive oil.

VARIATIONS Use cilantro instead of basil.

For a chunkier guacamole, remove the pit with the heel of a knife as directed. Use a sharp, thin-bladed knife to score the avocado flesh in a criss-cross pattern, being sure the knife goes all the way through to the skin. Invert the avocado over a bowl, pushing the skin through the flesh, and the avocado flesh will fall in dice.

EMBELLISHMENTS For a richer color, put the tomatoes through a food mill before using them. Drizzle each serving with Provençal Oil (page 28).

MARINATED SCALLOPS MAKES ABOUT 1 CUP, ENOUGH TO GARNISH 6 SERVINGS

These scallops operate on the same principle as a ceviche, a Peruvian dish in which the acid in the marinade "cooks" the fish or shellfish. The longer the scallops are dressed before serving, the more "well done" they'll be.

2/3 CUP BAY OR SEA SCALLOPS (ABOUT 6 OUNCES), PREFERABLY NANTUCKET BAY, MUSCLE REMOVED, WELL RINSED, AND SLICED THINLY HORIZONTALLY

1/2 TEASPOON FINELY DICED JALAPEÑO PEPPER, SEEDS REMOVED

1 TEASPOON FINELY SLICED BASIL

2 TABLESPOONS FRESHLY SQUEEZED LIME JUICE

1/2 TEASPOON KOSHER SALT

2 TEASPOONS FINELY DICED RED ONION

1 TABLESPOON FINELY DICED RED BELL PEPPER

1 TABLESPOON EXTRA VIRGIN OLIVE OIL

PUT the scallops in a mixing bowl. Add the other ingredients, stir gently, cover, and let marinate in the refrigerator for 20 minutes or up to 24 hours.

VARIATION These scallops would also be delicious on their own as an appetizer: Double the recipe and serve in chilled martini glasses on a bed of greens and/or guacamole, dressed with some of the marinade.

COLD "CAESAR SALAD" SOUP

SERVES 4

There are few surer ways of coming up with a new dish you know you'll like than mingling the ingredients of a classic in a new way, a principle that's used to dramatic effect here, in a soup made with the signature ingredients of a Caesar salad.

Soups fashioned from leafy greens are nothing new; spinach and escarole have been the basis of any number of examples. But you might be surprised at how well romaine works in this context and how naturally anchovy, lemon juice, Parmigiano-Reggiano, and black pepper fit in. The only thing missing is the raw egg yolk, which is omitted because it would make the soup excessively rich.

- 2 TABLESPOONS OLIVE OIL

- ²/₃ CUP SPANISH ONION, MEDIUM DICE

- 5 CLOVES GARLIC, CRUSHED AND PEELED

- 2 TEASPOONS PLUS I PINCH KOSHER SALT

- 3 CUPS WHITE CHICKEN STOCK (PAGE 45) OR LOW-SODIUM, STORE-BOUGHT CHICKEN BROTH

- I POUND ROMAINE LETTUCE (ABOUT I HEAD), CORED, CLEANED, AND COARSELY CHOPPED

- ¼ CUP PLUS 2 TABLESPOONS FINELY GRATED PARMIGIANO-REGGIANO (FROM ABOUT 2½ OUNCES CHEESE)

- 4 (PREFERABLY SALT-PACKED), ANCHOVY FILLETS (SOAKED, DRAINED, AND PATTED DRY; SEE PAGE II) (OPTIONAL)

- ¼ CUP PLUS 2 TABLESPOONS EXTRA VIRGIN OLIVE OIL

- 2 TABLESPOONS FRESHLY SQUEEZED LEMON JUICE

- PARMESAN AND BLACK PEPPER CROUTONS (RECIPE FOLLOWS)

POUR the olive oil into a large, heavy-bottomed pot and heat it over medium heat. Add the onion and garlic and a pinch of salt and cook until softened but not browned, approximately 4 minutes. Pour in the chicken stock and bring to a boil over high heat. Lower the heat and simmer until the onions are tender, approximately 15 minutes.

MEANWHILE, fill a large bowl halfway with ice water.

RAISE the heat to high, and return the stock to a boil. Add the romaine to the pot and let boil for 4 minutes. Remove the pot from the heat, add ¼ cup of the cheese, the 2 teaspoons salt, and the anchovies, if using, and puree the soup in a blender, in batches, until smooth. Slowly add some of the oil in a thin stream to thicken and enrich each batch. Transfer the soup to a stainless steel mixing bowl, set the bottom of the bowl into the ice water, and stir to cool the soup as quickly as possible.

THE soup can be made to this point, covered, and refrigerated for up to 3 hours. Stir in the lemon juice just before serving.

DIVIDE the soup among 4 chilled bowls. Garnish with the croutons and remaining 2 tablespoons cheese and serve.

THE REASON *The soup is pureed hot, then chilled:* Blending ingredients while hot results in a finer puree. Because the soup is made primarily of lettuce leaves, chilling it has the same effect as shocking cooked green vegetables in ice water, preserving its flavor and color.

EMBELLISHMENT Top each serving with a teaspoon of caviar, preferably Sevruga or Osetra, whose richness will nicely offset the clean, vegetal flavor of the lettuce.

PARMESAN AND BLACK PEPPER CROUTONS

There's just no reason to buy boxed croutons once you discover how easy it is to make your own. These croutons are a perfect topping to bean soups, minestrones, and just about any salad (or the salad as soup above). Note the cooking time instruction: these should be crispy on the outside but nicely chewy on the inside.

2 CUPS ¾ INCH CUBES COUNTRY BREAD OR BAGUETTE

I TABLESPOON EXTRA VIRGIN OLIVE OIL

I TABLESPOON UNSALTED BUTTER

I TEASPOON FINELY CHOPPED GARLIC

¼ TEASPOON KOSHER SALT PLUS A PINCH

2 TABLESPOONS FINELY GRATED PARMIGIANO-REGGIANO

½ TEASPOON FINELY CRACKED BLACK PEPPER

PREHEAT the oven to 325°F. Put the bread cubes into a mixing bowl and set them aside.

WARM the olive oil and melt the butter in a heavy-bottomed saucepan set over low heat. Add the garlic, along with a pinch of salt, and cook, stirring, until softened but not browned, 3 minutes. Pour the garlic butter over the bread cubes and stir to coat the cubes evenly. Sprinkle the cheese, pepper, and salt over the cubes and toss gently to evenly coat the cubes evenly.

POUR the croutons onto a cookie sheet or baking sheet, spread them out in a single layer, and bake them in the oven until golden-brown and crisp on the outside but still chewy inside, 5 to 6 minutes. Remove the baking sheet from the oven and serve the croutons warm or let cool. The croutons can be made in advance and kept at room temperature for up to 3 hours.

EMBELLISHMENT While still warm, toss the croutons with dried oregano or chopped fresh flat-leaf parsley.

CHILLED PEA SOUP WITH MINT CHUTNEY

SERVES 4

As with any ingredient so closely associated with one season, I recommend that you use only fresh peas to make this soup. The fresher the peas, the less sugar you need to use; if you're lucky enough to have just-picked ones, you might not need any sugar at all. For an especially sweet and refreshing soup, make this with sugar-snap peas, using the entire vegetable; puree the finished soup and strain out the fibrous pod remnants.

¼ CUP DOUBLE-SMOKED BACON, CUT INTO ¼-INCH DICE (FROM ABOUT 1¾ OUNCES BACON) (AVAILABLE FROM GOURMET STORES, SPECIALTY BUTCHERS, AND BY MAIL ORDER; SEE SOURCES, PAGE 318)

2 CUPS WHITE CHICKEN STOCK (PAGE 45) OR LOW-SODIUM, STORE-BOUGHT CHICKEN BROTH OR WATER

2 CUPS WATER

1¼ TEASPOONS KOSHER SALT

1⅓ POUNDS FRESH, SHELLED PEAS

2 TEASPOONS SUGAR, OR LESS (SEE HEADNOTE)

MINT CHUTNEY (RECIPE FOLLOWS)

FILL a large, wide bowl halfway with ice water.

PUT the bacon in a large, heavy-bottomed pot and cook over low heat until the fat is rendered and the bacon is cooked, approximately 7 minutes. Pour in the stock, add the 2 cups water and 1 teaspoon salt, and bring to a boil over high heat. Add the peas and let the stock return to a vigorous boil. Cook until the peas are tender, approximately 5 minutes.

DO the following in batches: Carefully pour the contents of the pot into a blender and blend at medium speed to make a smooth soup. (See safety note, page 137.) Pour the soup into a fine-mesh strainer set over a stainless steel bowl and press down on the solids with a rubber spatula or the back of a ladle to extract as much flavorful liquid as possible. Taste and season to taste with sugar. Set the bottom of the bowl into the ice water, and stir to cool the soup as quickly as possible. The soup can be made to this point, covered, and refrigerated for up to 8 hours.

DIVIDE the cold soup among 4 chilled bowls. Top each serving with 1 rounded tablespoon chutney. Serve.

TERMS AND TECHNIQUES *Double-smoked bacon:* All bacon is smoked and cured. Double-smoked bacon refers to bacon that is slowly smoked to emphasize the smoky flavor, sometimes focusing on a particular type of wood (such as applewood-smoked bacon).

THE REASON *No pepper is used:* Most recipes call for seasoning with salt and pepper, but the flavor of fresh peas is so delicate that I prefer not to introduce the heat of pepper to this soup.

EMBELLISHMENT Garnish each serving with pea tendrils.

MINT CHUTNEY MAKES ABOUT ¾ CUP

Usually a vehicle for fruits, chutney can also be a compelling way to use herbs. This would be a witty accompaniment for roasted lamb, playing on the mint jelly we all associate with it. Because the mint is cooked, it will lose its bright green color, but not its flavor.

⅔ CUP WHITE WINE VINEGAR

¼ CUP SUGAR

3 TABLESPOONS MINT LEAVES, THINLY SLICED, STEMS RESERVED

½ CUP FINELY CHOPPED SHALLOTS

KOSHER SALT

BLACK PEPPER IN A MILL

PUT the vinegar, sugar, mint stems, and shallots into a 1-quart, heavy-bottomed saucepan and bring to a boil over high heat. Lower the heat to low and cook, stirring, until the liquid has reduced by three-fourths, approximately 15 minutes.

WHEN the shallots are done cooking, set the mixture aside to cool. Use tongs to fish out and discard the mint stems. When the mixture is completely cool, add the sliced mint leaves and stir together. Season with salt to taste. The chutney can be covered and refrigerated for up to 3 days. Serve cold or at room temperature.

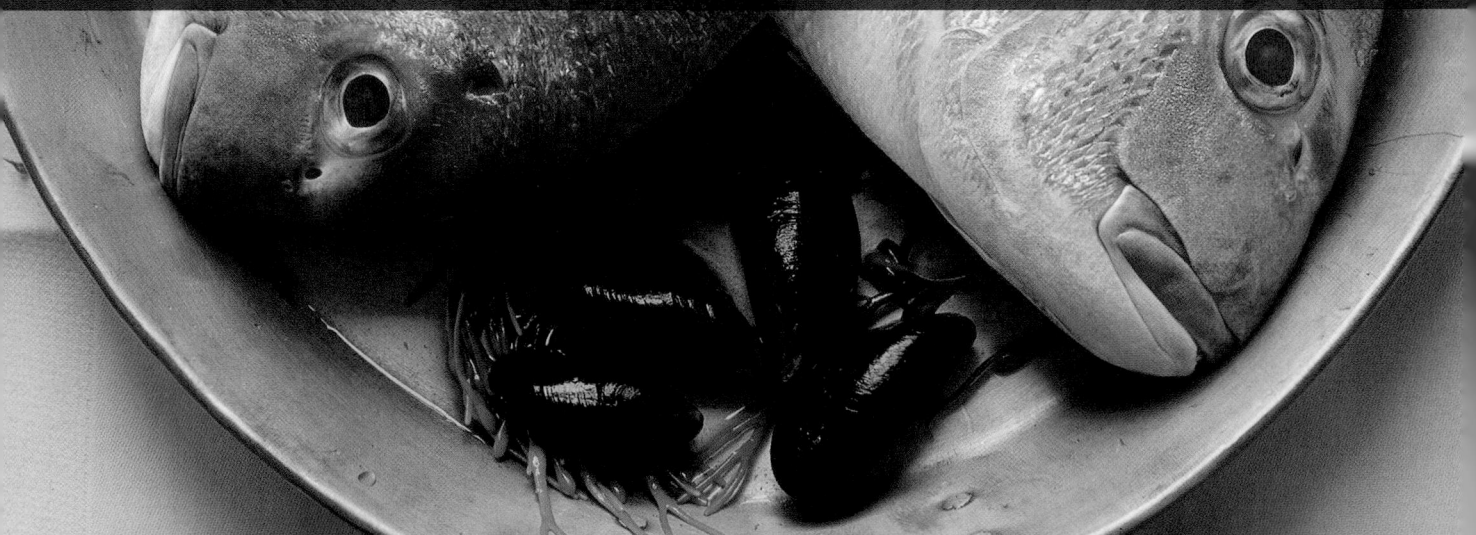

- COD WITH ARTICHOKES BARIGOULE *171* ·
- WILD SALMON WITH HORSERADISH CRUST *173* ·
- POACHED HALIBUT WITH LEMON MOUSSELINE, PISTACHIOS, AND DATES *176* ·
- RED SNAPPER WITH ZUCCHINI, PRESERVED TOMATOES, AND CAPERS *178* ·
- BAKED SEA BASS EN PAPILLOTE WITH FENNEL AND ORANGE-OLIVE BUTTER *181* ·

FISH AND SHELLFISH

- SAUTÉED SKATE WITH BLOOD ORANGE GRENOBLOISE *184* ·
- GRILLED TUNA WITH BASIL AÏOLI AND RAW TOMATO COULIS *186* ·
- DIVER SEA SCALLOPS WITH SALSIFY AND RED WINE BUTTER *188* ·
- LOBSTER WITH RHUBARB AND CHANTERELLES *191* ·
- MUSSELS WITH SHALLOTS, TOMATO, AND BASIL *193* ·
- SOFT-SHELL CRABS WITH MUSTARD SAUCE *194* ·

FISH AND SHELLFISH BRING OUT MY LOVE of Mediterranean cuisine. When I'm presented with a piece of fish, its flesh glistening with freshness, or a beautiful crab or lobster, still wet with sea water, I'm reminded of the small villages of France, where the catch of local fishermen determines dinner menus all over town.

In the same way, cooking fish today should be spontaneous. I'm sure your local market offers a varied selection on any given day, but you should leave yourself open to using the most appealing and fresh selections, perhaps calling ahead before settling on what dish you'll prepare for lunch or dinner. Because fish and shellfish are so delicate, obtaining the freshest catch possible is paramount.

That said, when perusing this chapter for inspiration, keep in mind that many of the components can be served with fish other than the ones with which I've presented them. So if, say, the Basil Aïoli and Raw Tomato Coulis paired with the tuna have caught your attention, and the market happens to have exquisitely fresh red snapper, by all means substitute one for the other. In other words, don't forget one of the best aspects of cooking at home: You're in charge of the kitchen and can alter the menu in any way you please.

COD WITH ARTICHOKES BARIGOULE

SERVES 4

Cod is a white fish, but not of the more delicate variety: It can take care of itself and works well with complex flavors. Think of Provence, where it's frequently cooked with tomatoes, olives, and other ingredients whose acid or salinity might overtake a less sturdy fish. I love serving artichokes with everything from poultry to lamb, but I think it's a more surprising choice with fish, especially here, where the barigoule is emulsified with extra virgin olive oil to make it into a light, flavorful, and healthful sauce.

CRUST MIXTURE

¼ CUP PARSLEY LEAVES (PACKED) PLUS ¼ CUP SNIPPED FLAT-LEAF PARSLEY

I TEASPOON MINCED FRESH ROSEMARY LEAVES

I CUP DRIED BREAD CRUMBS

½ TEASPOON MINCED GARLIC

KOSHER SALT

¼ CUP PLUS 3 TABLESPOONS OLIVE OIL

½ CUP PEELED, THINLY SLICED CARROT (FROM ABOUT I CARROT)

⅓ CUP THINLY SLICED FENNEL BULB (FROM ABOUT I MEDIUM FENNEL BULB, 2¾ OUNCES)

½ CUP THINLY SLICED ONION (FROM ABOUT ½ LARGE ONION)

4 WHOLE MEDIUM SIZED ARTICHOKES (3½ POUNDS), CLEANED DOWN TO THE HEART; HEARTS QUARTERED (PAGE 99)

4 CLOVES GARLIC, PEELED AND CRUSHED

I½ CUPS DRY WHITE WINE

I½ CUPS WHITE CHICKEN STOCK (PAGE 45) OR LOW-SODIUM, STORE-BOUGHT CHICKEN BROTH

4 SPRIGS THYME

3 BAY LEAVES

I LEMON, THINLY SLICED, SEEDS REMOVED PLUS I TABLESPOON LEMON JUICE

2 TABLESPOONS GARLIC CONFIT (PAGE 36) (OPTIONAL)

¼ CUP PLUS I TABLESPOON EXTRA VIRGIN OLIVE OIL

WHITE PEPPER IN A MILL

4 COD FILLETS, PREFERABLY CENTER CUT, 6 TO 7 OUNCES EACH

PUT the ¼ cup parsley leaves and the rosemary in the bowl of a food processor fitted with the steel blade and process to combine. Add the bread crumbs and garlic and process to fine crumbs. (Total processing time should be approximately 1½ to 2 minutes.) Transfer the mixture to a bowl, scraping down the sides of the processor bowl, and season with 1 teaspoon salt, or to taste. This is the crust for the cod; it can be covered and kept at room temperature for up to 3 hours.

PREHEAT the oven to 350°F. Pour ¼ cup olive oil into a heavy-bottomed, 4-quart pot and heat it over medium heat. Add the carrots, fennel, onions, artichokes, crushed garlic, and a pinch of salt, and cook, stirring occasionally, until slightly softened but not browned, approximately 5 minutes. Pour in the wine, bring to a boil over high heat, then lower the heat and let simmer until reduced by three-quarters, approximately 6 minutes. Pour in the stock and add the thyme, bay leaves, and lemon, and bring to a boil over high heat. Cover the pot and transfer to the oven. Cook until a thin-bladed knife pierces easily into the center of an artichoke, about 30 minutes. Remove the pot from the oven, but do not turn off the oven.

USE a ladle to skim off 1 cup of the cooking liquid, collecting it in a bowl. Use tongs to pick out and discard the lemon slices, bay leaf, and thyme sprigs. Set aside the vegetables in their liquid and keep warm.

POUR the skimmed cup of cooking liquid into a heavy-bottomed, 2-quart saucepan. Add the garlic confit (if using) and bring to a boil over medium heat. Lower the heat and let simmer until reduced by one quarter, approximately 6 minutes. Remove from heat. Use an immersion blender while gradually adding the extra virgin olive oil to the sauce to form a creamy, thick emulsion. (This can also be done in a standing blender.) Add the lemon juice and season with salt to taste and 4 turns of the pepper mill, or to taste.

PUT the bread crumb mixture in a shallow dish, and coat the cod fillets with the breading, pressing down gently to ensure the mixture adheres.

HEAT a 12 inch non-stick, ovenproof sauté pan set over medium heat. Add the remaining 3 tablespoons olive oil and heat it. Add the fillets and cook until the crust is golden-brown, approximately 2 minutes. Turn the fillets over, transfer the pan to the oven, and cook until golden-brown on the other side, approximately 4 minutes, or until cooked through.

MEANWHILE, use a slotted spoon to transfer the reserved vegetables to an 8-inch saucepan over low heat and cook until hot. (The liquid should evaporate over this time.) Toss the vegetables with the reserved sauce and gently warm over low heat, approximately 2 minutes. Add the remaining ¼ cup parsley and mix.

TO serve, divide the dressed vegetables and sauce among 4 shallow bowls. Place a cod fillet on top of the vegetables in each bowl and garnish with chopped parsley. Serve.

VARIATION You can make this without the crust mixture and the result will still be delicious.

EMBELLISHMENT Drizzle each serving with 1 to 2 tablespoons of Parsley Pistou (page 248). Add basil, Niçoise olives (pitted and halved), oven-dried tomatoes or tomato confit to the sauce as it's rewarmed with the vegetables just before serving.

WILD SALMON WITH HORSERADISH CRUST

SERVES 4

This is one of my better-known signature dishes, one that we've been serving at Picholine since the restaurant opened in 1993. The salmon's flavor is compounded with a breading made with gravlax (cured salmon), and the crème fraîche and cucumbers cut the heat of the horseradish. Try to make this dish from late summer through fall when wild Alaskan salmon is in season. I much prefer it to farm-raised salmon, which has been the source of some environmental concerns.

HORSERADISH CRUST MIXTURE

2 PACKED CUPS SMALL BREAD CUBES, CRUSTS REMOVED

1 TABLESPOON DIJON MUSTARD

3 TABLESPOONS FRESHLY GRATED HORSERADISH (FROM 2 OUNCES SALMON)

¼ CUP MINCED GRAVLAX (CURED SALMON) (FROM 2 OUNCES SALMON)

2½ TABLESPOONS UNSALTED BUTTER, SOFTENED AT ROOM TEMPERATURE

KOSHER SALT

1 ENGLISH CUCUMBER, 1½ POUNDS

¼ CUP CRÈME FRAÎCHE

4 WILD SALMON FILLETS, 6 TO 7 OUNCES EACH, CENTER CUT, SKIN REMOVED

2 TABLESPOONS CANOLA OIL

¼ CUP SALMON ROE

PUT the bread cubes in the bowl of a food processor fitted with the steel blade and pulse to fine crumbs. Add the mustard, horseradish, salmon, butter, and 1 tablespoon salt, and pulse until the mixture is well blended. Put the mixture between two pieces of wax paper and roll with a rolling pin to a thickness of ¼ inch. (If the mixture is too soft to roll, chill it briefly in the refrigerator to firm it up.) Divide the mixture into 4 rectangles, 1¾ inches wide and 4 inches long.

REFRIGERATE the crust for at least 30 minutes, up to 3 days, or freeze for up to 3 months. Let come to room temperature before proceeding.

PREHEAT the broiler. Peel and seed the cucumber. Slice the cucumber into ⅛-inch slices. Put the slices in a colander and toss with ½ teaspoon salt. Set aside for 2 hours at room temperature to let the water drain from the cucumbers. Remove the cucumbers from the colander and gently squeeze them to release any excess water. The cucumbers can be covered and refrigerated overnight.

HEAT an 8-inch sauté pan over medium heat. Add the cucumbers and crème fraîche and toss to coat. Cook just until warmed through, approximately 2 minutes.

SEASON the salmon on both sides with salt.

HEAT a 9-inch, ovenproof sauté pan over high heat. Add the oil and heat it. Add the salmon fillets to the pan and cook until very rare, 1 minute on each side. Remove the pan from the heat and let rest for 5 minutes. Remove the wax paper from the crust and use a spatula to set a horseradish rectangle on each piece of salmon. Broil on the highest rack in the oven until golden-brown, approximately 3 minutes.

TO serve, arrange some of the cucumbers in the center of each of 4 dinner plates. Top with 1 salmon fillet and spoon some roe around the edges of the cucumbers.

THE REASON *The cucumbers are salted:* Salting the cucumbers softens them without cooking and extracts some of their moisture, keeping them from making the crème fraîche runny.

EMBELLISHMENTS At Picholine, we make tournedos of salmon by cutting the fillet lengthwise down the center, tucking the tail end into the slit on the thicker end, and tying the piece around the equator with cooking string to hold it together in a round shape when cooked. (It looks like a tournedos of beef fillet, hence the name.) Try this for your next dinner party.

Make a fish herb blend of chopped chervil, chives, flat-leaf parsley, and yellow celery leaves and toss it with the cucumbers and crème fraîche.

POACHED HALIBUT WITH LEMON MOUSSELINE, PISTACHIOS, AND DATES

SERVES 4

Fine-flavored white-fleshed fish like halibut have a natural affinity for tart, acidic lemon. This dish maximizes that truth, pairing halibut with a creamy lemon mousseline and adding textural contrast with lemon-pistachio gremolata, a mixture based on the chopped lemon and herbs that traditionally tops the Italian veal dish *osso buco*. The lemon mousseline is similar to a sabayon, made with no cream, but instead finished with whipped crème fraîche.

LEMON MOUSSELINE

4 EGG YOLKS

2 TABLESPOONS FINELY GRATED LEMON ZEST

¾ CUP DRY WHITE WINE

½ CUP FRESHLY SQUEEZED LEMON JUICE

I TEASPOON HONEY

KOSHER SALT

WHITE PEPPER IN A MILL

LEMON-PARSLEY GREMOLATA

½ CUP SMALL BREAD CUBES, CRUSTS REMOVED

½ CUP SHELLED PISTACHIOS

I TEASPOON CHOPPED FLAT-LEAF PARSLEY

I TEASPOON MINCED GARLIC

¼ CUP ALL-PURPOSE FLOUR

2 EGGS, BEATEN

½ CUP FINE, DRIED BREAD CRUMBS

6 DATES, PITTED, HALVED, AND FLATTENED OUT

6 CUPS WATER

2 BAY LEAVES

5 SPRIGS THYME

I TABLESPOON BLACK PEPPERCORNS

4 HALIBUT STEAKS, CENTER CUT, 6 OUNCES EACH, I ¼ INCHES THICK

3 TABLESPOONS OLIVE OIL

2 TABLESPOONS CRÈME FRAÎCHE

FINE SEA SALT

MAKE the lemon mousseline: Put the egg yolks, 1 tablespoon lemon zest, ¼ cup wine, ¼ cup lemon juice, and the honey in the top of a double-boiler set over simmering water. Whisk vigorously until the yolks form pale, thick ribbons, 5 to 6 minutes. If the mixture gets too thick too fast, add some hot water to it. Season with salt and 3 grinds of pepper, or to taste. Cover and let rest in a warm area for up to 30 minutes.

MAKE the gremolata: Preheat the oven to 325°F. Spread out the bread cubes and pistachios in a single layer on two separate cookie sheets. Bake until the cubes are dry but not browned, and the nuts are lightly toasted, 4 to 6 minutes, shaking the cookie sheets periodically. (The cubes and nuts may finish at different times.) Remove the cookie sheets from the oven and let cool.

TRANSFER the cubes and nuts to the bowl of a food processor fitted with the steel blade. Add 1 tablespoon lemon zest, the parsley, and garlic, and season with salt and pepper. Process to a fine crumb, transfer to a bowl, and set aside while you make the rest of the dish.

PREPARE the dates: Put the flour, beaten eggs, and ½ cup bread crumbs in 3 separate shallow dishes. Coat the dates in flour, then eggs, then roll them in the bread crumbs. Set aside on a clean, dry plate.

PREPARE the halibut: Put the water in a heavy-bottomed, 4-quart pot and set over high heat. Add ½ cup white wine, ¼ cup lemon juice, the bay leaves, thyme, peppercorns, and 2 tablespoons salt. Bring to a boil over high heat, then lower the heat so the liquid is simmering. Carefully add the halibut steaks and poach for 2 minutes. Remove the pot from the heat and let poach off-heat for another 5 minutes.

MEANWHILE, heat the oil in a heavy-bottomed, 8-inch sauté pan over medium-high heat. Add the dates and cook until crispy on both sides, approximately 2 minutes per side. Drain on a paper-towel-lined plate and season with kosher salt. Keep warm.

TO serve, whip the crème fraîche in a small stainless steel bowl until stiff peaks form. Fold the crème fraîche into the mousseline with a rubber spatula. Divide the mousseline among 4 warm plates, spreading it out with the back of a spoon or ladle. Put a halibut steak on top of the mousseline on each plate and scatter the gremolata and some sea salt over the fish. Arrange 3 dates around the fish on each plate and serve.

TERMS AND TECHNIQUES *Crème fraîche:* Crème fraîche is a cultured cream that adds a lightly tangy flavor to a wide variety of dishes. It can be stirred or whisked into sauces, swirled atop soups, or added in a dollop atop a finished plate.

THE REASON *The halibut is partially poached off-heat:* If overcooked, halibut becomes especially dry, so it's important to take extra measures to avoid doing so. You can use this method for gently poaching any fish off-heat; it's especially successful with salmon.

RED SNAPPER WITH ZUCCHINI, PRESERVED TOMATOES, AND CAPERS

SERVES 4

This decidedly summery dish is one of the more simple-to-prepare main courses that I make. Red snapper is served alongside sautéed zucchini, oven-dried tomatoes, capers, and basil. It's a perfect choice for a last-minute meal that can be cooked quickly and still come out great. If the weather is right, grill the snapper and enjoy it outdoors.

---

2 TABLESPOONS SHERRY VINEGAR

½ CUP PLUS 3 TABLESPOONS EXTRA VIRGIN OLIVE OIL

1½ TABLESPOONS SMALL (NONPAREIL) CAPERS, RINSED AND DRAINED (IF USING LARGER CAPERS, CHOP THEM)

¼ CUP (PACKED) OPAL BASIL AND ¼ CUP SWEET BASIL (OR ½ CUP OF JUST 1 VARIETY), WASHED, DRIED AND VERY THINLY SLICED

12 PIECES OVEN-DRIED TOMATOES (PAGE 31)

KOSHER SALT

BLACK PEPPER IN A MILL

1 MEDIUM ZUCCHINI (½ POUND), CUT ON THE DIAGONAL INTO 8 EQUAL PIECES

4 SNAPPER FILLETS, 6 TO 7 OUNCES EACH, CENTER CUT, WITH SKIN

PUT the vinegar in a bowl and slowly whisk in 5 tablespoons oil to make a broken (non-emulsified) vinaigrette. Stir in the capers, the opal and sweet basil, and the tomatoes. Season with salt to taste and 3 grinds of pepper, or to taste.

PUT the zucchini in a small bowl, drizzle with 2 tablespoons oil, and season with salt and pepper. Toss gently to coat with the seasoning and oil. Heat a heavy-bottomed, 10-inch sauté pan over medium-high heat. Add the zucchini and cook until lightly golden, approximately 2 minutes per side. Transfer the zucchini to a bowl.

PAT the fillets dry and season on both sides with salt and 2 or 3 grinds of pepper, or to taste.

HEAT a nonstick, 12-inch sauté pan over medium heat. Add ¼ cup oil and heat the oil. Pat the skin side of the snapper dry with a paper towel. Add the snapper, skin side down, without crowding, and cook until the skin gets crispy, 3 to 4 minutes. Turn the fish over and cook for another minute.

DIVIDE the zucchini-tomato mixture equally among 4 dinner plates. Top with 1 fillet and spoon vinaigrette over each fillet, swirling it before taking each spoonful to ensure a good mix of ingredients on each serving. Serve.

THE REASON *The fish skin is patted dry before searing:* Patting the skin of a fish dry before searing helps it crisp in the pan by removing any excess moisture. You can also "squeegee" it dry by running the back (flat, dull side) of a kitchen knife along its length.

VARIATION Serve the fish with White Bean "Brandade" (page 204).

EMBELLISHMENT Add roasted or grilled peppers and/or fennel to this dish. Season the fish with Garlic Salt (page 21), rather than kosher salt, before cooking.

BAKED SEA BASS EN PAPILLOTE WITH FENNEL AND ORANGE-OLIVE BUTTER

SERVES 4

Using aluminum foil in place of parchment paper to cook dishes "en papillote" (a classic technique of bake-steaming fish and vegetables in a parcel to produce a sauce and aroma as they cook) has become so rampant, that I'd like to propose something radical: Actually use parchment paper. It's easy to find, even in supermarkets, and is much more attractive than aluminum when presented at the table.

Like many northeastern chefs, I have a soft spot for sea bass; it's locally fished from the Atlantic and has a mild, sweet flavor that is perfectly offset by the orange zest and diced olives in the compound butter. (If you're making this in other parts of the country, you can also use wild striped bass, sole, or snapper.) I prefer it with the skin on, but if you don't you can remove it and this dish will still be delicious.

This is a very convenient recipe for entertaining because you can assemble the parcels ahead of time and bake them in the oven just before you're ready to serve.

---

4 CUPS WATER

KOSHER SALT

I CUP ⅛- INCH- WIDE STRIPS FENNEL, FROM I MEDIUM BULB

4 PIECES PARCHMENT PAPER, 16 INCHES BY 24 INCHES

2 EGGS

I TABLESPOON COLD WATER

¼ CUP OLIVE OIL PLUS MORE FOR BRUSHING PARCHMENT PARCELS

BLACK PEPPER IN A MILL

4 BLACK SEA BASS FILLETS, 6 TO 7 OUNCES EACH, WITH SKIN

½ CUP TOMATO CONFIT (PAGE 79; OPTIONAL)

2 TABLESPOONS ORANGE-OLIVE BUTTER (PAGE 24), CUT INTO 12 THIN SLICES

4 SPRIGS THYME (OPTIONAL)

POUR the 1 quart water into a heavy-bottomed pot, add 1 teaspoon salt, and bring to a boil over high heat. Add the fennel and cook until tender, approximately 4 minutes. Drain the fennel, refresh under cold, running water, drain, and let dry.

ONE by one, fold the parchment pieces in half and cut them into half-heart-shaped pieces, 13 inches long at the longest point and 12 inches wide at the widest, starting at the bottom corner. In other words, when opened, the paper will be 13 inches long and 24 inches wide. (This will seem very large, but you will need all of that space.)

MAKE an egg wash by breaking the eggs into a small bowl and whisking with 1 tablespoon cold water.

PREHEAT the oven to 350°F. Rub oil over the right half of the upward-facing side of the parchment paper and season the paper with salt and a few grinds of pepper. (This will season the underside of the fish when you set it on the paper.)

PUT 1 fish fillet in the center of the right half of the paper, skin side up. Season with salt and pepper, then arrange some fennel, some tomato confit, if using, 3 slices of orange-olive butter, and a thyme sprig, if using, along the length of each fillet, stacking the ingredients neatly. Brush egg wash around the edges of the parcel. Seal the packet by making small, triangular folds along the edge in an overlapping pattern, starting at the top (rounded) end of the paper and finishing at the point. It's essential that the packets be very well sealed, so make as many small folds as possible, press down on them to compress the paper, and twist the pointed tip for good measure.

BRUSH the outside of the parcel with a light layer of egg wash, but do not brush the bottom.

PUT 2 sealed packets on each of 2 cookie sheets, and bake until the paper turns a nice golden-brown, 10 to 12 minutes. If you have two ovens, cook two parcels in each oven, which will allow maximum room for the paper to puff up when baked. If using one oven, be sure there's six inches of space between the top of the parcels on the bottom rack and the upper rack, and switch the pans from one rack to the other after 5 minutes to ensure even cooking.

THE paper should puff up and stay puffed; if it doesn't, then the paper wasn't sealed properly, but the fish will still be delicious.

PUT the parcels on a large tray or attractive cutting board and present to your guests at the table. Make an incision along the length of one parcel with a knife and twirl the paper towards the edges, gathering it around 2 forks, exposing the fish within. Carefully transfer the fish to a dinner plate and spoon the juices from the parcel over the fish. Repeat with the other parcels and serve.

THE REASON *The parcels are brushed with egg wash:* The egg wash on the outside of the parcel will harden as the packet cooks, helping the paper stand up, allowing moisture and flavor to circulate and infuse the fish. It also makes for a simple but beautiful presentation.

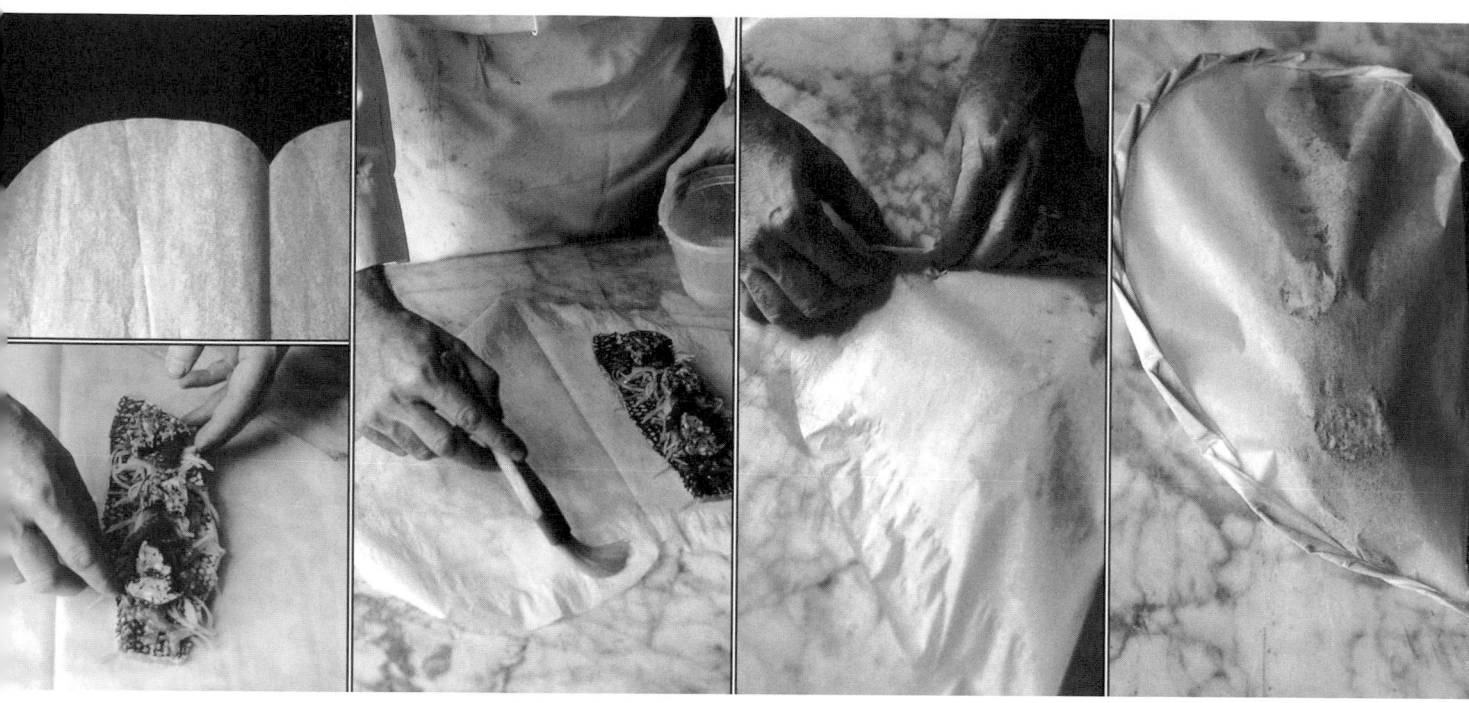

SAUTÉED SKATE WITH BLOOD ORANGE GRENOBLOISE

SERVES 4

This is a signature dish at Artisanal restaurant. It offers an important lesson about cooking skate; if you choose to sauté rather than poach it, you need to use more oil than usual, essentially shallow frying it so that the oil gets up into the fish's ridges.

When making the sauce, make sure that all of the ingredients other than butter are at room temperature. If you can't find blood oranges, use the juice of regular oranges or lemons instead.

I'm a firm believer in doing as much cooking ahead of time as possible, but this is one dish that should really be cooked *á la minute*. Make all of the components as quickly as possible and serve it right away.

¾ CUP SMALL CAULIFLOWER FLORETS (FROM ABOUT 3 OUNCES CAULIFLOWER)

1½ CUPS PLUS 1 TABLESPOON CANOLA OIL

KOSHER SALT

BLACK PEPPER IN A MILL

⅓ CUP ¼-INCH CRUSTLESS WHITE BREAD CUBES

½ CUP MILK

1 CUP WONDRA FLOUR (SEE PAGE 194) OR ALL-PURPOSE FLOUR

4 SKATE WINGS, 4 TO 5 OUNCES EACH, SKIN REMOVED BY FISHMONGER

½ CUP (1 STICK) CUBED COLD UNSALTED BUTTER PLUS 4 TABLESPOONS AT ROOM TEMPERATURE

20 BLOOD ORANGE SEGMENTS (FROM ABOUT 4 ORANGES) PLUS ½ CUP BLOOD ORANGE JUICE (FROM A THIRD ORANGE; NAVEL ORANGES CAN BE SUBSTITUTED)

1 TEASPOON FRESHLY SQUEEZED LEMON JUICE

1 TABLESPOON CAPERS, RINSED AND DRAINED

2 TABLESPOONS ROUGHLY SNIPPED FLAT-LEAF PARSLEY LEAVES

PUT the cauliflower in a bowl, toss with 1 tablespoon oil, and season with salt and 3 grinds of pepper, or to taste. Heat an 8-inch sauté pan over medium-high heat. Add the florets and sauté until golden brown, 3 to 4 minutes. Remove the pan from the heat and set aside.

HEAT a 10-inch sauté pan over low-medium heat. Add ½ cup oil and gently heat it. Add the bread cubes and cook them slowly until the oil starts to bubble around their edges and they turn a nice, even, golden color, approximately 9 minutes, tilting the pan as necessary to ensure even cooking. Add 2 tablespoons room-temperature butter and swirl it as it melts, continuing to cook the croutons to a deeper golden color and crunchy texture. Transfer the croutons to a clean paper towel to drain and season lightly with salt. Set aside.

PUT the milk and Wondra flour in separate shallow dishes. Dip each skate wing in milk, then dredge in Wondra flour, and gently shake off any excess flour.

IF possible, do the following in two pans in order to cook all 4 wings simultaneously: Heat a 12-inch sauté pan over medium-high heat. Add ½ cup of the oil and heat the oil. Add 2 skate wings and 1 tablespoon butter to the pan. Sauté the wings until crisp and dark golden-brown on both sides, 3 to 4 minutes per side. Use a fish spatula to transfer the wings to a clean, dry surface, and season with salt. Discard any oil and butter remaining in the pan and repeat with the remaining oil, skate, and butter.

HEAT a 10-inch sauté pan over medium-high heat. Add the cold butter, swirling the pan to keep it moving. When the butter has melted and turns brown, approximately 2 minutes, vigorously whisk in the blood orange juice and lemon juice to make a sauce. Add the capers, parsley, cauliflower florets, and orange segments. Toss in the croutons and season to taste with salt.

TO serve, spoon some sauce onto each of 4 dinner plates. Set a skate wing atop the sauce and serve.

GRILLED TUNA WITH BASIL AÏOLI AND RAW TOMATO COULIS

SERVES 4

 real tribute to the flavors of Provence, this recipe complements grilled tuna with tomato coulis and basil. This is a very easy and swift recipe that can be scaled down for a first course, or a smaller meal.

---

4 SUSHI-GRADE TUNA STEAKS, 6 TO 7 OUNCES EACH, 1¼ TO 1½-INCHES THICK

1 TABLESPOON OLIVE OIL

KOSHER SALT

BLACK PEPPER IN A MILL

1 TABLESPOON EXTRA VIRGIN OLIVE OIL

1 TEASPOON FRESHLY SQUEEZED LEMON JUICE

4 CUPS ARUGULA, WASHED AND THOROUGHLY DRIED

RAW TOMATO COULIS (RECIPE FOLLOWS)

HEAPING ¼ CUP BASIL AÏOLI (RECIPE FOLLOWS)

4 BASIL LEAVES, FOR GARNISH

PREPARE a grill for grilling, or preheat a grill pan over high heat. Rub the tuna steaks with olive oil and season them with salt and 3 grinds of pepper per side of each steak.

IN a small bowl, whisk together the extra virgin olive oil and lemon juice and season with salt and pepper. Set aside.

PUT the tuna on the grill and grill on both sides until medium-rare, 3 to 4 minutes per side for rare, or longer for more well done.

GENTLY toss the arugula with the lemon dressing. Spoon a generous ¼ cup of coulis onto the center of each of 4 dinner plates, using the bottom of the spoon to spread it out. Top with some arugula, then with a tuna steak. Finish with a generous tablespoon of aïoli and garnish with a basil leaf, standing it up in the aioli.

TERMS AND TECHNIQUES *Sushi-grade (sashimi-grade):* Sushi-grade refers to fish that is fresh enough and of a high enough quality to be eaten raw (sushi or sashimi). Use sushi-grade fish whenever you plan to cook fish to just rare or medium-rare, or if you plan to eat it uncooked.

EMBELLISHMENT Top each serving with a dollop of Oven-Dried Tomatoes (page 31). Serve the tuna and these accompaniments in tandem with the Heirloom Tomato Salad with Anchovy Toast (page 94).

RAW TOMATO COULIS MAKES 1⅓ CUPS

A coulis is a puree of fruits, vegetables, or other ingredients used as an easy sauce for fish or meat.

1½ POUNDS HEIRLOOM TOMATOES
    QUARTERED

1 TEASPOON CELERY SALT, PREFERABLY
    HOMEMADE (PAGE 19), OR KOSHER SALT
    TO TASTE

1 TABLESPOON SHERRY VINEGAR

1 TABLESPOON EXTRA VIRGIN OLIVE OIL

PUT the tomatoes, celery salt, and sherry vinegar in a food processor fitted with the steel blade and puree until smooth. With the motor running, slowly add the olive oil in a thin stream to form an emulsified mixture. Strain through a fine-mesh strainer set over a bowl pushing down on the solids to extract as much flavorful liquid as possible. Discard the solids.

THE coulis can be made up to 8 hours ahead of time and kept covered in the refrigerator.

VARIATION If you increase the volume, the coulis becomes a cold tomato soup.

EMBELLISHMENT For a richer color, put the tomatoes through a food mill before using them.

BASIL AÏOLI MAKES 1¼ CUP

You can make basil aïoli by simply stirring basil into the aïoli on page 30. But this recipe, designed expressly to go with the tuna dish on page 186, really emphasizes the basil flavor.

2 EGG YOLKS

2 GARLIC CLOVES, PEELED, OR 1 CLOVE
    FRESH GARLIC PLUS 1 TEASPOON GARLIC
    CONFIT (PAGE 36)

1 TABLESPOON FRESHLY SQUEEZED LEMON
    JUICE

1 TABLESPOON WATER

½ CUP BASIL LEAVES (LOOSELY PACKED),
    WASHED AND SPUN DRY IN A SALAD SPINNER

1 CUP OLIVE OIL

¾ TEASPOON KOSHER SALT

PUT the yolks, garlic, lemon juice, water, and basil in a food processor fitted with the steel blade. Turn on the motor and, with the motor running, slowly add the oil in a thin stream to make an emulsion. Transfer the aïoli to a bowl, scraping down the sides with a rubber spatula. Season with the salt. The aïoli can be made up to a day in advance and kept covered in the refrigerator for up to 2 weeks.

TERMS AND TECHNIQUES *Aïoli:* Aïoli is a garlicky mayonnaise used as a condiment in Provençal cuisine.

EMBELLISHMENT You can add tomato confit, chopped olives, and/or minced anchovy fillets to the aïoli. Add them after the oil, pulsing the processor just enough to incorporate them. This aïoli is also delicious stirred into fish soups and minestrones and served over vegetables.

DIVER SEA SCALLOPS with SALSIFY and RED WINE BUTTER

SERVES 4

Captured in a *beurre fondue* (literally translated as "melted butter"), or butter sauce, which softens its tannic punch, red wine is transformed into a surprisingly apt counterpart to meaty shellfish like scallops. It also proves to be a fine match for salsify, which some refer to as "oyster plant" because they think it tastes like an oyster. Personally, I think salsify has a pleasingly sweet flavor, more akin to artichoke, that stands up well to roasting and caramelizing to become an accompaniment to fish, game, or meat.

Harvested by hand off of day boats, diver sea scallops are the best, freshest scallops you can find. If your market doesn't carry them, purchase "dry" scallops rather than those stored in a milky white preservative.

---

2 TABLESPOONS CANOLA OIL

3 TABLESPOONS UNSALTED BUTTER

I CUP PEELED SALSIFY, DIAGONAL ½ INCH SLICES (FROM ABOUT 3 STALKS)

½ CUP WHITE CHICKEN STOCK (PAGE 45) OR LOW-SODIUM, STORE-BOUGHT CHICKEN BROTH

3 SPRIGS THYME

KOSHER SALT

12 LARGE DIVER SCALLOPS, MUSCLE REMOVED (ABOUT 1½ OUNCES EACH)

BLACK PEPPER IN A MILL

I TABLESPOON UNSALTED BUTTER

RED WINE BUTTER (RECIPE FOLLOWS)

PUT 1 tablespoon canola oil and 2 tablespoons butter in an 8-inch sauté pan and heat over medium heat. Add the salsify and sauté, lightly browning all sides, for 5 minutes Add the stock and thyme. Bring to a boil over high heat, then lower the heat and simmer until the salsify is tender to the tines of a fork, approximately 8 minutes. Season with ¼ teaspoon salt, remove the pan from the heat, and cover to keep warm.

WHILE the salsify is simmering, season the scallops with salt and 4 grinds of pepper, or to taste. Heat a 12-inch sauté pan over medium-high heat. Put 1 tablespoon butter and 1 tablespoon canola oil in the pan and heat them. Add the scallops to the pan and sear until lightly golden-brown on both sides and slightly opaque in the center, approximately 3 minutes per side.

TO serve, lift the salsify from its pan, letting any excess liquid run off, and divide among 4 dinner plates. Arrange 3 scallops on top of the salsify on each plate and drizzle with red wine butter.

RED WINE BUTTER MAKES 1 CUP

In addition to being a wonderful sauce for the scallops, this is also delicious over tuna or wild striped bass. It's also versatile enough to be served with beef or lamb.

¼ CUP SLICED SHALLOTS

1 SPRIG THYME

½ TABLESPOON BLACK PEPPERCORNS

2 TABLESPOONS RED-WINE VINEGAR

2 CUPS RED WINE

½ CUP RUBY PORT

8 TABLESPOONS (1 STICK) UNSALTED BUTTER, CUBED, COLD

KOSHER SALT

BLACK PEPPER IN A MILL

PUT the shallots, thyme, peppercorns, vinegar, wine, and port in a heavy-bottomed, 2-quart saucepan and set over mediu-high heat. Cook at a boil until reduced by three-quarters, approximately 10 minutes.

LOWER the heat and whisk in the butter, a cube at a time. Keep the butter sauce at a tepid temperature as you whisk. It should be just warm to the touch; if it overheats, the butter will break.

STRAIN the sauce into a double-boiler set over simmering water, season with salt and 4 grinds of pepper, or to taste, and keep covered and warm for up to 1 hour.

LOBSTER WITH RHUBARB AND CHANTERELLES

T he most elegant and luxurious of all shellfish, lobster demands to be served with other special ingredients. Here, it's paired with two of the real treasures of the spring: rhubarb, and one of the most prized of all mushrooms, chanterelles. The contrasting flavors and textures are a useful example of how to make every ingredient in a recipe count, coaxing the full potential out of each one.

---

4 MAINE LOBSTERS, 1¼ POUNDS EACH

12 CUPS WATER

5 SPRIGS THYME

4 BAY LEAVES

1 TABLESPOON BLACK PEPPERCORNS

½ CUP DRY WHITE WINE, PLUS MORE IF COOKING LOBSTER IN ADVANCE

1 LEMON, HALF VERY THINLY SLICED, HALF JUICED

KOSHER SALT

2 TABLESPOONS UNSALTED BUTTER, PLUS MORE IF COOKING LOBSTER IN ADVANCE

¼ CUP FINELY DICED SHALLOTS

2 CUPS CLEANED, TRIMMED, HALVED OR QUARTERED CHANTERELLES (FROM 4½ OUNCES CHANTERELLES)

BLACK PEPPER IN A MILL

RHUBARB MARMALADE (PAGE 43)

KILL the lobsters by driving a heavy knife right between their eyes and pulling the handle down like a lever; this will kill them instantly. Remove the tail and claws from their bodies.

POUR the water into a large, heavy-bottomed pot. Add the thyme, bay leaves, peppercorns, wine, lemon slices, and 2 tablespoons salt and bring to a boil over high heat. Add the lobster claws and cook for 5 minutes. Remove the claws with tongs or a slotted spoon. Return to a boil, add the tails, and immediately remove the pot from the heat. Let the tails steep for 7½ to 8 minutes. When cool enough to handle, but still warm, crack the claws and split the tail and remove the meat.

COOK the mushrooms: Heat the butter in an 8-inch sauté pan over medium heat. When the butter melts, add the shallots and a pinch of salt and sauté for 3 minutes. Lower the heat, add the mushrooms, and cook until tender, approximately 12 minutes. Season with salt, 3 grinds of pepper, or to taste, and a splash of lemon juice.

IF the lobster has cooled, rewarm it as the mushrooms cook. (See Terms and Techniques.)

DIVIDE the rhubarb marmalade among 4 dinner plates. Surround the marmalade with mushrooms. Put 1 lobster tail and 2 claws on top of the rhubarb on each plate and serve.

TERMS AND TECHNIQUES *Rewarming lobster:* To rewarm cracked lobster, put it in a baking dish, dab it with butter, drizzle with ¼ cup sweet white wine or water, and cook in an oven preheated to 225°F just until warmed through.

THE REASON Adding a splash of lemon juice to mushrooms brings out their woodsy flavor.

VARIATION You can cook the lobster in water if you don't have the necessary ingredients to make a court bouillon.

EMBELLISHMENT Garnish this dish with pea tendrils or mache.

MUSSELS WITH SHALLOTS, TOMATO, AND BASIL

SERVES 4

When a dish is created from just a few carefully selected ingredients, small enhancements can pay big dividends. This is a very simple, traditional, and familiar method of preparing mussels that's reinvigorated with the use of a sweet Alsatian wine, instead of a more conventional dry selection, and basil, a twist on the more familiar parsley. Where most compelling recipes rely on a contrast of sweet, sour, salt, and other tastes, this one is a symphony of sweetness—the wine, basil, and mussels each contributes its own distinct level, with enough variation of flavor and texture between the ingredients to be well balanced.

In addition to savoring the mussels, don't miss out on one of the great pleasures of Provençal dining: dunking hunks of bread into the broth, which I've supplemented here with chicken stock, making more of it to enjoy.

---

2 TABLESPOONS OLIVE OIL

3 TABLESPOONS FINELY CHOPPED SHALLOTS

I TABLESPOON CHOPPED GARLIC

2 POUNDS MUSSELS (ABOUT 60 MEDIUM MUSSELS), BEARDS REMOVED, RINSED CLEAN UNDER COLD, RUNNING WATER

¾ CUP WHITE ALSATIAN WINE, SUCH AS GEWURTZTRAMINER OR RIESLING

¼ CUP FRESHLY SQUEEZED LEMON JUICE

¼ CUP WHITE CHICKEN STOCK (PAGE 45) OR LOW-SODIUM, STORE-BOUGHT CHICKEN BROTH

¼ CUP PLUS 2 TABLESPOONS TOMATO CONFIT (PAGE 79) OR DICED PLUM TOMATOES

3 TABLESPOONS UNSALTED BUTTER

KOSHER SALT

BLACK PEPPER IN A MILL

3 TABLESPOONS THINLY SLICED BASIL LEAVES

POUR the olive oil into a heavy-bottomed, 8-quart pot and set it over medium-high heat. Add the shallots and garlic and cook, stirring often, until they release their flavors, approximately 1 minute. Add the mussels and continue to cook, stirring, for 2 minutes. Add the wine, lemon juice, stock, and tomato confit, and cover with a lid. Steam until the mussels have opened, 4 to 5 minutes. Discard any mussels that have not opened.

ADD the butter to the pot, season with salt and 6 grinds of pepper, or to taste, and gently toss to cause the butter and broth to come together in an emulsion. While tossing, add the basil. Divide the mussels and broth among 4 bowls, and serve.

EMBELLISHMENT Add a pinch of saffron threads and/or finely grated orange zest along with the shallots.

SOFT-SHELL CRABS WITH MUSTARD SAUCE

SERVES 4

 hen soft-shell crabs come into season each spring on the East Coast, there's not a more popular shell-fish in the world. Dredging the crabs in milk and flour and sautéing them will produce a light and crispy coating, like a delicate tempura. The mustard sauce is a perfect match for this preparation.

---

8 SOFT-SHELL CRABS (4½ TO 5 OUNCES EACH)

1 CUP MILK

½ CUP WONDRA FLOUR (SEE TERMS AND TECHNIQUES), OR ALL-PURPOSE FLOUR

KOSHER SALT

BLACK PEPPER IN A MILL

¼ CUP CANOLA OIL

4 TABLESPOONS UNSALTED BUTTER

MUSTARD SAUCE (RECIPE FOLLOWS)

IF cooking on the same day you purchase them, have your fishmonger clean the crabs for you. Otherwise, keep them alive for up to 1 day by wrapping them in damp newspaper or in hay if your fishmonger has some. (They are usually delivered to fishmongers in hay.) When ready to cook, rinse the crab under cold running water. Remove the gills (the feathery material located under the two sides of the shell), apron (the flap on the under belly), and pincers. Then snip off the face (front pincers and eyes).

PUT the milk and Wondra flour in two separate bowls wide and deep enough to hold 1 crab. Season the flour with salt and 4 grinds of pepper, or to taste, and mix well.

DIP the crabs on both sides in milk, then dredge in Wondra flour, shaking off any excess flour.

HEAT a 12-inch sauté pan over medium-high heat. Add 2 tablespoons oil and 2 tablespoons butter. The butter will sizzle and foam. When the foam begins to subside, add 4 crabs to the pan and cook until golden-brown and crispy on both sides, 2 to 3 minutes per side. (Crabs tend to "pop" open and spray their juices when cooked, so stand back from the pan as they get hotter.) Remove the crabs from the pan, set on a clean, dry surface, and keep warm. Repeat with the remaining butter and crabs.

TO serve, divide the mustard sauce among 4 plates. Top the sauce on each plate with 2 crabs and serve.

TERMS AND TECHNIQUES *Wondra flour:* Wondra flour, a combination of barley and wheat flour, crisps up especially well when fried, and doesn't clump up as other flours do.

THE REASON *The crabs are dipped in milk:* Milk helps the flour adhere to the crabs. Beaten egg or egg wash would be too heavy in texture and flavor.

MUSTARD SAUCE MAKES ABOUT 1½ CUPS

This sauce is delicious with anything you'd dress with mustard, such as chicken and roast pork.

- 1 TABLESPOON FRESHLY SQUEEZED LEMON JUICE
- 1 TABLESPOON WATER
- ½ POUND (2 STICKS) COLD UNSALTED BUTTER, CUT INTO CUBES
- 3 TABLESPOONS GRAIN MUSTARD, AT ROOM TEMPERATURE
- 2 TABLESPOONS DIJON MUSTARD
- ½ TEASPOON KOSHER SALT

PUT the lemon juice and water in a saucepan set over low heat. Heat the liquid to a simmer. Whisk in the butter, a cube at a time. Keep the butter sauce at a tepid temperature as you whisk. It should be just warm to the touch. Add the grain and Dijon mustards and season with the salt, or to taste.

THIS sauce can be made 1 hour ahead of time and kept warm.

POULTRY AND GAME BIRDS

ALTHOUGH OUR NATIONAL RECIPE REPERTOIRE HAS GROWN by leaps and bounds in the past few decades, Americans haven't really expanded their horizons on game birds. As a country we certainly love chicken, and turkey is the centerpiece of one of our most beloved holidays. I hope that we will soon embrace the vast array of birds that Europeans call on regularly in their cooking, such as duck, pheasant, and squab, which I learned to love while living abroad.

Perhaps because they are unfamiliar with them, many perceive these birds as difficult to cook. But they're actually no more challenging than chicken. And their flavors are quite varied—from the fullness of squab to the wild white meat of pheasant to the rich rewards of duck.

The recipes in this chapter were chosen to introduce those who have never cooked these birds to accessible recipes for doing so. If you already know and love them, you'll find several dishes that I hope become favorites in your homes as they have at my restaurants, including two rare Italian departures, a chicken tonnato salad from Artisanal and one of Picholine's long-standing signature dishes, duck risotto.

As a nod to reality, half of the recipes in this chapter are centered around chicken. We all love a great roast chicken, but here there are six recipes that show more creative ways to think about it.

A quick note about poultry: It's important to pay attention to doneness temperatures in any cooking, but especially with poultry. When in doubt, refer to the USDA guidelines, often featured right on the packaging label of many birds.

CHICKEN SCHNITZEL

SERVES 4

 uick and easy recipes are always a welcome addition to one's home-cooking repertoire, and it doesn't get much simpler, or more satisfying, than this. A chicken breast is breaded with a mixture of crumbs and Parmigiano-Reggiano, which adds crunch and cheesy flavor. (My kids love it because it's basically a sophisticated version of chicken fingers.) It's topped with a lemon, garlic, and caper sauce that's made right in the pan. This is delicious with steamed asparagus.

- ½ CUP ALL-PURPOSE FLOUR, SEASONED WITH SALT AND PEPPER

- 2 EGGS, WHISKED WITH 2 TABLESPOONS WATER

- 1 CUP PARMESAN CRUST (RECIPE FOLLOWS)

- 4 BONELESS SKINLESS CHICKEN BREASTS, ABOUT 4½ OUNCES EACH, TRIMMED OF FAT AND CARTILAGE, HALVED HORIZONTALLY

- 1 TEASPOON FRESHLY SQUEEZED LEMON JUICE

- 2 TABLESPOONS WATER

- 1¼ CUPS (2½ STICKS) COLD, CUBED UNSALTED BUTTER

- KOSHER SALT

- BLACK PEPPER IN A MILL

- ¼ POUND ROMA TOMATOES, PEELED (SEE PAGE 95), CORED, AND CUT INTO MEDIUM DICE

- 1 TEASPOON MINCED GARLIC

- 1 TABLESPOON CAPERS, RINSED AND DRAINED

- 1 CUP OLIVE OIL

PUT the flour in a large bowl, the eggs in another, and the Parmesan crust in a third. Individually dredge each breast half in flour, taking care to shake off any excess flour. Then dredge the breast in eggs. Finally, place the breast in Parmesan crust and coat evenly. Put the breasts on a baking sheet and chill in the refrigerator for 1 hour to firm them up.

MAKE the sauce: Put the lemon juice and water in a heavy-bottomed, 1-quart saucepan and set over low heat. Heat until warm. Whisk in the butter, 1 cube at a time, making sure the sauce stays warm as you make it. Remove the pan from the heat, and season with ½ teaspoon salt and a pinch of pepper. Add the tomatoes, garlic, and capers to the sauce, cover, and keep warm.

HEAT a 12-inch sauté pan over medium heat. Pour ½ cup olive oil into the sauté pan and heat. Add 4 breast halves to the pan and cook until the Parmesan crust is golden-brown, approximately 3 minutes. Turn the breasts over and continue to cook until golden-brown on the other side, approximately 3 more minutes. Season with salt and 4 grinds of pepper or to taste. Repeat with the other breasts, draining off the oil in the pan and adding the remaining oil between batches.

PUT 2 breast halves on each of 4 plates and serve.

THE REASON *Water is added to the eggs:* When using eggs as a binding or adhesive agent, whisk them with water to prevent too strong of an egg flavor in the dish.

VARIATIONS Serve the chicken breast with pasta, the salad from the Chicken Tonnato (page 200), or a simple arugula, tomato, and cucumber salad.

Make the sauce with olive oil instead of butter.

EMBELLISHMENTS The *beurre fondue,* or butter sauce, can be adapted with any number of flavoring agents, such as herbs.

PARMESAN CRUST MAKES ABOUT 1¼ CUPS

½ CUP ½-INCH CRUSTLESS WHITE BREAD CUBES

1 TABLESPOON FINELY GRATED LEMON ZEST

¾ CUP FINELY GRATED PARMESAN (FROM ABOUT 3 OUNCES CHEESE)

KOSHER SALT

BLACK PEPPER IN A MILL

PREHEAT the oven to 325°F. Spread the bread cubes out on a cookie sheet and bake until the bread turns hard but does not brown, approximately 8 minutes. Set aside and let cool. Put the bread in a food processor fitted with the steel blade and process to a medium-fine crumb. Transfer the crumbs to a bowl and stir in the lemon zest and Parmesan. Season with salt and 6 grinds of pepper, or to taste.

CHICKEN TONNATO

SERVES 4

My version of the classic Italian *vitello tonnato,* in which thin slices of veal are dressed with a tuna-mayonnaise sauce and served chilled, features thin slices of chicken breast in place of the veal. It's accompanied by a quick take on another popular Italian dish, the bread salad called *panzanella,* which is traditionally made with stale two- or three-day-old bread, but which you can have on demand by baking croutons instead.

---

4 BONELESS, SKINLESS CHICKEN BREASTS (5 TO 6 OUNCES EACH)

4 CUPS WHITE CHICKEN STOCK (PAGE 45) OR LOW-SODIUM, STORE-BOUGHT CHICKEN BROTH

½ CUP MAYONNAISE, PREFERABLY HOMEMADE (PAGE 32)

2 TABLESPOONS WATER

¾ CUP HIGH-QUALITY PRESERVED TUNA, FROM ITALY OR SPAIN, DRAINED OF EXCESS OIL

2 TABLESPOONS CAPERS, RINSED AND DRAINED

KOSHER SALT

WHITE PEPPER IN A MILL

1 CUCUMBER, PEELED, SEEDED, AND CUT INTO ½-INCH DICE (ABOUT 1 CUP DICE)

¾ POUND BEEFSTEAK OR HEIRLOOM TOMATOES, CUT INTO ½-INCH DICE (ABOUT 1½ CUPS DICE)

4 CUPS ARUGULA (FROM ABOUT 3 OUNCES ARUGULA), TOUGH STEMS DISCARDED, WASHED AND SPUN DRY

½ CUP FINELY JULIENNED RED ONION

½ CUP SHERRY VINAIGRETTE (PAGE 100)

½ CUP PITTED KALAMATA OLIVES (OPTIONAL)

1 CUP PARMESAN AND BLACK PEPPER CROUTONS (PAGE 165) (OPTIONAL)

FLEUR DE SEL

PREHEAT the oven to 325°F. Put the chicken breasts in a high-sided, 12-inch sauté pan with a lid. Pour in the stock, cover, and bring to a simmer over medium-high heat. Transfer the pan to the oven and poach until the chicken is cooked through (an instant-read thermometer inserted to the thickest part of a breast should read 160°F), approximately 20 minutes.

REMOVE the pan from the oven, drain the liquid from the pan, and let the chicken cool. Serve warm, or transfer to a clean plate or platter, cover, and refrigerate until cold, at least 2 hours, or up to 24 hours.

PUT the mayonnaise and water in the bowl of a food processor fitted with the steel blade. Add the tuna and capers, season with salt and 6 grinds of pepper, and process until all ingredients are well incorporated. The mayonnaise can be transferred to a bowl, covered, and refrigerated for up to 3 days.

PUT the cucumbers, tomatoes, arugula, onions, vinaigrette, olives, and croutons, if using, in a bowl and gently toss to coat all of the ingredients with the vinaigrette.

USE a sharp, thin-bladed knife to slice the chicken breasts horizontally as thinly as possible, as though you were slicing smoked fish.

DIVIDE the sliced chicken into 4 portions, fanning each portion out on a chilled salad plate. Season the chicken to taste with fleur de sel and a few grinds of pepper. Use an offset spatula to spread mayonnaise evenly over the chicken. Mound some bread salad in the center of the plate, and serve.

VARIATION Serve the salad on its own as a small meal or side dish, or top the salad with a grilled or seared tuna steak for a seafood alternative main course.

CHICKEN CURRY WITH BASMATI RICE AND FIGS

I am pretty much a classicist, but there are times when I pull together ingredients from disparate origins to get all the flavors I'm looking for in a dish, like in this recipe which I've never served in a restaurant but which is a favorite at home. Here, Indian stalwarts like curry and cilantro and Asian staples such as lemongrass and chili paste are cooked with the German wine Gewürztraminer; in this context, they seem made for each other, coming together in a complex sweet, spicy, and fragrant blend. A note on timing: You can make the rice while the chicken is in the oven.

¼ CUP PLUS I TABLESPOON CANOLA OIL

2 CHICKENS, 3 TO 3½ POUNDS EACH, CUT INTO 8 PIECES EACH (BREASTS HALVED CROSSWISE, 2 THIGHS, 2 LEGS TRIMMED BY REMOVING KNUCKLES AND CLIPPING WING, WING DISCARDED)

KOSHER SALT

⅓ CUP ALL-PURPOSE FLOUR

I CUP DICED ONION

2 TABLESPOONS CURRY POWDER

½ CUP TRIMMED, THINLY SLICED LEMONGRASS (FROM I STALK), OR I ADDITIONAL TABLESPOON MINCED GINGER AND I ADDITIONAL TABLESPOON LIME JUICE

¼ CUP ROUGHLY CHOPPED PEELED FRESH GINGER

PEEL OF I LIME, REMOVED IN STRIPS WITH A VEGETABLE PEELER WITH NO PITH

2 TEASPOONS GREEN THAI CHILI PASTE (OPTIONAL)

2 CUPS GEWÜRZTRAMINER OR RIESLING

2 CUPS WHITE CHICKEN STOCK (PAGE 45) OR LOW-SODIUM, STORE-BOUGHT CHICKEN BROTH

½ CUP COCONUT MILK

2 TABLESPOONS FRESHLY SQUEEZED LIME JUICE

3 TABLESPOONS SNIPPED CILANTRO LEAVES

BASMATI RICE AND FIGS (RECIPE FOLLOWS)

PREHEAT the oven to 350°F. Heat a small, heavy-bottomed Dutch oven over medium-high heat. Pour ¼ cup oil into the pan and heat it. Season the chicken generously with salt and coat with flour, shaking off any excess. Add the chicken pieces to the pan and cook, turning them with tongs, until golden on all sides, approximately 10 minutes total cooking time. (If necessary to avoid crowding the pan, do this in 2 or 3 batches.) Set the chicken pieces aside on a clean, dry plate. Discard any oil remaining in the pan.

RETURN the Dutch oven to the stovetop over medium heat. Add the remaining 1 tablespoon oil and heat it. Add the onions and a pinch of salt and cook until softened, approximately 4 minutes. (They may brown slightly due to the lingering fat from the chicken.) Add the curry, lemongrass, ginger, lime peel, and chili paste, if using, and cook, stirring, for 2 minutes. Add any remaining flour and cook, stirring, for 3 minutes. Add the wine, raise the heat to high, and bring to a boil. Lower the heat so the liquid is simmering, and continue to simmer until reduced by three-quarters, 7 to 8 minutes. Pour in the stock and coconut milk, stir, and return the chicken pieces to the Dutch oven. When the liquid comes to a simmer, cover and cook in the oven until the chicken is tender, approximately 45 minutes.

REMOVE the chicken pieces from the Dutch oven with tongs or a slotted spoon and set them aside. Strain the sauce into a bowl and discard the solids. Stir in the lime juice, cilantro, and 1 teaspoon salt. Add the chicken to the bowl and transfer to a serving platter. Serve hot, with the rice alongside.

BASMATI RICE AND FIGS

1 TABLESPOON CANOLA OIL

⅓ CUP FINELY DICED ONION

KOSHER SALT

1 CUP BASMATI RICE, RINSED AND DRAINED

½ CUP DRIED FIGS, QUARTERED

1½ CUPS WATER

PUT the oil in a 4-quart saucepan set over medium heat. Add the onions and a pinch of salt and cook, stirring, until softened, approximately 3 minutes. Add the rice and stir to coat rice with the oil. Add the figs, 1½ teaspoons salt, and water. Cover and bring to a boil. Lower the heat and cook for 20 minutes. Remove the pan from heat and let stand, covered, for 10 minutes. Before serving, fluff with a fork.

EMBELLISHMENT Steamed or sautéed bok choy works well with the flavors and textures in this dish.

CHICKEN COOKED UNDER A BRICK WITH WHITE BEAN "BRANDADE"

SERVES 4

T he phrase "chicken cooked under a brick" baffles many diners. Why would anyone want to cook chicken, or anything for that matter, under a brick? Well, the technique is an old European country one, in which a brick, wrapped in foil, is set over a chicken to weigh it down. If you've roasted only trussed whole chickens, then get ready: the difference in the finished dish will startle and delight you. Halving and pressing down the chickens as they cook ensures that as much skin as possible comes into direct contact with the pan, a foolproof way of getting the crispy, crackling skin that every cook dreams of.

I prefer to cook individual half-chickens with the bones in for a more rustic presentation and the best possible flavor, although you could certainly make this with boneless chicken.

The white bean "brandade" is an intensely flavored puree of white beans, lemon, anchovy, and garlic. The name is a play on the salt cod, whipped potato, and olive oil classic of French cuisine with anchovy standing in for the cod, and beans for the potato.

You will need four bricks wrapped in aluminum foil, two heavy 10-inch pans, or another ovenproof, heavy object wrapped in foil.

---

2 CUPS DRIED CANNELLINI BEANS OR OTHER WHITE BEANS

½ ONION, HALVED THROUGH THE ROOT END

I MEDIUM CARROT, PEELED, AND CUT CROSSWISE INTO 3 PIECES

I STALK CELERY, CUT CROSSWISE INTO 3 PIECES

6 SPRIGS ROSEMARY

I HEAD GARLIC, HALVED, EXCESS PAPERY SKIN REMOVED, PLUS I TEASPOON CHOPPED GARLIC

I TABLESPOON FINELY GRATED LEMON ZEST PLUS 3 TABLESPOONS FRESHLY SQUEEZED LEMON JUICE

2 TABLESPOONS (PREFERABLY SALT-PACKED) CHOPPED ANCHOVY FILLETS (FROM ABOUT 4 FILLETS, SOAKED, DRAINED AND PATTED DRY; SEE PAGE 11)

KOSHER SALT

BLACK PEPPER IN A MILL

¼ CUP OLIVE OIL

2 CHICKENS, 3 TO 3½ POUNDS EACH, CUT IN HALF

PUT the beans in a bowl and cover by 4 inches with room-temperature water. Cover and let soak overnight. (Alternately, you can quick-soak the beans: put them in a pot and cover them by 4 inches with water. Bring the water to a boil, turn off the heat, and cover the beans for 3 hours.) Drain.

PUT the beans in a heavy-bottomed pot and add the onion, carrot, celery, rosemary, garlic, and enough water to cover by 2 inches. Bring the water to a simmer, then cover and cook at a simmer until the beans are tender, approximately 90 minutes.

DRAIN the beans in a fine-mesh strainer set over a bowl, then pick out and discard the vegetables. Reserve the liquid. Transfer the beans to the bowl of a food processor fitted with the steel blade. Add the lemon zest, anchovy, salt and pepper to taste, and 2 tablespoons olive oil. Puree until smooth and the consistency of potato puree; if necessary, add some of the reserved cooking liquid to achieve the desired consistency.

PREHEAT the oven to 450°F. Heat two 12-inch ovenproof sauté pans over medium heat. Pour 2 tablespoons oil into each pan and heat the oil. Put 2 portions of chicken into each pan, skin-side down, and weight them down with the foil-wrapped bricks. Lower the flame and continue to cook until the skin becomes golden and crispy, approximately 5 minutes.

PUT the pans of chicken, with their bricks, in the oven and cook for 15 minutes. Remove the bricks, turn the chickens over with tongs or a spatula, and cook another 5 minutes. (An instant-read thermometer inserted to the thickest part of a half should read 160°F.) Remove the pans from the oven, turn the chickens over so they are skin side up, and let rest for 5 minutes.

DIVIDE the brandade among 4 dinner plates, top with 1 chicken portion, and serve.

VARIATIONS The chicken can also be served with mashed potatoes, Parlsey Pistou (page 248), or a quick sauce made by whisking Garlic Confit (page 36) into Dark Chicken Stock (page 46).

EMBELLISHMENT Use White Chicken Stock (page 45) rather than water to impart a richer flavor to the beans.

CHICKEN ɪɴ SALT CRUST ᴡɪᴛʜ DIABLO SAUCE

SERVES 4

ooking chicken in a salt crust causes it to bake and steam simultaneously, resulting in succulent, silky meat. The same technique is used to great effect with other meats such as beef, duck, and lamb, as well as fish, most notably salmon. Here, the chicken is topped with a spicy diablo sauce (the name means "devil," a nod to its spiciness) of jalapeño, vinegar, veal stock, and Dijon mustard. This recipe offers a powerful illustration of the concept of "carryover" cooking. Any piece of fish, poultry, or meat continues to cook after it's been removed from the heat, some more than others. It's always important to keep this in mind in order to get the perfect, desired doneness. Here, the chickens' temperature will rise at least 20 degrees because the crust traps so much heat.

Serve this with Potato Cake with Garlic and Parsley (page 259).

---

2 CLOVES GARLIC, CRUSHED

3 TABLESPOONS MINCED SAGE (OPTIONAL)

ABOUT 5 CUPS KOSHER SALT

BLACK PEPPER IN A MILL

2 CHICKENS, 3 TO 3½ POUNDS EACH

3 TABLESPOONS DIJON MUSTARD

3 CUPS ALL-PURPOSE FLOUR, PLUS MORE FOR DUSTING A WORK SURFACE

1 TABLESPOON CORIANDER SEEDS

ABOUT 1½ TEASPOONS CRUSHED BLACK PEPPERCORNS

2 CUPS WATER

NONSTICK COOKING SPRAY

DIABLO SAUCE

2 TABLESPOONS UNSALTED BUTTER

¼ CUP MINCED SHALLOTS

1 TEASPOON THYME LEAVES

1 BAY LEAF

1 TABLESPOON TOMATO PASTE

¼ CUP WHITE WINE VINEGAR

½ CUP DRY WHITE WINE

2 CUPS VEAL STOCK (PAGE 48) OR DARK CHICKEN STOCK (PAGE 46)

1 JALAPEÑO PEPPER, THINLY SLICED CROSSWISE, WITH ITS SEEDS

1 TABLESPOON DIJON MUSTARD

2 TABLESPOONS HEAVY CREAM (OPTIONAL)

¼ TEASPOON CAYENNE

PREHEAT the oven to 350°F. Put the garlic, 1 tablespoon sage, if using, 1 tablespoon salt, and 1 teaspoon ground pepper in a small bowl and mix them together. Season the inside of the chicken cavities with this mixture, truss the chickens with butcher twine (see Terms and Techniques), and brush the outside of each chicken with half the mustard.

PUT the remaining 2 tablespoons sage, 5 cups kosher salt, flour, coriander, 1½ teaspoons of the crushed peppercorns, and water in a bowl and mix them together, starting with a wooden spoon, then kneading by hand into a homogeneous dough.

SPREAD out a sheet of parchment paper or wax paper and coat it with nonstick cooking spray. Divide the dough into 2 equal pieces. Put half the dough on the paper and use your hands to work the dough into a ball, then roll it out with a rolling pin into a square shape with a thickness of about ¼ inch. Set aside. Repeat with the other piece of dough and another sheet of parchment paper.

PICK up the parchment and invert one piece of dough over one of the chickens to cause the dough to drape over the top of the chicken. Pull the dough over and around the bottom of the chicken to completely cover it, and seal it, molding the dough to the shape of the chicken. As you work, take care to gently tuck the dough into the chicken's curves and crevices to avoid tearing it. If you do happen to tear it, patch the hole with a small piece of dough taken from the end. Repeat with the other piece of dough and chicken.

PUT the chickens breast side up on a sturdy baking sheet. Bake until the salt crust is hard and golden-brown, and an instant-read thermometer inserted to the center of the chicken reads 135°F to 140°F, approximately 45 minutes. Remove the chickens from the oven and let rest for 20 minutes. The resting time is essential; the chickens will continue to cook to a true doneness of about 160°F. (If they do not, return them to the oven and bake until they reach 160°F.)

MAKE the sauce: Heat the butter in a large, heavy-bottomed pot over low heat. Add the shallots, thyme, bay leaf, and 1 pinch crushed black peppercorns and cook for 3 minutes. Add the tomato paste and continue cooking for 1 more minute. Add the vinegar and white wine. Bring to a boil and reduce by half, approximately 2 minutes. Pour in the stock, add the jalapeño, and cook at a simmer for 35 minutes, skimming any impurities that rise to the surface. Without allowing the liquid to reboil, whisk in the mustard, cream, if using, and cayenne and season with 1 teaspoon salt, or to taste. Strain the sauce though a fine-mesh strainer set over a bowl and set aside, covered to keep it warm.

BRING the chickens to the table and show them to your guests. Then return to the kitchen, and use the back of a heavy knife to crack the salt crust and peel it away carefully from the chickens, making sure not to tear the skin off the chicken. Once the chickens are free from the crust, carve each one into two portions, slicing and pulling the legs from the body first, then separating the breasts. Divide the chicken among 4 plates. Spoon about ¼ cup sauce over each serving and serve.

TERMS AND TECHNIQUES *The chicken is trussed:* Trussing a chicken or other bird with kitchen twine helps to maintain its shape during roasting, ensuring that it cooks evenly and looks as attractive as possible. To truss a bird, lay it on your cutting board, breast side up. Hold one end of a 3-foot piece of twine in each hand, overlap them to form a loop, and pass the twine under the bird, letting the loop catch on the ends of the legs. Tie the string to hold the legs together. Turn the bird over, tuck the wings under the twine, pull the twine taut, criss-cross, and pull taut again. Cut off any excess string.

THE REASON *The mustard sauce isn't boiled:* Boiling a sauce that includes mustard can cause the mustard to "break," turning the sauce gritty.

BREAST of CHICKEN with COMTÉ-SCALLION POLENTA

SERVES 4

ooking with cheese can be an excellent way to take advantage of its power. In this recipe, slices of Comté (reminiscent of the somewhat sharp quality of Gruyère) are stuffed into a pocket cut into the side of a chicken breast. When the breast is cooked, the cheese melts, infusing the entire piece with pungent flavor.

4 CHICKEN BREASTS, 6 OUNCES EACH, SKIN ON

3½ OUNCES COMTÉ CHEESE, CUT INTO 8 SLICES, 3 INCHES BY 1 INCH BY ¼ INCH THICK, AT ROOM TEMPERATURE

KOSHER SALT

BLACK PEPPER IN A MILL

3 TABLESPOONS OLIVE OIL

COMTÉ-SCALLION POLENTA (RECIPE FOLLOWS)

PREHEAT the oven to 350°F. Make a ½-inch deep pocket by slicing an incision along the length of each chicken breast, leaving ¼ inch of uncut flesh on each end.

PUSH 2 slices of cheese into each slit. Season the breasts with salt and 4 grinds of pepper per side of each breast.

HEAT a 12-inch sauté pan over low-medium high heat. Pour the oil into the pan and heat it. Add the chicken, flesh-side down, and lightly brown for 2 minutes. Turn the chicken over and lightly brown the skin side for 3 minutes. Put the pan in the oven and cook until the juices run clear when pierced with a thin-bladed knife, and an instant-read thermometer inserted into the center of the breast reads 160°F, 8 to 10 minutes.

REMOVE the pan from the oven and transfer the breasts to a wire rack, skin-side down to keep the cheese and juices from oozing out.

TO serve, spoon some polenta onto each of 4 plates and arrange 1 chicken breast alongside or lean it against the polenta.

EMBELLISHMENTS Finish the polenta by stirring in 2 tablespoons mascarpone cheese for a richer flavor and mouthfeel.

Drizzle the chicken with Parsley Pistou (page 248) or sauce the plate with Dark Chicken Stock (page 46).

If you'd like to round out this dish with a green vegetable, serve it with broccoli rabe sautéed in olive oil along with sliced garlic and crushed red pepper flakes.

For an accompaniment to the chicken (or to other poultry or lamb, especially braised lamb shank), replace the Comté with ½ cup crumbled fresh goat cheese (from about 3½ ounces cheese).

THE REASON *The chicken meat is only lightly browned, rather than seared:* Searing the flesh of poultry and game birds dries out the exterior, causing it to become hard and stringy, which distracts from the overall succulence of the bird.

VARIATIONS Substitute Gruyère or other hard mountain cheeses like Beaufort or Appenzeller for the Comté.

COMTÉ-SCALLION POLENTA SERVES 4

This is also delicious with other roasted poultry and meats.

4 CUPS WHITE CHICKEN STOCK (PAGE 45) OR LOW-SODIUM, STORE-BOUGHT CHICKEN BROTH OR WATER

½ CUP CORNMEAL

¼ CUP COARSELY GRATED COMTÉ (FROM ABOUT ¾ POUND CHEESE)

⅓ CUP SCALLIONS, WHITE AND LIGHT-GREEN PORTIONS, THINLY SLICED ON THE BIAS

1 TABLESPOON UNSALTED BUTTER

1 TEASPOON KOSHER SALT

BLACK PEPPER IN A MILL

POUR the stock into a saucepan and bring to a boil over high heat. Lower the heat to low and slowly whisk in the cornmeal, a little at a time. The polenta will thicken as you work in the cornmeal. Continue to simmer, stirring occasionally to avoid scorching, for 25 minutes. Remove the pot from the heat and whisk in the Comté, scallions, butter, and salt. Season with 4 grinds of pepper, or to taste. Cover with plastic wrap and set aside for up to 1 hour, or cool until ready to serve and reheat it. (If you reheat it, add some water or stock to replenish any liquid that might have evaporated during resting time.)

VARIATION After the polenta is cooked, make polenta cakes following directions for Panisse on page 272.

ROASTED DUCK À L'ORANGE WITH ORANGE MARMALADE AND TURNIP GREENS

SERVES 4

In the French classic duck *à l'orange,* the richness of the bird is complemented by the sweetness of oranges. The lessons of this dish reverberate throughout Western cooking; sweet accompaniments are often paired with other rich foods, such as the fruit compotes often served alongside foie gras, or even the all-American combination of peanut butter and jelly. Here, smoky bacon and bitter greens round out the flavors on the plate.

If you have an accommodating butcher, ask him or her to hang the ducks near the blower in the walk-in refrigerator for two to three days to dry them out as much as possible (see The Reason, page 214).

---

2 TABLESPOONS CLOVES

2 TABLESPOONS CORIANDER SEEDS

2 TABLESPOONS JUNIPER BERRIES

2 TABLESPOONS GROUND CARDAMOM

2 TABLESPOONS GROUND CINNAMON

2 TABLESPOONS GROUND STAR ANISE

2 TABLESPOONS GROUND ALLSPICE

2 QUARTS ORANGE JUICE, PREFERABLY FRESHLY SQUEEZED

6 QUARTS WATER

I CUP HONEY

2 BONELESS PEKIN (LONG ISLAND) DUCKS, ABOUT 4½ POUNDS EACH, INNARDS REMOVED

¼ CUP DUCK FAT (SEE SOURCES, PAGE 318) OR BUTTER

¼ CUP DICED SLAB BACON (FROM ABOUT 1½ OUNCES BACON)

I CLOVE GARLIC, THINLY SLICED

I POUND TURNIP GREENS, COARSELY CHOPPED, CLEANED, RINSED, AND DRIED

2 ORANGES, CUT INTO 6 WEDGES EACH

GENEROUS ¼ CUP ORANGE MARMALADE (PAGE 42)

PUT the cloves, coriander, and juniper in an 8-inch sauté pan and toast over low heat, shaking constantly, until fragrant but not browned, 2 to 3 minutes. Remove the pan from the heat and let the spices cool.

TRANSFER the spices to a spice or coffee grinder and grind together. Transfer to a bowl and add the cardamom, cinnamon, star anise, and allspice.

POUR the orange juice, water, and honey into a pot large enough to hold the ducks. Bring to a boil over medium-high heat. Prick the ducks all over with a fork, submerge them in the orange bouillon, cover, and simmer for 10 minutes, then remove them and pat them dry with paper towels. If you have the time, put the ducks on a cookie sheet and place uncovered in the refrigerator for up to three days to "air-dry".

WHEN ready to proceed, rub the spice mixture all over the ducks.

PUT 2 tablespoons duck fat and the bacon in a 12-inch sauté pan set over medium-low heat and cook until the fat is rendered from the bacon, approximately 4 minutes. Add the remaining duck fat and garlic and sauté until the garlic is pale golden, 1 minute. Add the turnip greens and cook until wilted and tender, approximately 12 minutes (they should release a lot of juice). Drain the cooked greens in a colander and let them cool there. Once they have cooled, firmly squeeze out any excess juice. Set aside.

PREHEAT the oven to 450°F. Stuff the pieces of 1 orange into each duck's cavity, crushing them and rubbing them into the sides of the birds. Put the ducks in a deep pan with a wire rack and roast for 20 minutes. Lower the heat to 350°F and cook until the skin becomes very crispy, 1 hour and 15 minutes. Remove the duck from the oven and let rest for 15 minutes. If the skin loses its crispiness during this time, reheat it briefly under the broiler. During the final few minutes of resting, or while the duck is under the broiler, gently reheat the greens in a saucepan set over low-medium heat.

TO serve, separate the breast and leg pieces, and divide the pieces among 4 dinner plates. Spoon a heaping tablespoon of orange marmalade and some turnip greens alongside the duck on each plate.

THE REASON *The duck is dried for up to three days:* The (optional) step of drying the duck in the refrigerator will help turn its skin super-crispy when roasted.

CONFIT DUCK WITH
CELERY ROOT–APPLE PUREE

SERVES 4

Confit means to preserve something in its own fat. In the days before refrigeration was a fact of life, confit was a means of preserving duck, pork, and other meats by drawing out the moisture and impurities to prevent spoilage. The finished legs are rich and tender and, true to their heritage, can be kept in the refrigerator for months, meaning a spontaneous, handcrafted meal is never more than a few minutes away.

A lot of duck leg confit recipes instruct you to trim too much fat, but you need enough to cover the skin, which will shrink and constrict during the confit process, so leave some overhang. You can always trim it later. You can double or even triple this recipe because the duck's flavor will improve with age. To store the confit duck legs, refrigerate them in airtight containers, making sure their fat comes up over them.

Serve the duck legs with Celery Root–Apple Puree (page 218), in a risotto (page 219), as the basis of a salad, or with hearty accompaniments such as Sweet Potato-Vanilla Puree (page 227), glazed root vegetables, or potatoes.

---

2 TABLESPOONS BLACK PEPPERCORNS

1 TABLESPOON CORIANDER SEEDS

1 TEASPOON JUNIPER BERRIES

1 TEASPOON DRIED THYME

3 BAY LEAVES

1 TABLESPOON DRIED SAGE

6 CLOVES GARLIC

½ TABLESPOON DRIED ROSEMARY

⅓ CUP PLUS 1½ TABLESPOONS KOSHER SALT

4 DUCK LEGS

6 CUPS RENDERED DUCK FAT (SEE SOURCES, PAGE 318)

CELERY ROOT-APPLE PUREE (RECIPE FOLLOWS)

PUT the peppercorns, coriander, and juniper berries in an 8-inch sauté pan and toast, shaking the pan constantly, until fragrant but not browned, 2 to 3 minutes. Remove the pan from the heat and let the spices cool.

TRANSFER the spices to a spice or coffee grinder and finely grind. Transfer to the bowl of a food processor fitted with the steel blade. Add the thyme, bay leaves, sage, garlic, rosemary, and salt and pulse 6 times to combine. Put the duck legs in a single layer in a baking dish or other shallow vessel, fat side down. Divide 1 tablespoon of the spice mixture among the legs, rubbing it in well. Cover with plastic wrap and another baking sheet.

Weigh down the top sheet with 2 to 2½ pounds of heavy food cans or another weight and refrigerate for 24 hours.

WASH the salt cure off the legs with cold running water and pat the legs dry.

PREHEAT the oven to 225°F. Put the duck fat in a 2-quart saucepan and melt it over low heat. Add the duck legs to the fat and bring the fat to a simmer over medium-high heat. Remove the pan from the heat, cover, and transfer to the oven. Cook until the duck is falling-apart tender, approximately 3 hours 15 minutes. Remove the pan from the oven, remove the lid, and let cool to room temperature. Carefully remove the duck legs from the fat using a slotted spoon. Alternatively, store the duck legs in the fat, refrigerated, for up to six months. Skim the duck fat from the pan and set it aside. Discard the liquid that remains at the bottom of the pan.

WARM a 12-inch sauté pan over medium heat. Add enough duck fat to submerge the legs up to the skin but not the exposed meat. Add the cooked duck legs, fat side down, and more fat if necessary to cover the desired portion. Crisp the skin for 4 minutes, then remove the pan from the heat, turn the legs over, and reheat the meat side for 2 minutes off heat. The duck should be hot throughout and have a crispy skin. Alternately, you can preheat the broiler, put the legs in an ovenproof baking dish or other shallow vessel, skin side up, and reheat for 4 minutes. This will crisp the skin and reheat the duck.

TO serve, mound some puree on each of 4 dinner plates and set 1 duck leg alongside the puree on each plate.

THE REASON *The spices are toasted:* Toasting spices releases their essential oils, intensifying the flavor.

VARIATION At home I create a quick Pekin duck–inspired dish by shallow-frying scallion pancakes in duck fat, spreading them with plum sauce and chili paste, and topping them with chopped confit duck and sliced scallions.

CELERY ROOT–APPLE PUREE SERVES 4

I enjoy eating root vegetable purees with game and meat. I love this side dish—in which the relatively light-textured but unmistakable flavor of celery root marries perfectly with tart apple—in the fall, especially with poultry such as pheasant, game such as venison, or Daube of Beef Short Ribs with Olives and Orange-Cumin Carrots (page 237).

8 CUPS WATER

I POUND CELERY ROOT, PEELED, QUARTERED, AND RUBBED WITH HALF A LEMON

½ CUP PEELED, DICED GRANNY SMITH APPLE

I TABLESPOON CRÈME FRAÎCHE, OR 2 TABLESPOONS HEAVY CREAM

KOSHER SALT

WHITE PEPPER IN A MILL

BRING the water to a boil in a 4-quart saucepan over high heat. Add the celery root and apple to the pot. Lower the heat and let simmer until the celery root is tender, stirring to prevent scorching, approximately 50 minutes.

DRAIN the celery root and apple. Return to the same pot and cook, stirring with a wooden spoon, over medium-high heat to evaporate any lingering moisture, approximately 3 minutes.

TRANSFER the celery root and apple to a blender and, with the motor running, add the crème fraîche. Blend until smooth, transfer to a bowl, and season to taste with salt and pepper.

THE REASON *The celery root is rubbed with lemon:* The acid in the lemon juice keeps the peeled celery root from turning brown when exposed to oxygen.

WILD MUSHROOM AND DUCK RISOTTO WITH SEASONAL VARIATIONS

T his dish is a classic at Picholine, where we serve it from a copper risotto pot that is left on the table, inviting diners to replenish their plates with additional servings, which they always do.

Here's a risotto-making tip: The only way to truly know if the rice is cooked is to taste it. To avoid tasting from your cooking spoon, dab a few grains onto the side of your hand and taste from there, or put a grain on your cutting board and cut it in half. As soon as the rice is al dente and there's no white (raw) portion visible in the center, the rice is done.

White truffle oil may be one of the most overused restaurant ingredients, but it adds a powerful aroma to this dish. Use only the indicated amount; it can overwhelm just about anything.

You can make this without the duck, or use it as a model for virtually any risotto you can think of.

---

3 CUPS WATER

I CUP FAVA BEANS (FROM 2 POUNDS FAVA BEANS IN THE POD)

2 TABLESPOONS OLIVE OIL

½ CUP WILD MUSHROOMS (CHANTERELLES, OYSTER, PORCINI), TRIMMED AND WIPED CLEAN WITH A DAMP CLOTH, THINLY SLICED

6 TABLESPOONS UNSALTED BUTTER, COLD

KOSHER SALT

BLACK PEPPER IN A MILL

¼ CUP PLUS 2 TABLESPOONS DICED ONION

½ TEASPOON MINCED GARLIC

2 CUPS CARNAROLI OR OTHER RISOTTO RICE SUCH AS ARBORIO OR VIALONE NANO

½ CUP DRY WHITE WINE

4 CUPS WHITE CHICKEN STOCK (PAGE 45) OR LOW-SODIUM, STORE-BOUGHT CHICKEN BROTH, SIMMERING IN A POT ON A BACK BURNER

½ CUP CONFIT DUCK LEG, I-INCH PIECES (PAGE 216, OR SEE SOURCES, PAGE 318)

I CUP GRATED PARMIGIANO-REGGIANO (FROM 3¾ OUNCES CHEESE)

I TEASPOON WHITE TRUFFLE OIL

FILL a large bowl halfway with ice water.

POUR the 3 cups of water into a 1-quart saucepan and bring to a boil over high heat. Add the fava beans and blanch for 1 minute. Transfer the favas to the ice water with a slotted spoon to shock them to stop the cooking. Strain and remove the outer skins. Set aside.

HEAT the oil in an 8-inch sauté pan set over medium heat. Add the mushrooms and cook until they begin to release their juices, approximately 4 minutes. Add 1 tablespoon of the butter and sauté for 2 more minutes. Season with salt and 3 grinds of pepper. Remove the pan from the heat and set aside.

MELT 2 tablespoons of the butter in a 4-quart saucepan set over medium low heat. Add the onions and a pinch of salt and cook until softened but not browned, approximately 4 minutes. Add the garlic and sauté for 1 minute. Add the risotto rice and stir to coat the rice with the butter, approximately 1 minute. Add the wine and continue to stir. Once the wine has been absorbed by the rice, add 1 cup of the chicken stock, stirring constantly. Once the stock has been absorbed by the rice, add another cup. Repeat the process with the remaining stock, stirring constantly. After you have added about half the stock, vigorously stir and agitate the rice for 30 seconds to release its starch content. When finished, the rice should be very thick and creamy and when stirred, should hold its shape for a moment before falling slightly. Fold the mushrooms, fava beans, and duck into the risotto.

REMOVE the pot from the heat and stir in the remaining 3 tablespoons butter, the Parmigiano-Reggiano, ¾ teaspoon salt, 6 grinds of pepper, and the truffle oil. Mix well, divide among individual plates or shallow bowls, and serve.

THE REASON *The risotto is stirred vigorously:* Stirring the risotto vigorously halfway through the cooking process releases its starch and helps it turn pleasingly creamy without losing its shape. Were you to do this later in the cooking process, when the rice is closer to being done, it would break the individual grains. This step also allows you occasionally to leave the risotto to cook rather than having you be a prisoner at the stove for the entire cooking time.

VARIATIONS By varying the vegetables in this dish, we never have to take it off Picholine's menu. You can adopt the same seasonal changes at home: Alter the mushrooms throughout the year, and replace the fava beans with corn in the summer, diced pumpkin in the fall, and diced squash in the winter.

ROASTED SQUAB WITH GLAZED ROOT VEGETABLES AND GOOSEBERRIES

I n the days of autumn, when game is not yet in season, squab is a good alternative for satisfying any cravings you might have. This dish is packed with other big flavors such as tart gooseberries, a perfect foil for the richness of the squab, and the creamy salsify, a somewhat uncommon root vegetable that's easy to find and makes a big impact at the table.

4 SQUABS, 14 TO 16 OUNCES EACH, INNARDS REMOVED

KOSHER SALT

BLACK PEPPER IN A MILL

6 CUPS WATER

½ POUND BABY TURNIPS, PEELED

½ POUND BABY CARROTS, PEELED

3 STALKS SALSIFY, PEELED AND CUT INTO 2-INCH PIECES

3 TABLESPOONS CANOLA OIL

5 TABLESPOONS UNSALTED BUTTER

1 TEASPOON RED-WINE VINEGAR

1 CUP PORT

2 CUPS VEAL STOCK (PAGE 48) OR DARK CHICKEN STOCK (PAGE 46)

2 TEASPOONS HONEY

¾ CUP GOOSEBERRIES OR GRAPES

PREHEAT the oven to 375°F. Season the squabs inside and out with salt and 6 grinds of pepper per bird. (You can mix the salt and pepper together in a dish before seasoning the birds.) Truss the squabs (see The Reason, page 209, for trussing instructions) and set them aside.

POUR the 6 cups water into a 2-quart pot, add 1 tablespoon salt, and bring to a boil over high heat. Fill a large bowl halfway with ice water.

ADD the baby turnips to the boiling water and cook until tender to a knife-tip, approximately 7 minutes. Use a slotted spoon to transfer the turnips to the ice water. When the water returns to the boil, add the baby carrots and cook until tender to a knife-tip, approximately 5 minutes. Transfer them to the bowl with the turnips. When the water returns to the boil, add the salsify pieces and cook until tender, approximately 6 minutes. Transfer them to the bowl with the other vegetables. Drain the cooked vegetables and set them aside.

HEAT a 12-inch ovenproof sauté pan over medium heat. Add the oil and 2 tablespoons butter. The butter will sizzle and foam. When the foam begins to subside, add the squabs to the pan, breast side down, and brown both sides of the breast for 2 minutes per side. Turn the squabs breast side up, transfer the pan to the oven, and roast the squabs, periodically tipping the pan and basting with the accumulated juices, until medium rare (an instant-read thermometer inserted to the thickest part of a squab should read 120 to 125°F, 7 to 8 minutes, or longer for more well done).

REMOVE the birds from the oven and place on a clean, dry surface. Tent with foil to keep warm and let rest for 8 to 10 minutes.

DRAIN the oil from the pan and return the pan to the stovetop over medium-high heat. Pour in the vinegar and deglaze. Pour in the port, bring to a simmer, and continue to simmer until reduced by half. Pour in the veal stock, bring to a simmer, and continue to simmer until it reduces and thickens enough to coat the back of a wooden spoon, approximately 15 minutes. Season to taste with salt.

MEANWHILE, put the remaining 3 tablespoons butter and the honey in a 10-inch sauté pan and set over medium heat. When the butter has bubbled and the bubbling begins to subside, add the vegetables and sauté until the liquid reduces to a syrupy glaze and the vegetables are hot. Add the gooseberries and toss or stir to combine well. Season with salt and 4 grinds of pepper, or to taste. Remove the pan from the heat, cover, and keep warm.

TO serve, debone the squabs by cutting a slit along the length of the breastbone and gently cutting the meat away from the bone as you pull the two apart, taking care to maintain the shape of the squab. Spoon some sauce into the center of each of 4 dinner plates. Divide the glazed vegetables evenly among the plates, and set a squab on top of the vegetables on each plate. Serve.

VARIATION The glazed vegetables from this dish can be served with other meats and game.

EMBELLISHMENT Drizzle the finished dish with Autumn Spice Oil (page 29) and/or serve it with an accompaniment of Fig Chutney (page 40).

PHEASANT WITH MADEIRA AND VANILLA SWEET POTATO PUREE

SERVES 4

To me, pheasant exists in a very pleasing middle ground between chicken and game; it has a fuller flavor than chicken but doesn't overwhelm other ingredients. If you can get it, make this recipe with wild pheasant, which has an even richer flavor.

---

4 YOUNG PHEASANTS (SOLD AS "BABY" PHEASANTS), ABOUT I POUND EACH, INNARDS REMOVED (SEE SOURCES, PAGE 318)

KOSHER SALT

FRESHLY GROUND BLACK PEPPER

3 TABLESPOONS CANOLA OIL

4 TABLESPOONS UNSALTED BUTTER

¾ CUP MADEIRA

I CUP VEAL STOCK (PAGE 48) OR DARK CHICKEN STOCK (PAGE 46)

I TABLESPOON SHERRY VINEGAR

VANILLA SWEET POTATO PUREE (RECIPE FOLLOWS)

SEASON the pheasant inside and out with salt and pepper and truss them. (See The Reason, page 209, for trussing instructions.)

PREHEAT the oven to 400°F. Heat a heavy-bottomed, ovenproof 12-inch sauté pan over medium heat. Add the oil and butter. The butter will sizzle and foam. When the foam begins to subside, add the pheasants to the pan, breast-side down, and brown both sides of the breasts for 3 minutes per side. Angle the pheasants to cook the other side of the breasts for 2 minutes. Turn the pheasants breast side up. (To avoid puncturing the skin, put a meat fork in the pheasant's cavity to do this, or use tongs, putting one tong in the cavity and the other outside.) Put the pan in the oven and roast the pheasants, periodically opening the oven door, tipping the pan toward you, and spooning some of the juice over the pheasant. Continue cooking until an instant-read thermometer inserted to the thickest part of the pheasant reads 160°F and/or the juices run clear when the bird is pierced with a sharp, thin-bladed knife, 7 to 9 minutes.

REMOVE the pan from the oven, set the pheasants on a clean, dry surface, tent them with foil to keep them warm, and make the sauce.

POUR off any oil remaining in the pan and set the pan over medium heat. Add the Madeira and use a wooden spoon to scrape up any flavorful bits stuck to the bottom of the pan. Bring to a boil and reduce by three-fourths, approximately 2 minutes. Lower the heat to medium-low, pour in the stock, and simmer until the sauce reduces enough to coat the back of a wooden spoon, 10 to 12 minutes. Stir the vinegar into the sauce and season to taste with salt.

AS the sauce reduces, carve the pheasants as you would roasted chicken, separating the leg–thigh pieces from the breasts, then separating the legs and thighs.

SPOON some sauce over the surface of 4 dinner plates. Spoon some puree in a mound on each plate. Divide the pheasant among the plates, setting the meat alongside the puree, and serve.

THE REASON *Oil and butter are used:* Using a combination of oil and butter allows you to cook at a high heat and still enjoy the flavor of butter. Because oil has a higher smoking point, it keeps the butter from browning too soon in a hot pan.

The pheasant is basted as it roasts: Because pheasants, like turkeys, have a relatively low fat content, basting is essential to making sure they don't dry out in the oven.

The sauce is spooned on the plate, before the pheasant: When you have a beautifully browned, roasted piece of meat, you don't want to obscure its visual appeal with a sauce. If, on the other hand, the fish or meat you're serving doesn't look particularly special (poached salmon is a good example), spoon the sauce over it to enhance its appearance.

VARIATION You can make this recipe with pheasant breasts, or use older, larger pheasants. Just be sure to adjust the quantity and cooking time accordingly.

EMBELLISHMENT Add sage leaves and/or juniper berries to the pan with the butter to augment flavor while basting. A piece of bacon added to the sauce would lend a nice, smoky undercurrent. You might also replace the canola oil with Autumn Spice Oil (page 29).

VANILLA SWEET POTATO PUREE

SERVES 4 Fiery orange sweet potato and vanilla-infused cream make for a rich side dish that echoes the marshmallow-topped yams many of us grew up with. The puree balances the somewhat gamey flavor of the pheasant and is also great for a holiday feast, especially Thanksgiving. If you're in a kitschy mood you can even serve it in a casserole with little marshmallows on top.

To make this and other purees more refined, push them through a fine-mesh strainer set over a bowl, which will grant them a smoother texture and mouthfeel. I do this with all purees and find that it's always worth the trouble.

This is also a good accompaniment for pork.

1½ POUNDS SWEET POTATOES, CLEANED AND LEFT A BIT DAMP

½ CUP PLUS 3 TABLESPOONS HEAVY CREAM

⅓ VANILLA BEAN, SPLIT LENGTHWISE AND SEEDS SCRAPED

1 TEASPOON GRATED ORANGE ZEST (OPTIONAL)

2 TABLESPOONS UNSALTED BUTTER, AT ROOM TEMPERATURE

KOSHER SALT

WHITE PEPPER IN A MILL

PREHEAT the oven to 350°F. Put the potatoes on a baking sheet and bake in the oven until tender to a fork tip, about 1 hour. Remove from oven and let cool until warm enough to handle, 10 to 15 minutes. Peel and discard the skin. Put the potatoes in the bowl of a food processor fitted with the steel blade.

MEANWHILE, pour the cream into a 2-quart pot, add the vanilla bean and orange zest, if using, and set it over medium heat. Bring to a simmer and cook for 5 minutes. Remove from heat. Use tongs to fish out and discard the vanilla bean. Pour the mixture over the potatoes in the processor and add the butter.

PUREE the potato mixture until smooth. Season with salt and 4 grinds of pepper, or to taste. Keep covered and warm until ready to serve.

THE REASON *The sweet potato is baked rather than boiled:* To concentrate the flavor of the potato, I bake it here to extract as much moisture as possible.

EMBELLISHMENT Add some Autumn Spice Oil (page 29) when pureeing to punch up the seasonal character of this puree.

- GRILLED PORTERHOUSE WITH BÉARNAISE SAUCE *231*
- SIRLOIN STEAKS WITH A CARAWAY CRUST *233*
- POACHED FILET OF BEEF WITH HORSERADISH CREAM *234*
- DAUBE OF BEEF SHORT RIBS WITH OLIVES AND ORANGE-CUMIN CARROTS *237*
- LAMB WITH BOULANGÈRE POTATOES *240*
- GRILLED LAMB CHOPS WITH ANCHOVY BUTTER *242*

MEATS AND GAME

- GRILLED PORK CHOP WITH APRICOT CHUTNEY *243*
- PORK STEAK WITH SAGE, PUMPKIN, AND PRUNES *244*
- LAMB STEAK WITH ORZO AND PARSLEY PISTOU *247*
- RABBIT AU RIESLING WITH RUTABAGA "SAUERKRAUT" *249*
- VENISON AU POIVRE WITH RED CABBAGE CONFIT *252*
- VENISON CHOPS WITH BANYULS VINEGAR AND SQUASH-PRUNE GRATIN *254*

MEATS AND GAME ARE MORE VERSATILE than they are often given credit for, lending themselves to grilling in the summer, or slow cooking in the fall and winter. In this chapter you'll find a full range of preparations, including one that poaches filet mignon. As with the fish and poultry chapters, if you are drawn to a particular sauce or accompaniment, by all means use it with a type of meat other than the one I have chosen.

Attention to a few details before and after the actual cooking will give you the best results with meats and game. Before cooking, let the meat come to room temperature, allowing it to cook evenly. On the other side of the process, meats need to rest between the time they are cooked and the time they are served. When meat is cooked, the juices collect in the center of the meat. A period of "rest" after cooking allows them to redistribute throughout, along with their moisture and flavor. With larger cuts such as leg of lamb, the resting time can be rather drastic, as long as 30 minutes, because it takes longer for those juices to settle; with most of the recipes in this chapter, it's fairly short, just 5 or 10 minutes. But it is essential.

An ever-expanding selection of meats is available in supermarkets today, but to ensure an artisanal experience at home, I recommend finding a reliable butcher shop, or even ordering meats by mail (see Sources, page 318). In recent years, companies such as D'Artagnan in New Jersey, Jamison Farm in Latrobe, Pennsylvania, and Niman Ranch in Northern California have arrived on the scene, ready to deliver cuts of the meats in this chapter, most of them produced according to meticulous guidelines of everything from grazing to aging that ensure superlative quality, right to your door. Although this can be a pricier option, if you've never tried it, you should; there's no easier way to take your cooking to the next level than by discovering new, superior ingredient sources.

GRILLED PORTERHOUSE WITH BÉARNAISE SAUCE

SERVES 4

The typical aging time for beef is three weeks. I prefer beef that has been aged for about six weeks; it has a more mineral flavor than non-aged steaks. I also recommend dry versus wet aging; extracting moisture concentrates the flavor. You won't find dry-aged beef in the supermarket, but you can find it at gourmet shops, certain butcher shops (some of which do their own aging), and by mail order from specialty meat companies. Each of these sources will proudly tell you the minimum or maximum amount of time they age their beef.

You can make this with a smaller sirloin, varying the grilling times as indicated in the recipe. You can also serve this with many of the accompaniments in the Side Dishes chapter. My favorites are Creamed Spinach (page 260), Potato Cake with Garlic and Parsley (page 259), Porcini and Onion Tart (page 264), or Macaroni and Cheese (page 271).

4 PRIME DRY-AGED PORTERHOUSE STEAKS, 1½ POUNDS EACH, AT LEAST 1 INCH THICK

2 TABLESPOONS OLIVE OIL

KOSHER SALT

BLACK PEPPER IN A MILL

BÉARNAISE SAUCE (RECIPE FOLLOWS)

PREPARE an outdoor grill for grilling, letting the coals burn down until covered with white ash.

RUB each side of the steaks with oil, then generously season with salt and 6 grinds of pepper. Press down on the salt and pepper to form a uniform crust.

SET the steaks on the grill over high heat, lower the cover and grill for 5 minutes on each side for rare to medium-rare (an instant-read thermometer inserted to the thickest part of a steak should read 120°F to 125°F), or longer for more well done. (You can also make this dish with a 1-pound, 1-inch-thick sirloin, cooking it for 6 to 7 minutes per side.) The meat should caramelize and develop a crust. Remove the steaks from the grill and let rest for 5 minutes.

TO serve, place 1 steak on each of 4 dinner plates and serve with the sauce.

THE REASON *When grilling, you should pay extra attention to doneness cues:* When grilling any meat from a recipe, bear in mind that a number of factors influence the rate of doneness, such as the intensity of the heat and the proximity of the meat to the flame. So don't take the cooking times in the recipe as gospel; use an instant-read thermometer to test for doneness.

BÉARNAISE SAUCE MAKES ABOUT 1 CUP

When cooking at home, I use an unusual method, designed to save time, for making béarnaise sauce: Instead of making a reduction with the vinegar and tarragon, I blanch the herb, then chill it and chop it, a technique that keeps the leaves bright green and preserves their color. This sauce is also wonderful on chicken and fish.

14 TABLESPOONS (1 STICK PLUS 6 TABLESPOONS) UNSALTED BUTTER

2 CUPS WATER

½ CUP (LOOSELY PACKED) TARRAGON LEAVES

3 EGG YOLKS

2 TEASPOONS FRESHLY SQUEEZED LEMON JUICE

¾ TEASPOON KOSHER SALT

¼ TEASPOON CAYENNE

PUT the butter in a tall, narrow saucepan and melt it over low-medium heat. Spoon off the milk solids that collect on top. Remove from heat, and allow to rest for 10 minutes. The butter will separate. Carefully collect the thicker top layer into a separate container. This is clarified butter.

BRING the 2 cups water to a boil in a small saucepan over high heat. Fill a large bowl halfway with ice water. Add the tarragon to the boiling water and blanch it for 20 seconds. Drain the leaves in a fine mesh strainer and dip the strainer into the ice water to cool the leaves and stop the cooking. Drain again and squeeze the excess water from the leaves by hand. Chop the leaves finely and set aside. You should have about 2 teaspoons chopped leaves.

IN a large bowl set over a pot of simmering water, whisk the egg yolks and 2 teaspoons lemon juice with a small, flexible balloon whisk, until pale, thick ribbons form, 1 to 2 minutes. Don't whisk too vigorously; you don't want to let too much air into the mixture. However, if the eggs start to scramble, remove the bowl from the heat and whisk vigorously to cool.

SLOWLY whisk in the clarified butter, in a slow steady stream, scraping down the sides, and fully incorporating the butter. (It is important not to let the sauce get too hot or too cold; use the back of a finger to check the temperature of the sauce; it should feel warm to the touch.) Remove the pan from the heat, whisk in the salt, tarragon, and cayenne, and serve.

SIRLOIN STEAKS WITH A CARAWAY CRUST

SERVES 4

**A** prime sirloin, well cooked, is something special on its own. Coated with a crust of butter, rye bread, caraway seeds, and mustard, it takes on a nuance rarely associated with beef. Serve this with French fries, roasted potatoes, Potato Cake with Garlic and Parsley (page 259), or seasonal vegetables.

¼ CUP OLIVE OIL

4 PRIME SIRLOIN STEAKS, 10 OUNCES EACH, 1½ INCHES THICK

KOSHER SALT

BLACK PEPPER IN A MILL

1½ TABLESPOONS CARAWAY SEEDS

3 TABLESPOONS UNSALTED BUTTER, CHILLED

2 (PACKED) CUPS CRUSTLESS RYE BREAD CRUMBS, PULSED TO FINE IN THE BOWL OF A FOOD PROCESSOR FITTED WITH THE STEEL BLADE

3 TABLESPOONS DIJON MUSTARD

POSITION a rack 4 inches from the heating element of the broiler. Preheat the broiler. Grease a cookie sheet with 2 tablespoons olive oil and set it aside.

SEASON each side of the sirloins generously with salt and several grinds of pepper per side of each steak. Set aside.

PUT the caraway seeds in an 8-inch sauté pan and toast them over medium heat until fragrant, approximately 2 minutes.

ADD 2 tablespoons butter to the bowl of a food processor fitted with the steel blade. Add the caraway seeds, bread crumbs, mustard, ½ teaspoon salt, and ¼ teaspoon pepper. Pulse until all ingredients are well incorporated and the mixture is spreadable.

HEAT a 12-inch sauté pan over medium-high heat. Add olive oil and 1 tablespoon butter. When the butter has bubbled and the bubbling begins to subside, add the sirloins. Cook for 4 minutes and turn over. Cook another 4 minutes. Remove the steaks from the pan and arrange them on the greased cookie sheet without crowding. Let cool, then spread the caraway crust evenly on one side.

BROIL for 2 to 3 minutes for rare to medium rare (an instant-read thermometer inserted to the thickest part of a steak will read 120°F to 125°F), a bit longer for more well done, careful not to burn the crust.

PUT 1 steak on each of 4 dinner plates and serve.

POACHED FILET OF BEEF WITH HORSERADISH CREAM

Beef à la Ficelle is a classic dish in which filets of beef are lowered into a cauldron of simmering broth and gently poached, not unlike a *pot au feu*—without the long cooking time. This recipe uses the same technique, but omits the string. If you're looking for a way to cook beef without the added fat of oil or butter, this recipe could become your best friend. The gently flavored beef can be part of a spread, with condiments like cornichons, grain mustard, and so on, or it can be served as a sliced filet, presented here with an enlivening horseradish sauce.

---

2 QUARTS WHITE BEEF STOCK (PAGE 47) OR LOW-SODIUM, STORE-BOUGHT BEEF BROTH

1 TEASPOON THYME LEAVES

1 HEAD GARLIC, SPLIT

4 MEDIUM LEEKS, WHITES AND LIGHT GREEN PARTS ONLY (FROM ABOUT 12 OUNCES LEEKS), SPLIT LENGTHWISE, WELL RINSED, AND TIED INTO A BUNCH WITH BUTCHER STRING

4 FILETS OF BEEF, 6 TO 7 OUNCES EACH, TWINED AROUND THE EQUATOR WITH BUTCHER STRING

COARSE SEA SALT

BLACK PEPPER IN A MILL

1 CUP HORSERADISH CREAM (RECIPE FOLLOWS)

POUR the stock into a 3-quart saucepan. Add the thyme and garlic and bring to a boil over high heat. Lower the heat so the liquid is simmering, add the leeks, and cook until tender to a knife-tip, approximately 12 minutes, turning them over every few minutes to ensure even cooking. Remove the leeks from the stock using a slotted spoon and keep warm.

TURN the heat up to high, bring the liquid back to a boil, then add the beef filets and cook at a simmer. Adjust the heat as necessary to keep the liquid from returning to a boil, for 6 to 7 minutes for rare to medium rare (an instant-read thermometer inserted to the center of a filet will read 120°F to 125°F), or longer for more well done. Remove the filets with tongs or a slotted spoon and let rest on a clean, dry surface for 5 minutes. Season the reserved leeks and beef with sea salt and 3 grinds of pepper, or to taste.

TO serve, arrange 4 leek halves on each of 4 shallow bowls and top with a filet. Spoon some broth into the bowl and serve, passing the horseradish cream on the side. Serve.

VARIATIONS Serve the beef with Parsley Pistou (page 248) or Red Wine Butter (page 189) instead of Horseradish Cream. It would also be well complemented by any of the compound butters on pages 22 to 25.

EMBELLISHMENT Add root vegetables to the liquid along with the leeks and add them to the plate with the beef.

HORSERADISH CREAM MAKES 1 CUP

You can make this with prepared horseradish and skip the chilling time, because the flavors will need less time to develop.

2/3 CUP HEAVY CREAM

1 TEASPOON SHERRY VINEGAR

1 TEASPOON DIJON MUSTARD

KOSHER SALT

BLACK PEPPER IN A MILL

2 TABLESPOONS FRESHLY GRATED HORSERADISH, OR 1 TABLESPOON PREPARED HORSERADISH (IF USING PREPARED, OMIT THE VINEGAR)

PUT the heavy cream in a small bowl and whisk until the cream thickens enough so that light ribbons form with the whisk's motion. Add the vinegar and mustard and season with salt and 3 grinds of pepper, or to taste. Continue to whisk until soft peaks form. (The mixture will hold its shape in a peak but flop over when the whisk is lifted.) Fold in the horseradish.

COVER and keep refrigerated for 2 hours, or up to 6 hours. If you refrigerate it closer to 6 hours, the cream will exude some water. Drain it off, using a spatula to hold the cream in the bowl, then whisk the cream to refresh it.

DAUBE of BEEF SHORT RIBS with OLIVES and ORANGE-CUMIN CARROTS

SERVES 4

**M**ost chefs feel like they were ahead of the curve with at least one dish in their career, and that's how I feel about short ribs. They're all the rage now, but I've been serving them at Picholine since we opened in 1993. It's one of my favorite cuts of meat—they are rich and succulent and easy to cook.

This version is based on the Provençal daube, or stew, of beef. The alcohol is cooked out of the wine and the beef is marinated for 24 to 48 hours. It's very hearty, with the wine's full-bodied, fruit-forward essence dominating.

Like many stews, this dish can be made a day or more ahead of time to further develop its flavor. It's a perfect make-ahead dinner for Saturday night parties or Sunday night family dinner.

¼ CUP PLUS I TABLESPOON OLIVE OIL

½ CUP CELERY, LARGE DICE

½ CUP PEELED CARROTS, LARGE DICE

I CUP ONION, LARGE DICE

KOSHER SALT

2 CUPS PORT

3 BOTTLES (750 ML EACH) RED WINE

2 HEADS GARLIC, HALVED CROSSWISE, EXCESS PAPERY SKIN REMOVED

4 PIECES BONE-IN BEEF SHORT RIBS (ABOUT 6 POUNDS TOTAL WEIGHT), 4 INCHES LONG, TRIMMED OF EXCESS FAT

8 SPRIGS THYME

3 BAY LEAVES

6 FLAT-LEAF PARSLEY LEAVES, STEMS ATTACHED

½ MEDIUM LEEK (CUT LENGTHWISE), WHITE AND LIGHT GREEN PARTS ONLY, WELL RINSED

I CUP ALL-PURPOSE FLOUR

6 TO 7 CUPS VEAL STOCK (PAGE 48) OR LOW-SODIUM, STORE-BOUGHT BEEF BROTH

ORANGE PEEL FROM HALF AN ORANGE, (USE A VEGETABLE PEELER; REMOVE ALL PITH) OR 3 STRIPS DRIED ORANGE PEEL (PAGE 35)

6 (PREFERABLY SALT-PACKED) ANCHOVY FILLETS (SOAKED, DRAINED, AND PATTED DRY; SEE PAGE II) (OPTIONAL)

⅓ CUP NIÇOISE OLIVES, PITTED AND HALVED (OPTIONAL)

BLACK PEPPER IN A MILL

2 TABLESPOONS UNSALTED BUTTER

ORANGE-CUMIN CARROTS (RECIPE FOLLOWS)

HEAT 3 tablespoons of the oil in a large saucepan over medium heat. Add the celery, carrots, onions, and a pinch of salt, and cook, stirring until softened but not browned, approximately 10 minutes. Add the port, red wine, and garlic and bring the liquid to a boil. Lower the heat and simmer for 5 minutes to cook out the alcohol to help prevent the meat from "burning". Remove the pot from the heat and let cool completely.

PUT the short ribs in a container and pour the liquid over the ribs. Cover and refrigerate for 1 to 2 days. (Be sure the container is small enough that the liquid completely covers the ribs.)

SET the thyme sprigs, bay leaves, and parsley against the cut side of the leek half and tie the bundle together with butcher string. Remove the short ribs from the marinade and pat dry. Strain the marinade through a fine-mesh strainer into a Dutch oven or large, heavy-bottomed pot and bring to a boil over high heat reserving the vegetables. Lower the heat and let simmer until the liquid is reduced by two-thirds, approximately 2 hours.

MEANWHILE, pour the remaining 2 tablespoons oil into a 12-inch sauté pan and heat it over medium-high heat. Dredge the ribs in flour, and sear the short ribs two at a time, approximately 3 minutes per side. As they are done, transfer them to the Dutch oven with the reduced liquid.

PREHEAT the oven to 325°F. Add enough stock to cover the ribs, the orange peel, the anchovies, if using, and the leek and herb bundle, and bring to a simmer over high heat. Cover the Dutch oven and transfer to the oven. Cook until the beef is tender and pulling away from the bone, 2½ to 3 hours. Remove the pot from the oven, transfer the meat to a platter, and set it aside.

STRAIN the liquid through a fine-mesh strainer set over another pot. Set the sauce over medium heat, add the olives, if using, bring to a simmer, and let simmer until it reduces enough to coat the back of a wooden spoon, approximately 1 hour, skimming any foam and oil that rise to the surface. (You should have about 5 cups liquid.) Season with salt and pepper, then whisk in the butter to enrich and emulsify the sauce, round out the flavor, and give it a beautiful sheen.

REMOVE the bones from the short ribs and cut each piece in half. Divide the carrots evenly among 4 dinner plates and place 1 piece of beef on top. Ladle about ¼ cup sauce over the ribs and serve.

THE REASON *A bottle of wine is significantly reduced:* Reducing a relatively high quantity of wine results in a deep, intense flavor.

EMBELLISHMENTS Add the olive pits to the liquid as the daube cooks to deepen the olive flavor, then remove them at the end. Or tie them in a cheesecloth bundle before cooking, making it easier to extract them.

Serve this with Parsnip Puree (page 273), Celery Root and Apple Puree (page 218), or Macaroni and Cheese (page 271).

ORANGE-CUMIN CARROTS SERVES 4

Serve this with fish, meat, or poultry.

- 1 TEASPOON WHOLE CUMIN SEEDS
- 4 TABLESPOONS UNSALTED BUTTER
- 2 CUPS YOUNG CARROTS, PEELED AND CUT DIAGONALLY BETWEEN 1/8 INCH AND 1/4 INCH THICK
- 1/2 CUP FRESHLY SQUEEZED ORANGE JUICE
- 2 TEASPOONS FRESHLY SQUEEZED LEMON JUICE
- KOSHER SALT
- BLACK PEPPER IN A MILL

PREHEAT the oven to 350°F. Put the cumin seeds in a sauté pan and toast over low heat, shaking constantly, until fragrant but not browned, 2 to 3 minutes. Remove the pan from the heat and let the seeds cool.

MELT the butter in a saucepan set over medium-low heat. Add the carrots, orange juice, and cumin seeds. Bring the mixture to a simmer, cover, and transfer the pan to the oven. Cook until the carrots are tender to the tines of a fork, approximately 18 minutes. Add in the lemon juice and season with salt and 3 grinds of pepper, or to taste. Pour off any excess liquid, or use it to make a sauce (see Embellishment). The carrots can be cooled, covered, and refrigerated for up to 24 hours.

EMBELLISHMENT Make a glaze for the carrots by simmering the juices they give off when cooked in a saucepan until thick enough to coat the back of a wooden spoon. Toss the glaze with the carrots just before serving.

LAMB WITH BOULANGÈRE POTATOES

SERVES 10 TO 12

This rustic dish is a classic of the French countryside. *Boulangère* refers to dishes featuring a garnish of onions and potatoes. The most common version features lamb, as this dish does, which is roasted atop the potatoes, allowing the flavors to seep down from the lamb into what becomes its side dish. This dish is meant to serve a large group, and it will make quite an impression at the table and in people's memories as well.

6-POUND BONELESS LEG OF LAMB, EXCESS FAT AND SINEW TRIMMED

I CUP OLIVE OIL

3 TABLESPOONS KOSHER SALT

BLACK PEPPER IN A MILL

3 TABLESPOONS MINCED GARLIC

I TABLESPOON CHOPPED THYME LEAVES

3 TABLESPOONS FINELY SLICED FLAT-LEAF PARSLEY

2 TABLESPOONS UNSALTED BUTTER, AT ROOM TEMPERATURE

2 POUNDS ONIONS, PEELED, HALVED, AND THINLY SLICED

5 POUNDS IDAHO POTATOES, CUT CROSSWISE INTO ¼-INCH-THICK SLICES AND RESERVED IN COLD WATER

5 CUPS WHITE CHICKEN STOCK (PAGE 45) OR LOW-SODIUM, STORE-BOUGHT CHICKEN BROTH

PREHEAT the oven to 350°F. Spread the lamb out on your work surface with the inside facing up. Drizzle with ¼ cup olive oil and rub over the surface. Season generously with salt and pepper and scatter the garlic, thyme, and parsley over the surface. Roll the lamb up as taut and evenly as possible and tie it with kitchen twine at 2-inch intervals.

HEAT a large, heavy-bottomed roasting pan over two burners on medium-high heat. Add ¼ cup oil and heat it. Rub the butter over the outside of the lamb and season the outside of the lamb generously with salt and pepper, and sear the lamb well on all sides. Transfer the lamb to a clean, dry surface.

CAREFULLY pour off any oil remaining in the pan. Add ¼ cup fresh oil and heat it. Add the onions and a pinch of salt and cook, stirring, until tender but not browned, approximately 4 minutes. Drain the potatoes and add them to the pan. Add the stock, 1 tablespoon garlic, 1 tablespoon salt, and 1 teaspoon pepper. Stir and spread the potatoes out evenly in the pan.

SET the lamb on top of the potatoes and roast in the oven until an instant-read thermometer inserted to the thickest part of the lamb reads 110°F to 115°F for rare to medium rare, or longer for more well done, approximately 1 hour 20 minutes.

REMOVE the pan from the oven, and let rest for 25 minutes, keeping the potatoes and lamb covered and warm during this time.

TO serve, slice the lamb and arrange it on a platter. Serve the potatoes reheated if necessary alongside in a bowl, or on the platter.

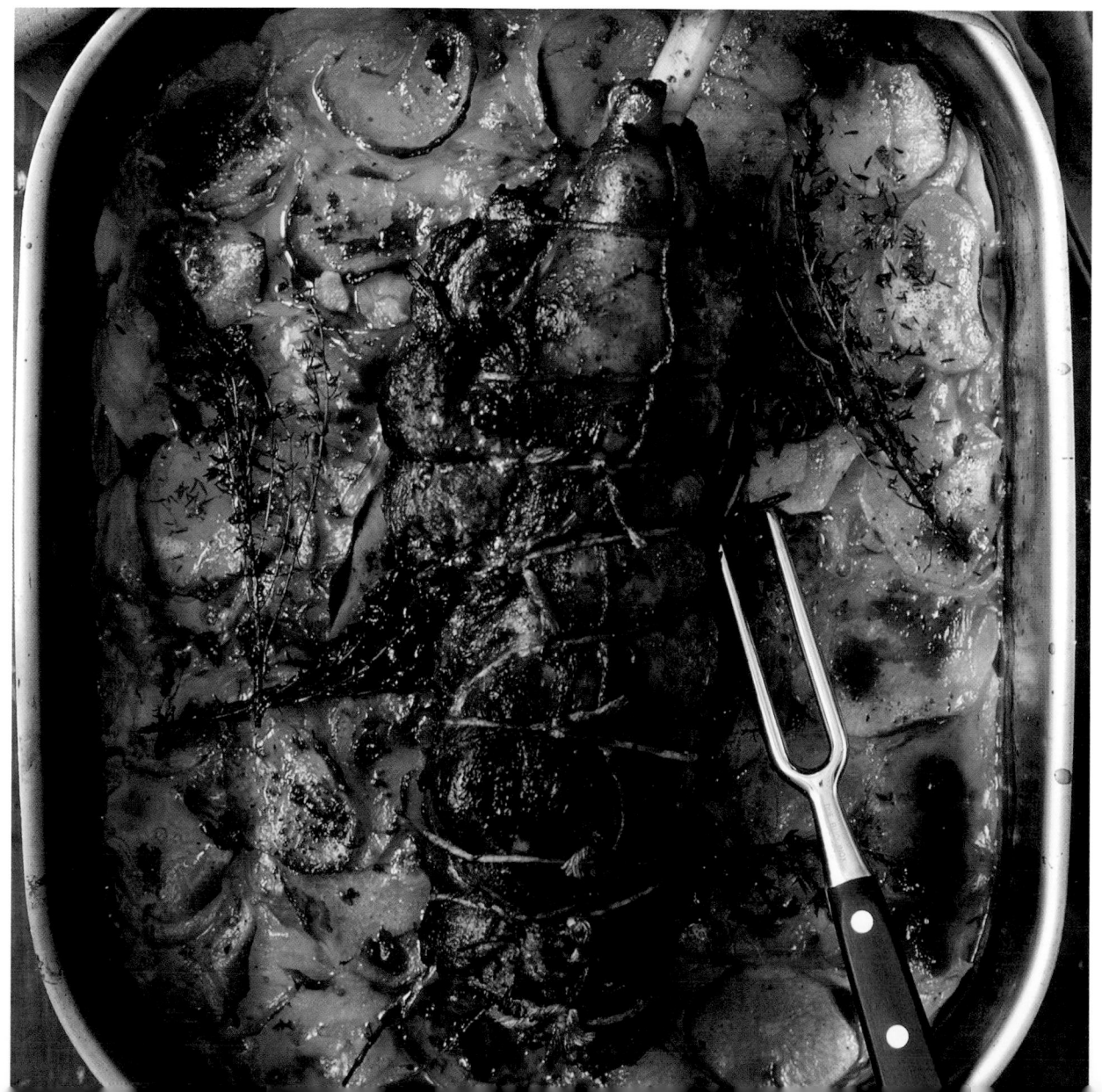

GRILLED LAMB CHOPS WITH ANCHOVY BUTTER

SERVES 4

amb gets a triple dose of flavors here, most of them time-honored partners for this elegant meat: First, it is marinated in oil, rosemary, lemon, and garlic. Then, it is grilled. Finally, a Provençal butter is set on top of the individual chops, releasing the potent qualities of anchovy, shallots, parsley, and rosemary. Serve this with grilled vegetables like peppers and zucchini, and/or with Panisse (page 272).

¼ CUP OLIVE OIL

2 TABLESPOONS ROSEMARY LEAVES

1 LARGE LEMON, THINLY SLICED

6 CLOVES GARLIC, CRUSHED

12 DOMESTIC OR AUSTRALIAN LAMB CHOPS, 2 TO 3 OUNCES EACH, TRIMMED OF EXCESS FAT

KOSHER SALT

FRESHLY GROUND BLACK PEPPER

12 SLICES ANCHOVY BUTTER (PAGE 24), ¼ INCH THICK EACH

PUT the oil, rosemary, lemon slices, and garlic in a large plastic bag, such as a freezer bag, add the lamb, seal the bag, and shake to coat on both sides with the marinade. Let marinate for 1 hour at room temperature, then refrigerate for at least 3 hours or up to 8 hours, but no longer or the lemon will begin to cure the meat. Take out 1 hour before cooking.

WHEN ready to cook and serve the lamb, prepare an outdoor grill for grilling, letting the coals burn down until covered with white ash. (Alternately, you can cook the lamb indoors in a sauté pan.)

REMOVE the lamb chops from the marinade, letting any excess marinade run off. Put the chops on a plate and season them with salt and pepper. Place the chops on the grill and cook for approximately 2½ minutes per side for rare, or a bit longer for more well done. (An instant-read thermometer inserted into the thickest part of the chops will red 120°F to 125°F.) Just before serving, give the chops a final turn to briefly reheat the downward-facing side for just a few seconds to keep the meat warm enough to melt the butter when it is placed on top.

TRANSFER each chop to a plate, top with 1 slice of butter, and serve.

THE REASON *Australian lamb is worth seeking out:* Australian and New Zealand lamb are grass fed, resulting in a milder flavor. There are some American producers (like Jamison Farm and Niman Ranch; see Sources, page 318) who grass feed their lambs, but they are the exception, not the rule.

GRILLED PORK CHOP WITH APRICOT CHUTNEY

SERVES 4

 ork no longer has to be cooked to death to be safe to eat. In the days of trichinosis, that was the case, but today, there's no reason to cook pork beyond medium or even medium-rare, as I recommend you do here, where it's paired with a classic fruit accompaniment.

2 TABLESPOONS CANOLA OIL, PLUS MORE FOR GRILLING THE CHOPS

8 APRICOTS, QUARTERED, PITS REMOVED

⅓ CUP ONION, SMALL DICE

½ CUP WHITE WINE VINEGAR

⅓ CUP SUGAR

½ STICK CINNAMON

1 SPRIG ROSEMARY

KOSHER SALT

BLACK PEPPER IN A MILL

4 BONE-IN, FRENCHED CENTER CUT PORK CHOPS, 10 OUNCES EACH

PREPARE an outdoor grill for grilling, letting the coals burn down until covered with white ash.

HEAT 2 tablespoons oil in an 8-inch sauté pan over medium-high heat. Add the apricots and lightly caramelize them, shaking the pan to keep them from scorching or sticking, approximately 6 minutes. Turn them over with a spatula, press down gently to flatten them, and cook another 6 minutes. Lower the heat and cook until tender, approximately 6 minutes more, stirring periodically. Set aside.

PUT the onion, vinegar, sugar, cinnamon, and rosemary in a small saucepan and season with salt and pepper. Cook over low-medium heat, stirring occasionally, until reduced to a light syrup, approximately 20 minutes. Add the apricots and cook in the syrup, over medium-high heat, for 12 minutes. Remove and discard the cinnamon stick and rosemary.

LIGHTLY oil the chops on both sides and season on both sides with salt and 3 grinds of pepper.

PLACE the chops on the grill and sear, partially covered, on both sides, approximately 4 minutes per side, or until an instant-read thermometer inserted to the center of the meat reads 140°F to 145°F for medium, or longer for more well done. Remove the chops from the grill and let rest for 5 minutes.

PUT 1 chop on each of 4 plates, spoon some chutney alongside, and serve.

VARIATION The chutney is also a perfect sweet foil for game, poultry, foie gras, and cheese.
EMBELLISHMENT Serve this with Mustard Sauce (page 195) spooned over the pork.

PORK STEAK WITH SAGE, PUMPKIN, AND PRUNES

SERVES 4

 here are times when the alchemy that occurs among a relatively modest assemblage of ingredients produces sublime results. That's certainly the case in this dish, in which sage, pumpkin, and prunes come together in a perfectly balanced accompaniment for pork.

KOSHER SALT

BLACK PEPPER IN A MILL

½ TEASPOON GROUND ALLSPICE

¼ TEASPOON GROUND STAR ANISE

¼ TEASPOON GROUND CINNAMON

¼ CUP PLUS 2 TABLESPOONS CANOLA OIL

4 BONELESS PORK STEAKS, CUT FROM THE LOIN, 6 TO 7 OUNCES EACH, 1½ INCHES THICK

¼ CUP (PACKED) PRUNES (DRIED PLUMS), CHOPPED INTO ¼-INCH PIECES

2 TABLESPOONS ARMAGNAC (OPTIONAL)

½ CUP (1 STICK) PLUS 3 TABLESPOONS UNSALTED BUTTER, SOFTENED AT ROOM TEMPERATURE, CUT INTO TABLESPOON-SIZED PIECES

2 CUPS PEELED CHEESE PUMPKIN, CUT INTO ¼-INCH DICE

10 SAGE LEAVES, MINCED

PUT 1½ teaspoons salt, ½ teaspoon pepper, the allspice, star anise, and cinnamon in a bowl and stir them together. Whisk in 2 tablespoons of the oil. Rub the mixture on both sides of each pork steak.

PUT the prunes in a bowl. If using the Armagnac, pour it over them and set aside to soak.

HEAT 2 tablespoons of the oil and 2 tablespoons of the butter in a 10-inch sauté pan set over medium heat. Add the pumpkin and cook, tossing and stirring every few minutes, until lightly caramelized on all sides, 15 to 18 minutes. Toss in the prunes. Remove the pan from the heat and season with salt and 4 grinds of pepper, or to taste.

PREHEAT the oven to 350°F. Heat a 12-inch sauté pan over medium-high heat. Add the remaining 2 tablespoons oil and 1 tablespoon of the butter to the pan and heat them. Add the pork steaks and sear until nicely browned, approximately 4 minutes on each side. Turn over again, transfer the pan to the oven, and cook until the pork reaches an internal temperature of 140°F to 145°F, 8 to 10 minutes for medium, or longer for more well done. Remove the pan from the heat, transfer the pork to a clean, dry surface, and let rest for 5 minutes.

WHILE the pork is resting, heat a sauté pan over medium-high heat. When the pan is hot, add the remaining ½ cup butter and cook until it melts and turns to brown, approximately 4 minutes. Remove the pan from the heat, and stir in the sage leaves.

TO serve, divide the pumpkin and prunes evenly among 4 plates. Top each portion with a steak and drizzle with brown butter.

VARIATIONS The pumpkin and prune mixture is also delicious with venison. The combination can also be served as dessert if you leave out the salt and pepper and season it with sugar instead. Try some over vanilla ice cream for an autumnal treat.

EMBELLISHMENT Instead of the canola oil, use 2 tablespoons Autumn Spice Oil (page 29) to cook the pork.

LAMB STEAK WITH ORZO AND PARSLEY PISTOU

 **T**his is a very flexible summer recipe: You can make it with any cut of lamb, such as the loin or loin chop. The gentle flavor of lamb and potent tang of goat cheese offer alternating flavors that really hit your palate and the gutsiness of the parsley pistou pulls all the elements of the dish together.

4 CUPS WATER

KOSHER SALT

¾ CUP ORZO

½ CUP OLIVE OIL

¼ CUP ONION, ¼-INCH DICE

¼ CUP EGGPLANT, ¼-INCH DICE

¼ CUP ZUCCHINI, ¼-INCH DICE

OVEN-DRIED TOMATOES (PAGE 31) (OPTIONAL)

¼ CUP CRUMBLED GOAT CHEESE (FROM ABOUT 1 OUNCE CHEESE), AT ROOM TEMPERATURE

BLACK PEPPER IN A MILL

8 LAMB LOIN CHOPS, 3 TO 3½ OUNCES EACH, TRIMMED OF ANY EXCESS FAT OR SINEW

PARSLEY PISTOU (RECIPE FOLLOWS)

POUR the water into a 3-quart stockpot. Add 1 tablespoon salt and bring to a boil over high heat. Add the orzo and cook until al dente, approximately 12 minutes.

MEANWHILE, heat 1 tablespoon oil in an 8-inch sauté pan set over medium heat. Add the onion and cook until softened and translucent, approximately 5 minutes. Transfer the onion to a bowl and wipe out the pan. Add another tablespoon oil and cook the eggplant over medium-high heat until softened, approximately 8 minutes. Add the eggplant to the bowl with the onion and set aside. Add another tablespoon of oil to the pan and cook the zucchini and tomatoes, if using, until softened, 3 to 4 minutes.

WHEN the orzo is ready, use a Pyrex measuring cup to scoop out about ¼ cup cooking liquid. Drain the orzo and transfer it to a large bowl. Add the goat cheese and about 2 tablespoons of the reserved cooking liquid. Mix together with a wooden spoon to melt the cheese into an emulsified mixture. Gently stir in the vegetables and tomatoes and season with salt and 6 grinds of pepper, or to taste. Cover and keep warm.

PREPARE an outdoor grill for grilling, letting the coals burn down until covered with white ash.

RUB the lamb pieces with 2 tablespoons of olive oil and season on both sides with salt and 5 grinds of pepper, or to taste.

COOK the lamb partially covered over medium-high heat for approximately 3 minutes per side for rare to medium-rare. (An instant-read thermometer inserted into the thickest part of the steaks will read 120°F to 125°F.) Remove from grill.

TO serve, divide the orzo among 4 dinner plates. Place two chops on top of the orzo on each plate and drizzle parsley pistou over and around the lamb.

TERMS AND TECHNIQUES Most restaurant chefs use what is commonly referred to as the "hand test" to determine how cooked a piece of meat is by comparing the feel of the meat to a part of your hand: Well-done meat will feel similar to the firm center of your palm, while rare meat feels more or less like the fleshy part at the base of your thumb.

THE REASON *Orzo's cooking liquid is added back into the dish:* When pasta is cooked, it releases some of its starch into the cooking liquid. That liquid can then be used to thicken and bind the ingredients in a pasta sauce, or to help melt and emulsify a cheese.

VARIATION The orzo can be made with other summer vegetables and served as part of just about any grilled meal. It can also be served cold as a salad on its own.

PARSLEY PISTOU MAKES ¾ CUP

Pistou is the French version of pesto, but with no pine nuts. Using parsley is a good, year-round alternative to basil, which is only in season during the summer. This is delicious stirred into soups and pasta or served with lamb, beef, and fish dishes.

I CUP FLAT-LEAF PARSLEY

⅔ CUP OLIVE OIL

¾ TEASPOON CHOPPED GARLIC

I TEASPOON KOSHER SALT

I TABLESPOON FINELY GRATED PARMIGIANO-REGGIANO

PICK and wash the parsley leaves and dry them in a clean, dry cloth. Put the parsley, oil, garlic, and salt in a blender and pulse to combine. It should remain a bit chunky and leafy; do not overmix it into a smooth paste. Stir in the cheese. Set aside. This pistou can be covered and refrigerated for up to 3 days.

EMBELLISHMENT Blend a few cloves of Garlic Confit (page 36) into the pistou to make it creamier and give it a greater depth of flavor.

RABBIT au RIESLING with RUTABAGA "SAUERKRAUT"

SERVES 4

One of my signature dishes, Rabbit au Riesling has been enormously popular at Artisanal restaurant since it first opened. Inspired by the classic coq au vin, or chicken in red wine sauce, this recipe features tender rabbit legs marinated in Riesling for one to two days, then slow-cooked in a light braising liquid. The result is falling-apart-tender leg meat that pairs perfectly with the sweet and tangy Rutabaga "Sauerkraut."

¼ CUP PLUS I TABLESPOON OLIVE OIL

I TABLESPOON BLACK PEPPERCORNS

¼ CUP DICED ONION

¼ CUP DICED CARROT

¼ CUP DICED CELERY

I HEAD GARLIC, HALVED HORIZONTALLY, EXCESS PAPERY SKIN REMOVED

I BOTTLE (ABOUT 3½ CUPS) RIESLING WINE

4 BAY LEAVES

I½ CUPS FLOUR

8 RABBIT LEGS (SEE SOURCES, PAGE 318)

ABOUT 2½ CUPS WHITE CHICKEN STOCK (PAGE 45) OR LOW-SODIUM, STORE-BOUGHT CHICKEN BROTH

ABOUT 2½ CUPS VEAL STOCK (PAGE 48)

4 SPRIGS THYME

I TABLESPOON UNSALTED BUTTER

I TEASPOON KOSHER SALT

BLACK PEPPER IN A MILL

RUTABAGA "SAUERKRAUT" (RECIPE FOLLOWS)

POUR 2 tablespoons of the oil into a saucepan and heat it over medium heat. Add the peppercorns, bay leaves, onion, carrot, celery, and garlic. Cook until the vegetables are soft and lightly caramelized, approximately 10 minutes. Pour in the wine, add the bay leaves, bring to a boil, and reduce for 5 minutes to cook out the alcohol. Remove the pan from the heat and let it cool.

ARRANGE the rabbit legs in a single layer in a baking dish or other shallow vessel. Pour the liquid over the legs. Cover and refrigerate for 1 to 2 days.

WHEN ready to proceed, preheat oven to 350°F. Remove the rabbit legs from the marinade and pat them dry. Heat a heavy-bottomed pot or Dutch oven over medium heat. Pour the remaining 3 tablespoons oil into the pot and heat it. Dredge the legs in flour. Add the rabbit legs in a single layer and lightly brown them, approximately 3 minutes per side. Add the Riesling marinade, bring to a boil, and then simmer until reduced by half, approximately 6 minutes. Add the chicken stock, veal stock, and thyme and bring to a boil over high heat. Reduce the heat so the liquid is simmering. Cover the pot and transfer it to the oven. Braise, until the legs are tender, approximately 1 hour 20 minutes. Remove the legs from the liquid and set them aside.

RETURN the pot to the stovetop over medium-low heat and reduce the liquid at a simmer (do not let it boil), skimming any impurities that rise to the surface, until thick enough to coat the back of a wooden spoon, approximately 1 hour. Strain the sauce through a fine-mesh strainer set over a bowl. Whisk in the butter and salt, and season with pepper to taste.

DIVIDE the rutabaga among 4 dinner plates. Place 2 rabbit legs on each plate and spoon some sauce over the legs. Serve.

TERMS AND TECHNIQUES *Caramelized:* Caramelizing refers to browning vegetables, meats, or other ingredients, letting their natural sugars turn nicely dark and flavorful.

THE REASON *The sauce is not allowed to boil while reducing:* To keep sauces from becoming cloudy, always reduce them at a simmer, skimming often to clarify them. The exceptions to this rule are sauces or dishes, like bouillabaisse, for which an emulsification is desired.

RUTABAGA "SAUERKRAUT" SERVES 4

My executive chef, David Cox, devised this smart take on sauerkraut. Rather than the conventional cabbage, which takes weeks to ferment, he uses grated rutabaga, slow-cooking it in a flavorful blend of duck fat, wine, and vinegar. It's a beguiling dish that tastes of sauerkraut at first, but reveals a series of subtleties as it's consumed—an exception to my usual preference for clean, easily identified flavors.

1 TEASPOON CARAWAY SEEDS

1 TABLESPOON UNSALTED BUTTER

¼ CUP DUCK FAT (SEE SOURCES, PAGE 318) OR UNSALTED BUTTER

¼ CUP THINLY SLICED ONION

KOSHER SALT

1¼ POUNDS RUTABAGA, GRATED (3 CUPS)

½ CUP DRY WHITE WINE

¼ CUP SHERRY VINEGAR

½ CUP WHITE CHICKEN STOCK (PAGE 45) OR LOW-SODIUM, STORE-BOUGHT CHICKEN BROTH

BLACK PEPPER IN A MILL

PUT the caraway seeds in an 8-inch sauté pan and toast over low heat, shaking constantly, until fragrant but not browned, 2 to 3 minutes. Remove the pan from the heat and let the caraway seeds cool.

PREHEAT oven to 350°F. Put the butter and duck fat in a 2-quart pot and melt it over medium heat. Add the onions and a pinch of salt and sauté until softened but not browned, approximately 4 minutes. Add the rutabaga and caraway seeds and cook, stirring occasionally, for 5 minutes. Pour in the white wine and sherry vinegar, raise the heat to high, bring to a simmer, and continue to simmer until reduced by two-thirds, 6 to 7 minutes.

POUR in the stock, bring it to a boil, cover the pot, and transfer to the oven. Cook until the rutabaga is tender, approximately 1 hour 10 minutes. Season with salt and 6 grinds of pepper, or to taste.

SERVE warm, or let cool, cover, and refrigerate for up to 3 days. Reheat before serving.

VENISON AU POIVRE WITH RED CABBAGE CONFIT

SERVES 4

A u poivre means "peppered" and most people associate it with steak au poivre, which can take two forms: pepper-crusted steak, or steak with a pepper sauce. Contemporary chefs have borrowed the idea of steak au poivre for seafood dishes, like tuna au poivre. Those have become so common that you can get the most surprising results by peppering another type of meat. Venison au poivre, a dish we serve regularly at Picholine restaurant, makes great use of the pepper, which registers more powerfully against the gentle flavor of farm-raised venison than it does against beef.

Don't cook the venison beyond medium; it's very lean and will dry out.

6 JUNIPER BERRIES

3 CLOVES

2 TABLESPOONS WHOLE BLACK PEPPERCORNS

1 TABLESPOON WHOLE WHITE PEPPERCORNS, OR AN ADDITIONAL TABLESPOON BLACK PEPPERCORNS

8 ALLSPICE PODS

4 VENISON LOINS, 6 TO 7 OUNCES EACH

2 TABLESPOONS CANOLA OIL

2 TABLESPOONS UNSALTED BUTTER

COARSE SEA SALT

RED CABBAGE CONFIT (RECIPE FOLLOWS)

PREHEAT the oven to 350°F. Put the juniper berries, cloves, black and white peppercorns, and allspice in an 8-inch sauté pan and toast over low heat, shaking constantly, until fragrant but not browned, 2 to 3 minutes. Remove the pan from the heat and let the spices cool.

TRANSFER the spices to a spice or coffee grinder and grind them into a coarse mixture. Put the spices on a platter or in a wide shallow bowl. Roll the loins in the peppercorn mixture, pressing down firmly to form a crust.

PUT the oil and butter in a 12-inch ovenproof sauté pan over medium-high heat and heat them. The butter will sizzle and foam. When the foam begins to subside, add the venison loins and sear them for 1 minute. Turn them over and transfer the pan to the oven. Roast until an instant-read thermometer inserted to the center of a loin reads 120°F to 125°F for rare. Remove the pan from the oven and let the venison rest on a clean, dry surface for 3 to 4 minutes.

SLICE each loin crosswise into 3 equal pieces. Sprinkle the exposed meat with salt. Evenly divide the red cabbage among 4 dinner plates. Place 1 venison loin on top of the cabbage and serve.

VARIATION You can use a variety of peppercorns such as white, black, green, Szechuan, and pink. This would also be very good with Madeira Sauce (page 225).

EMBELLISHMENTS Instead of the canola oil, use 2 tablespoons Autumn Spice Oil (page 29) to cook the venison.

Make a quick pan sauce by deglazing the venison's pan with ½ cup red wine. Bring to a boil over high heat and continue to boil until reduced by three-quarters. Add ½ cup Veal Stock (page 48), bring to a boil, and reduce by half. Swirl in a tablespoon of butter and season to taste with salt and pepper.

RED CABBAGE CONFIT MAKES ABOUT 2 CUPS

This side dish takes its cue from the technique for confit (a classic preparation in which meat, especially duck, is slow-cooked in its own fat), simmering cabbage in a combination of butter and duck fat that's punched up with aromatics like thyme and juniper berries. It's delicious with venison and with roasted pork.

¼ CUP PLUS 2 TABLESPOONS DUCK FAT (SEE SOURCES, PAGE 318)

3 TABLESPOONS UNSALTED BUTTER

¼ CUP FINELY DICED CARROT

¼ CUP FINELY DICED ONION

¼ CUP FINELY DICED CELERY ROOT

¼ CUP FINELY DICED APPLEWOOD SMOKED BACON OR OTHER SMOKED BACON (FROM ABOUT 1¼ OUNCES BACON)

¼ TEASPOON THYME LEAVES

1¼ POUNDS RED CABBAGE, CORE REMOVED, SHREDDED (ABOUT 8 CUPS SHREDDED)

2 TABLESPOONS HONEY

¼ TEASPOON GROUND JUNIPER BERRIES

3 TABLESPOONS RED-WINE VINEGAR

1 CUP WHITE CHICKEN STOCK (PAGE 45) OR LOW-SODIUM, STORE-BOUGHT CHICKEN BROTH OR WATER

KOSHER SALT

BLACK PEPPER IN A MILL

PREHEAT the oven to 300°F. Put the duck fat and butter in a 4-quart saucepan and melt it over low heat. Add the carrot, onion, celery root, and bacon and cook, stirring, until the bacon has rendered much of its fat, and the vegetables are tender but still holding their shape, 6 to 7 minutes. Add the thyme, cabbage, honey, and juniper berries, and continue to cook gently, stirring, for 4 minutes. Add the vinegar and stock, bring to a boil, then lower the heat and simmer for 10 minutes.

COVER the pan and transfer it to the oven. Cook until the cabbage is tender, approximately 2½ hours. Remove the pan from the oven and season with 1 teaspoon salt and 6 grinds of pepper, or to taste. Serve hot.

EMBELLISHMENT Add some roasted, peeled, and sliced chestnuts along with the carrot, onion, and celery root. (See page 154 for instructions on roasting and peeling chestnuts.) Add ½ cup diced apple.

VENISON CHOPS WITH BANYULS VINEGAR AND SQUASH-PRUNE GRATIN

SERVES 4

My affection for the rich and complex Banyuls vinegar led me to showcase it in this dish. A sauce is fashioned in the pan in which venison chops have been seared and roasted. When the vinegar, robust red wine, and veal stock come together, the result is layer upon layer of flavors, all of them well matched to the tender venison and the sweet notes and soft texture of the squash and prune gratin.

---

4 DOUBLE VENISON CHOPS, ABOUT 10 OUNCES EACH

KOSHER SALT

BLACK PEPPER IN A MILL

3 TABLESPOONS CANOLA OIL

4 TABLESPOONS UNSALTED BUTTER

2 TABLESPOON BANYULS VINEGAR

1 CUP FULL-BODIED RED WINE, LIKE SHIRAZ

2 CUPS VEAL STOCK (PAGE 48)

SQUASH-PRUNE GRATIN (PAGE 268)

PREHEAT the oven to 400°F. Season the venison generously with salt and about 4 grinds of pepper per side of each chop. Heat a heavy-bottomed, 12-inch, ovenproof sauté pan over medium-high heat. Pour the oil and 3 tablespoons butter into the pan and heat them. The butter will sizzle and foam. When the foam begins to subside, put the venison in the pan with the curved bone side down, and sear until well browned, approximately 5 minutes.

TURN the chops over, transfer the pan to the oven, and roast, basting with the butter and oil in the pan every 5 minutes, until an instant-read thermometer inserted to the center of a chop reads 120°F to 125°F for rare, 12 to 15 minutes. Remove the pan from the oven, transfer the venison to a clean, dry platter, and let it rest for 8 to 10 minutes, loosely covered.

POUR off and discard any fat that remains in the pan. Return the pan to the stovetop over medium-high heat. Pour in the vinegar and deglaze by scraping up any flavorful bits stuck to the pan. Pour in the red wine, bring it to a boil, and continue to boil until it reduces by three-quarters, approximately 8 minutes. Pour in the stock and bring it to a boil. Lower the heat and simmer until reduced by half, approximately 15 minutes. Swirl in the remaining 1 tablespoon of butter and season with salt and 4 grinds of pepper, or to taste.

TO serve, cut each double chop into 2 pieces, by slicing between the bones. Spoon some sauce onto each of 4 dinner plates. Put a slice of gratin toward the "6 o'clock" edge of the plate and set 1 chop on each side of the gratin, crossing the bones over the gratin. Or serve the meal family style, passing the venison on a platter, the sauce in a sauceboat, and the gratin in its baking dish.

EMBELLISHMENT Chestnut Spaetzle (page 274) gets along great with the flavors in this dish.

SIDE DISHES AND ACCOMPANIMENTS

SIDE DISHES AND ACCOMPANIMENTS are valuable kitchen commodities: Having a repertoire at your disposal is a way to make even a last-second meal a bit special. Set a vegetable or potato dish alongside fish or meat and even the most simply prepared protein seems more exciting and appealing. The home cook who knows how and when to deploy the right ones is never more than a few minutes away from being able to prepare and serve a memorable meal, even on short notice.

Side dishes offer a chance to appreciate the role of proportion in a meal. Because they are enjoyed in relatively small portions, these little recipes can be more intensely flavored than other components of a meal. They also illustrate the importance of planning your time in the kitchen. Home cooks often focus on the main course, to the exclusion of side dishes. Many of the side dishes that follow can be prepared as the main course is simmering on the stove or roasting in the oven, or well in advance, making a fully composed meal a surprisingly user-friendly proposition.

ASPARAGUS WITH LEMON-PARMESAN BUTTER

SERVES 4

The lemon in this dish is the perfect complement to asparagus, giving an extra lift to the vegetable's fresh flavor. Serve this alongside shellfish such as Soft-Shell Crabs with Mustard Sauce (page 194), grilled or roasted fish, or chicken dishes such as Chicken Schnitzel (page 198).

KOSHER SALT

I POUND JUMBO ASPARAGUS (ABOUT 16 STALKS), PEELED, BOTTOMS TRIMMED

I TABLESPOON FRESHLY SQUEEZED LEMON JUICE

¾ CUP (1½ STICKS) COLD UNSALTED BUTTER, CUBED

¼ CUP GRATED PARMIGIANO-REGGIANO (FROM ABOUT I OUNCE CHEESE)

½ TABLESPOON GRATED LEMON ZEST

BLACK PEPPER IN A MILL

FILL a heavy-bottomed, 12-inch sauté pan halfway with cold water. Sprinkle with 2 tablespoons salt and bring to a boil over medium-high heat. When the water boils, carefully arrange the asparagus in the pan in a single layer with all the tips facing the same way. Move the pan so the tip end is just off the heat. Cook until the asparagus are al dente, approximately 7 minutes.

MEANWHILE, put the lemon juice in a 1-quart saucepan and bring to a simmer over low heat. Use an immersion blender or whisk to blend in the butter, one cube at a time. Keep the butter sauce at a tepid temperature as you blend; it should be just warm to the touch. If the mixture gets too cold, return the pan to the heat over very low heat for a few seconds, taking care not to overheat it, which will cause the butter to break. Slowly whisk in the Parmigiano-Reggiano and lemon zest, and season with salt and pepper.

REMOVE the asparagus from the water with tongs or a slotted spoon and drain. Transfer to a plate or platter and sauce with the lemon-parmesan butter. Serve.

THE REASON *The asparagus tips are cooked slightly off-heat:* This helps the tips and thicker stalk end cook at the same rate.

TERMS AND TECHNIQUES *Al dente:* Al dente is an Italian culinary phrase that means "to the tooth." It's a degree of doneness where ingredients, usually pasta, rice, or vegetables are cooked, but still firm to the bite.

EMBELLISHMENTS Add capers or small croutons to the butter sauce.

POTATO CAKE WITH GARLIC AND PARSLEY

SERVES 4

P otato cakes strike a resonant chord with Francophile chefs like me, echoing both the bistro culture we adore as well as classic—and in some cases world-renowned—renditions. The most famous is that served at L'Ami Louis in Paris—a restaurant also widely acclaimed for its roasted chicken—where they cook the potatoes in generous amounts of goose fat. This version is almost as rich, freshened up at the last second with a scattering of fresh parsley and garlic that perfumes the hot potatoes, announcing them as they make their way to the table.

Serve this with Breast of Chicken with Comté-Scallion Polenta (page 211), leaving out the polenta, Grilled Lamb Chops with Anchovy Butter (page 242), or Grilled Steak with Béarnaise Sauce (page 231). It's also, of course, a fine accompaniment to roasted chicken.

1¼ POUNDS IDAHO POTATOES, PEELED

1 TABLESPOON KOSHER SALT

BLACK PEPPER IN A MILL

2 TABLESPOONS CANOLA OIL

1 STICK UNSALTED BUTTER, CUT INTO 8 PIECES

¼ CUP SLICED FLAT-LEAF PARSLEY

2 TEASPOONS CHOPPED GARLIC

PREHEAT the oven to 400°F. Julienne the potatoes, preferably with a mandoline, and gather them in a large mixing bowl. Season with the salt and 6 grinds of pepper, or to taste. Toss well.

POUR the oil into a heavy-bottomed, ovenproof, 8-inch sauté pan and heat it over high heat, until the oil is shimmering but not smoking. Add the potatoes and use a spatula to press them down in an even layer, then use the spatula to tuck the edges down, forming a neat, uniform rim.

ARRANGE 4 pieces of butter around the edge of the potato cake. Use a spatula to lift the edges of the cake, tilting the pan as necessary, to help the butter seep under the potatoes as it melts. Lower the heat to medium. Again, pat down the potatoes, and tuck down the edge to maintain its uniform shape. Cook for 2 minutes. Transfer the pan to the oven and cook for 10 minutes.

REMOVE the pan from the oven and invert the cake onto a plate. Put the remaining 4 pieces of butter in the pan and melt them over high heat. Return the cake to the pan, cooked-side up. Set the pan over medium heat and cook for 2 minutes. Transfer the pan to the oven and cook for 15 minutes.

REMOVE the pan from the oven and carefully transfer the cake to a cutting board. Cut the cake into quarters, serve on the cutting board, or transfer to a plate, sprinkle evenly with chopped parsley and garlic, and serve.

CREAMED SPINACH

SERVES 4

A steakhouse favorite for good reason, creamed spinach is one of the ultimate pairings with grilled beef (page 231), a rare case where two rich components serve to enhance each other, with no acidic or sweet elements offering relief. Here, Parmigiano-Reggiano and mascarpone cheese are added for a more complex flavor. This also pairs very well with most fish, poultry, and other meats.

---

12 CUPS WATER

KOSHER SALT

1½ POUNDS SPINACH, STEMS REMOVED, WELL WASHED IN SEVERAL CHANGES OF COLD WATER, AND SPUN DRY (WASH IN THE SAME MANNER AS MUSHROOMS, PAGE 128)

2 TABLESPOONS UNSALTED BUTTER

¼ CUP ONION, SMALL DICE

¼ CUP HEAVY CREAM

¼ CUP MASCARPONE, OR ADDITIONAL HEAVY CREAM

¼ CUP GRATED PARMIGIANO-REGGIANO (FROM 1 OUNCE CHEESE)

GRATED FRESH NUTMEG

WHITE PEPPER IN A MILL

FILL a large bowl halfway with ice water.

POUR the water into a 4-quart pot, add 1 tablespoon salt and bring to a boil over medium-high heat. Add the spinach and cook for 2 minutes. Transfer the spinach to the cold water to shock it and preserve its color, then drain the spinach in a colander, and squeeze out all excess water.

WIPE out the pot, add the butter, and melt it over medium heat. Add the onions and 1 teaspoon salt and cook until the onions are softened but not browned, approximately 4 minutes. Add the spinach, cream, mascarpone, Parmigiano-Reggiano, and nutmeg to taste, and cook, stirring, for 2 to 3 minutes until the mixture is hot. Season with salt and 6 grinds of pepper, or to taste.

THE spinach can be made up to 1 hour in advance and kept warm in a covered double boiler set over simmering water. Or you can let the spinach cool, transfer it to a baking dish, cover it, and refrigerate for up to 24 hours. Reheat in an oven preheated to 300°F until warmed through, approximately 15 minutes, and serve.

EMBELLISHMENT For a casserole-type presentation, top the spinach with extra grated Parmigiano-Reggiano and finish it under the broiler.

Serve this dish with the Potato Cake on page 259.

WILD MUSHROOMS WITH CHESTNUTS AND BRUSSELS SPROUTS

SERVES 4

This intensely autumnal side dish single-handedly makes the case for cooking with seasonal vegetables. Because of its unmistakable seasonality, it's a natural complement to fall dishes such as Pheasant with Madeira and Vanilla Sweet Potato Puree (page 225) and dishes featuring game. It's also a perfect side dish to add to your Thanksgiving Day menu.

¼ CUP OLIVE OIL

3 TABLESPOONS UNSALTED BUTTER

3 TABLESPOONS FINELY DICED SHALLOTS

KOSHER SALT

¾ POUND WILD MUSHROOMS (SUCH AS OYSTER OR CHANTERELLE), CLEANED, TRIMMED, LARGER ONES HALVED OR QUARTERED SO ALL PIECES ARE A UNIFORM SIZE

BLACK PEPPER IN A MILL

SPLASH FRESHLY SQUEEZED LEMON JUICE

2-INCH PIECE CELERY, SLICED

4 SPRIGS THYME

¾ CUP WHITE CHICKEN STOCK (PAGE 45) OR STORE-BOUGHT, LOW-SODIUM, CHICKEN BROTH

I CUP FRESH CHESTNUTS (ABOUT 6 OUNCES), PEELED (SEE PAGE 154), OR DEFROSTED, FROZEN CHESTNUTS

I CUP WATER

2 TABLESPOONS PANCETTA, CUT INTO SMALL DICE

12 BRUSSELS SPROUTS, SLICED THINLY ON A MANDOLINE OR WITH A VERY SHARP, THIN-BLADED KNIFE

POUR 3 tablespoons olive oil and 1 tablespoon butter into a 12-inch sauté pan and heat it over medium-low heat. Add the shallots and a pinch of salt and sauté until softened but not browned, 2 to 3 minutes. Add the mushrooms and sauté until the mushrooms release their juices, 10 to 12 minutes. Season with salt and 5 grinds of pepper, or to taste, sprinkle with the lemon juice, mix, and set aside.

PUT the celery, thyme, stock, chestnuts, remaining 2 tablespoons butter, and water in a heavy-bottomed, 2-quart saucepan and bring to a boil over medium heat. Lower the heat, cover, and simmer for 15 minutes. Remove the chestnuts from the pot with a slotted spoon and set aside, covered to keep warm. Reserve the liquid.

PUT the pancetta in the same 12-inch pan and heat it over medium-high heat until it gives off enough fat to coat the bottom of the pan. Add the Brussels sprout slices and cook until lightly browned, approximately 2 minutes, shaking the pan. Add the mushrooms and chestnuts and toss to warm through. Season with salt and about 4 grinds of pepper, or to taste. Transfer to a bowl and serve.

PORCINI AND ONION TART

A celebration of my favorite mushroom, this tart can be served with just about any fish, poultry, or meat dish you like. My favorite pairing is with a grilled porterhouse steak (page 231).

Note that porcini mushrooms vary quite a bit. Depending on where they come from, they will be either soft and supple, or firm and dry, or something in between. The softer ones take less time to cook, so if cooking firmer, drier porcini, you may need to add some water (or stock) to keep them from scorching before they soften.

½ CUP PLUS 1 TABLESPOON OLIVE OIL

2 CUPS THINLY SLICED ONION (FROM ABOUT 1 MEDIUM ONION)

1¾ CUPS LEEKS, WHITE AND LIGHT GREEN PARTS, WELL RINSED AND DICED (FROM ABOUT 2 MEDIUM LEEKS)

KOSHER SALT

¼ CUP CRÈME FRAÎCHE PLUS 2 TABLESPOONS

BLACK PEPPER IN A MILL

2 CUPS CLEANED, SLICED PORCINI MUSHROOMS (FROM ABOUT 8 OUNCES MUSHROOMS), STEMS PEELED, STEMS AND CAPS SLICED INTO ¼-INCH-THICK SLICES AND RESERVED SEPARATELY

1 TABLESPOON UNSALTED BUTTER

SPLASH FRESHLY SQUEEZED LEMON JUICE

4 SHEETS PHYLLO DOUGH, 12 INCHES BY 17 INCHES EACH (IF FROZEN, LET THAW TO REFRIGERATOR TEMPERATURE)

2 TABLESPOONS MELTED BUTTER

1 TABLESPOON THINLY SLICED CHIVES

PREHEAT the oven to 375°F. Heat ¼ cup plus 2 tablespoons of the oil in a heavy-bottomed, 3-quart saucepan set over medium heat. Add the onions, leeks, and a pinch of salt, and cook until they're very tender and lose their texture, but do not let them brown, approximately 20 minutes. If the mixture becomes dry, add a few drops of water, as needed. Fold in the crème fraîche. Season with 1 teaspoon salt and 3 grinds of pepper, or to taste, and set aside, covered to keep it warm.

PUT 3 tablespoons of the oil in a 10-inch sauté pan and heat it over medium-high heat. Add the mushroom stems and cook over medium heat until tender, approximately 2 minutes. Add the mushroom caps and unsalted butter and cook until tender, approximately 3 more minutes. Season the mixture with salt and pepper and sprinkle with the lemon juice. Set aside.

LAY one sheet of phyllo on a flat surface, use a pastry brush to dab lightly with melted butter, top with another sheet, and repeat, stacking the sheets and dabbing each one with butter. Cut the phyllo into 5-inch rounds with a biscuit cutter.

SHAPE the dough circles into 4-inch-round by 1-inch-deep nonstick molds or ring molds set on a cookie sheet. The phyllo should fit inside and come ½ inch up the sides. Fill the molds to a height of ¼ inch with pie weights or beans and blind bake until the phyllo is golden-brown, 6 to 7 minutes. Remove the weights; set aside.

MEANWHILE, combine the leek mixture and the porcini mushrooms and gently reheat them.

CAREFULLY transfer 1 tart shell to each of 4 plates and spoon some of the leek-porcini mixture into each one. Garnish with chives and serve.

EMBELLISHMENT Garnish each tart with sliced, sautéed porcini mushrooms.

CRUSHED CAULIFLOWER

SERVES 4

Although it has its own unmistakable character, cauliflower also takes on other flavors well too. Here, it anchors a simple but very satisfying side dish of Parmesan cheese, olive oil, and butter, letting the qualities of each one shine. It's a smart alternative to potato puree and is especially good with roasted poultry and seafood.

6 CUPS WATER

KOSHER SALT

I POUND CAULIFLOWER, SEPARATED INTO MEDIUM-SIZED FLORETS

2 TABLESPOONS UNSALTED BUTTER

2 TABLESPOONS OLIVE OIL

¼ CUP FINELY GRATED PARMIGIANO-REGGIANO

WHITE PEPPER IN A MILL

POUR the water into a large, heavy-bottomed pot, add 1½ tablespoons salt, and bring to a boil over high heat. Add the florets and cook until tender, approximately 10 minutes. Drain.

RETURN the florets to the pot over low-medium heat and cook for 3 minutes to evaporate any excess liquid. Add the butter, oil, and cheese. Break up the florets and incorporate the other ingredients with a potato masher, and season generously with salt and pepper.

TRANSFER the crushed cauliflower to a bowl and serve hot.

VARIATION Substitute cheddar cheese for the Parmesan.

BUTTERNUT SQUASH AND PRUNE GRATIN

 ratins are usually made with combinations of starchy and creamy elements, like potatoes, milk, and cheese. This gratin is lighter and sweet, thanks to the squash and the layer of prunes at its center. The sweetness balances the richness of poultry and wild game.

I POUND BUTTERNUT SQUASH, PEELED, HALVED LENGTHWISE, SEEDS REMOVED, CUT INTO ¼-INCH SLICES

KOSHER SALT

WHITE PEPPER IN A MILL

½ CUP PRUNES, CUT INTO MEDIUM DICE

I CUP HEAVY CREAM

¾ CUP WHITE CHICKEN STOCK (PAGE 45) OR LOW-SODIUM, STORE-BOUGHT CHICKEN BROTH

½ CUP CRÈME FRAÎCHE

2 EGG YOLKS

PREHEAT the oven to 350°F. Use a pastry brush to butter an 8-inch by 8-inch baking dish.

PUT the squash slices in a large bowl, season with salt and 6 grinds of pepper, or to taste, and gently toss. Arrange half the squash slices in the bottom of the baking dish and season. Top with the prunes, in a single layer, then cover with the remaining squash.

PUT the cream and stock in a bowl and whisk them together. Season with salt and pepper. Pour the mixture over the gratin, gently shake the dish to help the cream seep down to the bottom, and gently press down on the squash slices to settle them evenly. Cover the gratin loosely with foil and poke a few holes in the foil with the tines of a fork. Bake for 55 minutes, or until tender when tested with the tip of a knife. Remove from the oven and let cool slightly.

WHILE the gratin is still warm, put the crème fraîche in a bowl, add the yolks, and whisk vigorously until well incorporated. Season with salt and 4 grinds of pepper, or to taste, and spread over the gratin evenly. Bake, uncovered, until golden-brown, approximately 15 minutes. Remove from the oven and let rest for 10 to 15 minutes before serving (it's a little wet and loose when right out of the oven).

CUT rounds with a 3½-inch cookie cutter (as shown) or spoon out onto plates.

MACARONI AND CHEESE

SERVES 4

I s it any surprise that a cheese lover like me has a soft spot for macaroni and cheese? Italian in origin, it has become a popular side dish for barbecued foods in the American South. At Artisanal restaurant, we make our own version with a variety of cheeses and offer it as an à la carte accompaniment. Serve it with grilled and roasted meats and poultry, or on its own as a main course treat for kids.

8 CUPS WATER

5 ½ TABLESPOONS BUTTER

¾ CUP DRIED BREAD CRUMBS

¼ CUP PARMIGIANO-REGGIANO

¼ CUP PLUS 2 TABLESPOONS ALL-PURPOSE FLOUR

3 CUPS MILK

KOSHER SALT

WHITE PEPPER IN A MILL

2 ½ CUPS GRUYÈRE OR COMTÉ, GRATED (FROM 5 ½ OUNCES)

½ CUP MASCARPONE

1 ½ CUPS DRY ELBOW MACARONI

PREHEAT the oven to 350°F. Pour the water into a 3-quart pot and bring to a boil over high heat.

IN a small saucepan, melt 2½ tablespoons of the butter over low heat. Add the bread crumbs and Parmigiano-Reggiano, toss well, and set aside.

PUT the remaining 3 tablespoons butter in a 2-quart, heavy-bottomed saucepan and melt it over low heat. Add the flour and cook for 5 minutes, whisking constantly, but not letting the flour brown. Pour in the milk and cook for 5 minutes, whisking or stirring with a wooden spoon. Add 4½ teaspoons salt, 4 grinds of pepper, and the Gruyère and mascarpone, and continue to whisk until the cheese is melted and incorporated. Remove the pot from the heat.

ADD 1 tablespoon of salt and the elbow macaroni to the boiling water and cook until al dente, approximately 8 minutes. Drain the macaroni in a colander and add it to the pot with the cheese sauce. Mix well with a wooden spoon.

POUR the macaroni mixture into an 8-inch by 8-inch baking dish. Sprinkle the breadcrumb mixture evenly over the top of the macaroni and cheese. Bake until golden brown and bubbly, 30 to 35 minutes. Serve hot.

EMBELLISHMENT For a main-course pasta dish, double the recipe and add prosciutto and/or peas.

PANISSE
CHICKPEA CAKES

SERVES 4

A classic of Provençal gastronomy, the panisse is a little chickpea cake that is lightly fried and served alongside just about anything. In their native home, they're a popular street food, prepared like crepes by the purveyors of small carts, and rolled and eaten. They are sometimes eaten on their own as a midafternoon snack and are especially good with fish and lamb.

---

3 TABLESPOONS OLIVE OIL

2 TABLESPOONS GARLIC CONFIT (PAGE 36), OR 1 TEASPOON MINCED FRESH GARLIC

2½ CUPS WHITE CHICKEN STOCK (PAGE 45) OR LOW-SODIUM, STORE-BOUGHT CHICKEN BROTH OR WATER

¾ CUP CHICKPEA FLOUR (SEE SOURCES, PAGE 318)

½ CUP ALL-PURPOSE FLOUR

KOSHER SALT

BLACK PEPPER IN A MILL

POUR 1 tablespoon of the oil into a heavy-bottomed, 2-quart saucepan and heat it over medium heat. Add the garlic confit and stock and bring to a simmer over high heat. Slowly whisk the chickpea and all-purpose flour into the simmering stock and continue to whisk until the mixture thickens and is smooth, with no lumps whatsoever, approximately 8 minutes. Lower the heat and continue to cook until it takes on the consistency of loose mashed potatoes, approximately 5 more minutes.

POUR the mixture into an 8-inch by 8-inch Pyrex dish (it should come up to a depth of about ½ inch). Brush the top with 1 tablespoon olive oil and let cool, then cover and refrigerate for 2 hours or up to 24 hours.

WHEN ready to proceed, cut the chickpea cake into four rounds with a 3½-inch cookie cutter. Line a large plate or platter with paper towels and set it aside.

DUST the rounds with all-purpose flour on both sides, shaking off any excess.

HEAT the remaining tablespoon olive oil in a heavy-bottomed, 10-inch, nonstick sauté pan set over medium-high heat. Add the rounds and cook until lightly golden, approximately 3 minutes per side. Drain on the paper towel-lined plate, season with salt and 5 grinds of pepper, or to taste, and serve.

PARSNIP PUREE

SERVES 4

ere's a less starchy alternative to potato puree that makes use of an underrated root vegetable. The grated orange zest punches up the lively flavor of the parsnips. Serve it alongside any dish you'd pair with mashed potatoes. It's especially good with game.

---

2 CUPS MILK

4 CUPS WATER

¾ POUND PARSNIPS, PEELED AND CUT INTO 2-INCH PIECES

¼ CUP HEAVY CREAM

I TEASPOON FINELY GRATED ORANGE ZEST

I TABLESPOON UNSALTED BUTTER

KOSHER SALT

WHITE PEPPER IN A MILL

POUR the milk into a 4-quart saucepan. Add the water and parsnips and bring to a simmer over medium heat. Cook at a simmer until the parsnips are tender when tested with the tines of a fork, approximately 45 minutes. Use tongs or a slotted spoon to remove the parsnips from the cooking liquid and discard the cooking liquid.

PUT the cream in a small saucepan, add the zest, and heat it over medium heat, to simmer.

PUT the parsnips in a blender and, with the motor running, add the butter, then gradually add the cream. Transfer the puree to a bowl, and season with salt and 4 grinds of pepper or to taste. Serve hot, or let cool and reheat.

CHESTNUT SPAETZLE

SERVES 4

T hese tender little dumplings, which are quickly boiled, then lightly sautéed, are as common in European dining as they are rare in the United States. Their nutty character underscores game and roasted meats with autumnal flavor. You can use chestnut flour to make other flour-based foods, such as fresh pasta; just be sure to mix them well because chestnut flour has relatively little gluten, so it needs more time to bind.

ABOUT 12 CUPS WATER

KOSHER SALT

3 WHOLE EGGS, BEATEN

½ CUP ALL-PURPOSE FLOUR

1 CUP CHESTNUT FLOUR

3 TABLESPOONS MILK

CANOLA OIL (OPTIONAL)

2 TABLESPOONS UNSALTED BUTTER

BLACK PEPPER IN A MILL

POUR the water into a heavy-bottomed, 8-quart pot (you should be able to set a colander in the top of the pot with 3 inches of space from the bottom of the colander to the surface of the water; adjust water quantity as needed). Add 1 tablespoon salt and bring the water to a boil over high heat. Meanwhile, fill a large bowl halfway with ice water.

PUT the eggs in a large bowl and whisk in the all-purpose flour and chestnut flour, 1½ teaspoons salt, and the milk. Mix until smooth and slightly elastic, about 5 minutes.

SET a shallow perforated pan or colander over the boiling water. Put half of the batter in the pan and use a rubber spatula to press the batter through the holes, causing it to fall into the water in teardrop-shaped pieces. Cook the spaetzle in the water until it rises to the top, approximately 1 minute. Remove the spaetzle from the pot with a slotted spoon and transfer them to the ice water. Repeat with the remaining batter.

CLEAN the colander and drain the spaetzle in it. If preparing the spaetzle in advance, toss it with a few tablespoons of oil and set aside for up to 24 hours.

SET a heavy-bottomed, nonstick, 10-inch sauté pan over medium-high heat. Add 2 tablespoons of butter and melt it. Add the spaetzle and cook, tossing constantly, until golden-brown all over, approximately 10 minutes. Season with salt and 4 grinds of pepper, or to taste. Serve.

SIDE DISHES AND ACCOMPANIMENTS

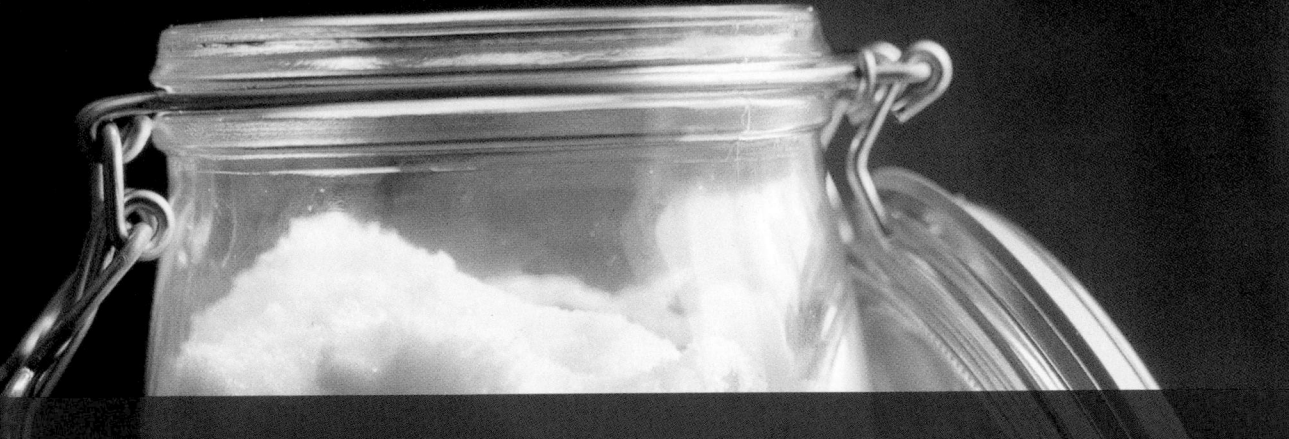

DESSERTS

ARTISANAL COOKING DOESN'T END after the last savory course has been served. The artisanal philosophy extends to the dessert course as well. I believe that desserts should follow the same principles that the rest of the recipes in this book do, fitting into your life, accommodating any situation, and leaving you with time to spend at the table.

Accordingly, this chapter features desserts that range from small-form treats like macaroons, to ice creams and sorbets that can be made ahead of time and frozen for weeks, to a chocolate fondue that can be festively shared at the table, to plated affairs for more elaborate or formal occasions.

Many of these desserts feature more than one component; often the principal one supported by a sauce or an ice cream. While I encourage you to serve them as they are presented here, you can often leave out the supporting element, or purchase a store-bought one instead. The headnotes to the individual recipes offer guidance on this.

Homemade desserts are often left out of home-cooked meals, usually because it seems like a reasonable way to save time. I humbly propose that it's actually fairly easy to make room for your own artisanal desserts in your life.

If you set aside a pantry day as I recommend on page 10, make an ice cream or sorbet or two, a compote, and perhaps some chocolate sauce. Or set your sights on an ambitious dessert to enjoy midweek. Or refrigerate, or freeze, the components and serve later on in the week. That will facilitate your day-to-day cooking, and also streamline your efforts when you entertain.

COCONUT MACAROONS

SERVES 6 TO 8

niversally popular, these chewy, coconut cookies couldn't be easier to make. They are also a dessert for your artisanal pantry, because they can be made and stored for up to three days. Have some on hand and you'll always be ready for company, even if all you do is set them out simply with coffee or tea. Make these part of a plated dessert by serving them with Chocolate Sorbet (page 305).

NONSTICK COOKING SPRAY

5 LARGE EGG WHITES, AT ROOM TEMPERATURE

½ CUP SUPERFINE SUGAR

2 CUPS PLUS 1 TABLESPOON UNSWEETENED SHREDDED DRIED COCONUT

1 TEASPOON FINE SEA SALT

PREHEAT the oven to 350°F. Spray a baking sheet with nonstick cooking spray, and set it aside.

PUT the egg whites, sugar, coconut, and salt in a large mixing bowl and whisk until well blended. Transfer the mixture to a pastry bag fitted with a ½-inch star tip and pipe 1-inch wide by ½-inch high round disks onto the baking sheet. You can also use a tablespoon if you don't have a pastry bag; the macaroons won't look as precise, but will taste just as good.

BAKE the macaroons until golden-brown, 26 to 28 minutes. Remove the sheet from the oven and let the macaroons cool completely on the sheet.

THE macaroons can be eaten right away, stored in an airtight container at room temperature for up to 3 days, or frozen for up to 3 months (defrost and thaw them at room temperature).

CHOCOLATE FONDUE WITH RASPBERRY MARSHMALLOWS

SERVES 4 TO 6

 ondue isn't just a mode of enjoying cheese; it's also a fun, communal way to share chocolate. Here's my recipe for fondue, along with one of my favorite dipping accompaniments: addictively delicious Raspberry Marshmallows. This is especially popular among kids.

If you make the (optional) Pecan Shortbread Cookies (page 317), you'll have your own, adult version of S'mores.

---

1 CUP FINELY CHOPPED UNSWEETENED CHOCOLATE

½ CUP HEAVY CREAM

⅓ CUP SUGAR

½ TEASPOON FINE SEA SALT

4 TABLESPOONS UNSALTED BUTTER

3 TABLESPOONS LIGHT CORN SYRUP

2 TABLESPOONS GRAND MARNIER (OPTIONAL)

RASPBERRY MARSHMALLOWS (RECIPE FOLLOWS)

PECAN SHORTBREAD COOKIES (PAGE 317) (OPTIONAL)

POUR the cream into a fondue pot and light the heating element. Add the sugar and salt and bring to a boil. Add the chocolate, stirring to melt it. Stir in the butter, corn syrup, and Grand Marnier, if using.

SERVE at once with marshmallows and shortbread cookies and any other accompaniments. (See Embellishments.)

VARIATION If you don't have a fondue pot, make the fondue in a 1 quart saucepan and transfer to a heatproof bowl for serving. (You will need to return the fondue to the heat periodically if not consumed within 8 to 10 minutes.)

EMBELLISHMENTS This fondue can also be served with a variety of the following: strawberries, sliced bananas, dried apricots, miniature cream puffs, marshmallows, wafers, pound cake, sliced pears, orange segments, or ladyfingers.

RASPBERRY MARSHMALLOWS

In addition to complementing chocolate fondue, these can also add a sophisticated flourish to ice cream sundaes. You can also toast them over a campfire, or cut them into smaller cubes and use them to garnish the chocolate soup on page 313, or hot chocolate.

⅓ CUP PLUS 1 TABLESPOON FRESH OR DEFROSTED FROZEN RASPBERRY PUREE

4 TEASPOONS UNFLAVORED GELATIN POWDER

½ TEASPOON RASPBERRY EXTRACT (OPTIONAL)

1 CUP CONFECTIONERS' SUGAR

1 CUP CORNSTARCH

⅓ CUP WATER

1 CUP PLUS 1 TABLESPOON SUGAR

1 TABLESPOON LIGHT CORN SYRUP

1 LARGE EGG WHITE

PUT the raspberry puree, gelatin, and extract (if using) in a bowl and stir to combine. Set aside while the gelatin softens.

PUT the confectioners' sugar and cornstarch in a bowl and stir to combine. Spread half the mixture evenly over a 16-inch by 14-inch by 1-inch-high cookie sheet.

POUR the water, sugar, and corn syrup into a medium saucepan and bring to a boil over high heat. Cook until the mixture reads 121°C on a candy thermometer. As it cooks, set a small pot of water to simmer on another burner and brush down the sides of the sugar–corn syrup pot with a 1- to 2-inch pastry brush to keep the sugar from sticking to the sides of the pot.

PUT the egg white in the bowl of a standing mixer fitted with the whisk attachment. Whisking on high speed, pour the still-hot sugar mixture into the egg white in a slow, steady stream along the side of the bowl. Add the raspberry puree-gelatin mixture and the raspberry extract and continue to whisk for 15 minutes.

SPREAD the marshmallow mixture out on the prepared cookie sheet. Sprinkle the remaining cornstarch-sugar mixture evenly over the top of the marshmallows. Let rest for at least 3 hours. Cut into squares or other shapes.

The marshmallows can be eaten right away, or refrigerated in an airtight container for up to 3 days.

THE REASON *A specific temperature is indicated in the recipe:* When making candies, different temperatures indicate different stages of melting sugar, from softball to firmball to hardball. In this case, we're trying to attain the "hardball" stage, when a drop of boiling syrup dropped in cold water will form a rigid ball, hard but still pliable. (Technically, the hardball stage is 250°F or 121°C.) When such a temperature is included in a recipe, it's essential that it be followed as closely as possible.

FROZEN CHOCOLATE MOUSSE TERRINE WITH HAZELNUT SAUCE

MAKES ONE 9-INCH BY 5-INCH TERRINE, ENOUGH TO SERVE ABOUT 8

F rozen desserts can be lifesavers when entertaining because they allow you to avoid that last, time-consuming disappearance into the kitchen at the height of the evening's conversation. This frozen terrine can be prepared up to one month ahead of time and the sauce can be made up to three days early. Best of all, it's appropriate to even the most special and formal of occasions. You can leave out the sauce and this will still be delicious.

---

12 OUNCES BITTERSWEET CHOCOLATE, FINELY CHOPPED

¾ CUP (1½ STICKS) UNSALTED BUTTER

8 LARGE EGG WHITES, AT ROOM TEMPERATURE

⅔ CUP PLUS 3 TABLESPOONS SUPERFINE SUGAR

11 LARGE EGG YOLKS PLUS 5 LARGE EGG YOLKS IN A SEPARATE BOWL

2⅔ CUPS MILK

½ CUP HAZELNUT PASTE (AVAILABLE AT SPECIALTY STORES AND GOURMET MARKETS, OR SEE SOURCES, PAGE 318)

LINE a 9-inch by 5-inch rectangular loaf pan with 2 pieces of plastic wrap, extending the plastic 3 inches over the sides of the pan.

IN a double boiler set over simmering water, melt the chocolate and butter, stirring them into a uniform mixture. Remove the chocolate from the double boiler and let the mixture cool for 5 minutes.

MEANWHILE, put the egg whites in the bowl of a standing mixer fitted with the whisk attachment. Whisk on medium speed until the whites begin to form soft, foamy peaks, then gently sprinkle in 3 tablespoons sugar and mix on high speed. Continue to beat until the whites hold their shape, but do not overmix.

ONE by one, whisk 6 of the egg yolks into the chocolate mixture. Whisk ⅓ of the beaten egg whites into chocolate mixture. Using a spatula, gently fold in the remaining egg whites.

POUR the chocolate mousse into the prepared loaf pan. Cover the surface with plastic wrap and freeze for 6 hours or up to 1 month.

WHEN ready to proceed, fill a large bowl halfway with ice water.

PUT the milk and hazelnut paste in a medium saucepan and bring to a boil over low heat.

IN a bowl, whisk the remaining 5 egg yolks and remaining ⅔ cup sugar together until pale yellow ribbons form.

REMOVE the milk mixture from the heat and whisk one-third of it slowly into the egg yolks. Pour the tempered egg yolk mixture into the milk mixture and return the saucepan to the stovetop. Cook over medium-low heat until the custard thickens enough to coat the back of a wooden spoon, approximately 8 minutes. Do not let it boil.

STRAIN the sauce through a fine-mesh strainer set over a bowl. Set the bottom of the bowl in the ice water and stir the mixture to chill it as quickly as possible. Cover the hazelnut sauce with plastic wrap and chill in refrigerator for at least 1 hour and up to 3 days.

CUT the terrine, while still frozen, into slices, about 1 inch each. Serve each slice on its own plate, drizzling some of the hazelnut sauce around it.

THE REASON *A small amount of hot liquid is whisked into eggs before the rest is added:* This technique, known as tempering, increases the temperature gradually, keeping the eggs from hardening into scrambled eggs, which would happen if the temperature increased dramatically when the hot liquid is added.

VARIATION Omit the sauce and serve this with fresh raspberries and whipped cream.

EMBELLISHMENTS Top the slices with walnuts, pistachios, or other nuts, and/or add some raspberries or currants to the plate.

PUMPKIN BREAD PUDDING WITH POACHED FALL FRUITS

SERVES 4

 t doesn't get much more autumnal than this: slices of bread are dipped in a spiced pumpkin custard and then sandwiched with poached fruits. If you're looking for a dessert to add to your Thanksgiving buffet, this just might become your next family favorite.

¼ CUP DRIED CHERRIES

½ CUP DRIED APRICOTS

½ CUP PRUNES

¼ CUP GOLDEN RAISINS

½ CUP DRIED FIGS

½ VANILLA BEAN, SPLIT LENGTHWISE

THREE 1-INCH STRIPS ORANGE ZEST (USE A VEGETABLE PEELER; REMOVE ALL PITH) OR DRIED ORANGE PEEL (PAGE 35)

1 CUP PORT

2 CUPS ZINFANDEL OR OTHER HEARTY RED WINE OR WATER

½ CUP SUGAR

2 TABLESPOONS ORANGE JUICE

2 LARGE EGGS

1½ CUPS MILK

8 OUNCES CANNED PUMPKIN PUREE

½ CUP LIGHT BROWN SUGAR

½ TEASPOON GROUND CINNAMON

¼ TEASPOON FRESHLY GRATED NUTMEG

¼ TEASPOON FINE SEA SALT

½ TEASPOON PURE VANILLA EXTRACT

EIGHT ¼-INCH-THICK SLICES BRIOCHE OR WHITE BREAD

4 TABLESPOONS UNSALTED BUTTER, AT ROOM TEMPERATURE

PREHEAT the oven to 325°F. Put the dried cherries, dried apricots, prunes, golden raisins, dried figs, vanilla bean, orange zest, port, Zinfandel, sugar, and orange juice in a medium saucepan. Bring the mixture to a simmer over medium heat, then lower the heat and cook at a low simmer, stirring occasionally, for 20 minutes. Remove the pan from the heat and set aside to cool.

PUT the eggs in a large bowl and whisk them together well. Whisk in the milk. Add the pumpkin, brown sugar, cinnamon, nutmeg, salt, and vanilla extract and whisk to incorporate.

CUT the bread slices into 8 rounds using a 3-inch cookie cutter. Dip the rounds in the custard to coat them.

GENEROUSLY butter four 3-inch ramekins. Put 1 disk of soaked bread in the bottom of each dish, top with a ¼-inch layer of poached fruits, then with 3 tablespoons of custard. Top with another layer of bread and fill each dish with custard. Put the ramekins in a baking dish. Fill the dish with hot water, halfway up the sides of the ramekins.

BAKE the bread pudding until it sets (a toothpick inserted to the center of a pudding will come out clean), 35 to 45 minutes.

SERVE the bread puddings warm or at room temperature in their molds with the remaining poached fruit alongside. They can also be refrigerated and served cold.

VARIATION You can make one large bread pudding in a baking dish and serve individual portions from the dish. Just be sure to cook the pudding long enough for it to pass the toothpick test included in the recipe.

PECAN PRALINE CHEESECAKE

Rich, creamy cheesecake is deeply satisfying on its own; when you add a variety of flavors and textures, it takes on a complexity most people don't expect from this universal crowd pleaser. In this dessert, a cream cheese filling is baked on a crust of pecan-shortbread crumbs and topped with pecan praline crunch. This cake hits all the right buttons—the decadent look, the smooth texture, the desired sweet-mildly tart taste, plus the surprise elements—and it's quite likely that your entire cake will be gone within minutes.

---

2 3/4 CUPS PLUS 2 TABLESPOONS CONFECTIONERS' SUGAR

2 3/4 CUPS PLUS 2 TABLESPOONS UNSALTED BUTTER

1 CUP ALL-PURPOSE FLOUR, PLUS MORE FOR DUSTING A WORK SURFACE

1 TABLESPOON GROUND CINNAMON

6 EGGS

1 3/4 CUPS CHOPPED PECANS

2 TABLESPOONS LIGHT CORN SYRUP

3 TABLESPOONS WATER, PLUS WATER FOR A WATER BATH

3/4 CUP GRANULATED SUGAR

1 TEASPOON FINE SEA SALT

1/4 TEASPOON BAKING POWDER

4 1/2 CUPS PLUS 3 TABLESPOONS CREAM CHEESE

PINCH NUTMEG

1 1/2 CUPS SOUR CREAM

1 VANILLA BEAN, SPLIT LENGTHWISE, SEEDS SCRAPED

1 CUP PLUS 2 TABLESPOONS HALF-AND-HALF

PUT ¾ cup confectioners' sugar and 1 cup plus 2 tablespoons butter in the bowl of a standing mixer fitted with the paddle attachment. Paddle on medium speed until smooth. Add 1 cup flour and the cinnamon and continue to mix on medium speed until well incorporated. Add 1 egg and 1/2 cup chopped pecans and continue to mix until incorporated.

WRAP the dough in plastic wrap and refrigerate for at least 30 minutes or up to 1 hour.

WHILE the shortbread dough chills, make the pecan praline: Put the corn syrup, 3 tablespoons of water, and the sugar in a small saucepan and heat to 300°F (tilt the pan and use a candy thermometer to check it) over medium heat. Stir in 1¼ cups butter. Add the salt and baking powder and mix well with a wooden spoon. Add the remaining 1¼ cups pecans and mix quickly to incorporate. Pour the praline onto a nonstick cookie sheet and set aside to cool.

PREHEAT the oven to 325°F.

FLOUR a work surface. Remove the dough from the refrigerator and roll it out with a rolling pin to a thickness of about ½ inch; the shape of the dough is not important. Put the dough on a nonstick cookie sheet. Bake until light golden, 10 to 12 minutes. Remove from the oven and let cool.

SET a 9-inch round piece of parchment paper in the bottom of 9-inch springform pan and wrap the base of the pan with foil.

WHILE the shortbread is cooling, make the cheesecake filling: Put the cream cheese and remaining 2 cups plus 2 tablespoons of confectioner's sugar in the bowl of a standing mixer fitted with the paddle attachment. Mix on low speed until smooth. Add the nutmeg, sour cream, vanilla seeds, and half-and-half to the mixture. Then add 5 eggs, one at a time, scraping the sides of the bowl after each addition, and mix well. Set aside.

BREAK the shortbread into pieces. Put them in the bowl of a food processor fitted with the steel blade and process to fine crumbs.

PUT the remaining ½ cup butter in a small saucepan and melt it over medium heat. Add 3 cups of shortbread crumbs to the melted butter and stir together until moist and sticky; this is your crust. Press the crust evenly in the bottom of the springform pan with your hands. Bake for 10 minutes.

BREAK the pecan praline into 1-inch pieces. Set aside 1 cup of the pieces. Put the remaining pecan praline pieces in a food processor and process to a fine crumb.

POUR the cream cheese filling over the crust in the pan and sprinkle the pecan praline crumbs evenly over the surface. Put the springform pan in a roasting pan and fill the roasting pan halfway up the side of the springform pan with warm water. Bake until the filling sets (a toothpick inserted to the center of the cake will come out clean), approximately 50 minutes. Turn the oven off and leave the cheesecake in the oven for another 25 minutes.

REMOVE the pan from the oven, remove the springform pan from its water bath, and let cool to room temperature. Wrap with plastic wrap and refrigerate for at least 5 hours or up to 3 days, or freeze for up to 1 month.

TO serve, cut the cake into individual portions, set each portion on a dessert plate, and garnish with the reserved pecan praline pieces.

THE REASON *The cake rests in the turned-off oven:* This allows it to gradually come to room temperature. If you were to simply remove it from the oven after the baking time, it would crack due to the rapid change in temperature.

APPLE TARTE TATIN WITH CHEDDAR CHEESE CRUST

At Artisanal Fromagerie and Bistro, we delight in referencing the associations diners have with cheese, whether by making gourmet grilled cheese sandwiches or creating a new version of a *croque monsieur*. This dessert applies an American tradition—topping apple pie with a slice of cheddar cheese—to a French classic. *Tarte tatin* is the original "upside down" cake, a tart of caramelized apples that is cooked in a sauté pan and inverted. Here, the crust is made with grated cheddar cheese, fusing two of the most beloved desserts of the United States and France with a success the United Nations can only dream of.

- 1¼ CUPS ALL-PURPOSE FLOUR, PLUS MORE FOR DUSTING WORK SURFACE
- PINCH FINE SEA SALT
- ½ TEASPOON BAKING POWDER
- PINCH CAYENNE PEPPER
- ½ CUP PLUS 2 TABLESPOONS GRATED FARMHOUSE CHEDDAR, SUCH AS GRAFTON FOUR-STAR CHEDDAR (FROM ABOUT 3¼ OUNCES CHEESE)
- ¾ CUP PLUS 2½ TABLESPOONS COLD UNSALTED BUTTER, CUT INTO CUBES

- 3 TABLESPOONS ICE COLD WATER
- 1 TEASPOON PLUS ¼ TEASPOON WHITE WINE VINEGAR
- ¾ CUP SUGAR
- 6 RED DELICIOUS APPLES, PEELED, CORED, AND QUARTERED
- 1 TEASPOON PURE VANILLA EXTRACT
- ¼ CUP BRANDY (OPTIONAL)

PUT the flour, salt, baking powder, cayenne, and cheese in a medium bowl and stir together until well incorporated. Add ½ cup plus ½ tablespoon butter to the mixture. Using a pastry cutter, work the butter into the mixture until the mixture resembles coarse corn meal. Add the cold water and vinegar and continue to mix until the dough comes together. Do not overmix.

FORM the dough into a ball and wrap in plastic wrap. Refrigerate for 1 hour or up to 24 hours.

PREHEAT the oven to 375°F. Put the remaining 6 tablespoons butter and the sugar in a 10-inch sauté pan and cook over medium-high heat. Once the sugar has caramelized, add the apples and sauté for 20 minutes, turning the apples every other minute with tongs or a wooden spoon until dark amber. Add the vanilla extract and brandy, if using, leaning away from the pan to avoid any possible flare-ups. Cook for 2 more minutes.

LET the apples cool in the pan for 10 minutes, then use tongs to arrange the apples in a circular pattern in the same sauté pan, starting at the outside and working in toward the center seed side up. The slices are too thick to overlap, but they should touch each other and be arranged as neatly and consistently as possible.

FLOUR a work surface and roll the dough out to a thickness of $\frac{1}{4}$ inch. Cut one round out of the dough, just over 10 inches in diameter, so that it can be neatly draped over the apples. Drape the dough over the apples in the sauté pan. (See Terms and Techniques.)

BAKE until the crust is golden-brown and cooked through, approximately 35 to 40 minutes. Remove the tart from the oven and let cool for 15 minutes. (If the caramel hardens too much, place the sauté pan on the stovetop over low heat to warm and loosen it slightly.)

CAREFULLY invert the tart onto a platter by placing a platter or cake plate over the pan and holding the two together. Invert them to transfer the tarte to the plate. Cut into slices and serve. The tart tatin can also be refrigerated and served room temperature or cold.

TERMS AND TECHNIQUES *Topping a tart with dough:* With the dough spread out before you on your work surface, set a rolling pin on the dough and starting at the end closest to you, roll it away from you, spooling the dough onto the pin. Then set the dough-wrapped pin on the side of the tart furthest from you and roll the pin back your way; the dough will unspool and top the tart.

EMBELLISHMENTS Serve the tarte tatin with vanilla ice cream, whipped crème fraîche, or slices of cheddar cheese.

CHOCOLATE MOCHA TART WITH SALTED CARAMEL ICE CREAM

SERVES 4

This dessert is my answer to one of the most popular restaurant desserts of the modern era: the flourless, molten chocolate cake. It's also a wonderful example of how well salty and sweet flavors pair: Caramel complements both coffee and chocolate extremely well. It's also delicious with Cherry Ice Cream (page 309), Red Wine-Port Ice Cream (page 310), or vanilla ice cream. Or you can omit the ice cream and serve it with Crème Chantilly (page 299) or crème fraîche.

¾ CUP (1½ STICKS) UNSALTED BUTTER, AT ROOM TEMPERATURE

¾ CUP ALL-PURPOSE FLOUR, PLUS MORE FOR FLOURING A WORK SURFACE

¼ CUP HAZELNUT FLOUR

2 TABLESPOONS COCOA POWDER

1 TABLESPOON SUPERFINE SUGAR

¼ TEASPOON FINE SEA SALT

2 LARGE EGG YOLKS

4 CUPS WATER

2 TEASPOONS MILK

6½ OUNCES BITTERSWEET CHOCOLATE

2 TABLESPOONS LIGHT CORN SYRUP

1 TABLESPOON INSTANT ESPRESSO

2 LARGE EGGS

SALTED CARAMEL ICE CREAM (PAGE 311)

PUT 8 tablespoons of the butter, the flour, hazelnut flour, cocoa powder, sugar, and salt in the bowl of a standing mixer fitted with the paddle attachment. Paddle on low speed to blend. Add the egg yolks and paddle until well incorporated, but do not overmix.

WRAP the dough in plastic wrap and refrigerate for at least 30 minutes or up to 24 hours.

PREHEAT the oven to 350°F. Lightly flour a work surface. Remove the dough from the refrigerator and roll it out to a thickness of ⅛ inch. Cut four 4-inch rounds out of the dough and place them on a cookie sheet. Put the sheet in the refrigerator for 30 minutes.

REMOVE the chilled dough from the refrigerator and press it into 4-inch tart molds (¾ inch high). Line a baking sheet with parchment paper and put the molds on the baking sheet. Line each mold with parchment paper, extending the paper ¼ inch over the top of the shells. Top with pie weights or dried beans. Blind bake the shells in the oven until firm, approximately 25 minutes.

REMOVE the shells from the oven and let cool to room temperature. Do not turn off the oven.

POUR the water into a 2-quart saucepan and bring to a simmer over medium heat. Put the milk, chocolate, and remaining ¼ cup butter in a stainless-steel bowl and set over the simmering water. Stir until the chocolate and butter melt together.

POUR the corn syrup into a small saucepan and warm it over medium heat. Stir in the espresso until dissolved. Meanwhile, put the eggs in the bowl of a standing mixer fitted with the whip attachment. Remove the pan from the heat. Start mixing the eggs on high speed, then pour the espresso mixture slowly into the beating eggs and beat on high speed for 8 minutes.

REMOVE the pie weights from the shells and pour the chocolate mixture into the shells. Bake until just set, 7 to 10 minutes. (For a more gooey center, bake them for a little less time.)

TO serve, set 1 tart on each of 4 dessert plates. Serve warm, with a scoop of Salted Caramel Ice Cream alongside.

VARIATION You can make one large tart, baking it for a longer period of time until set, but the individual tarts are stunning, so if you have small tart molds I urge you to use them here.

EMBELLISHMENT Sprinkle some Malden sea salt over each serving.

TOMATO TART with BASIL ICE CREAM

This sly summer variation of a fruit tart reminds us that, tomatoes—usually employed as a vegetable in savory courses—are technically a fruit. Here they are the centerpiece of a sweet, herbaceous tart, complemented by ricotta cheese and their old friend basil, present in a surprising ice cream. Don't skip the ice cream with this dessert; it really completes the tart.

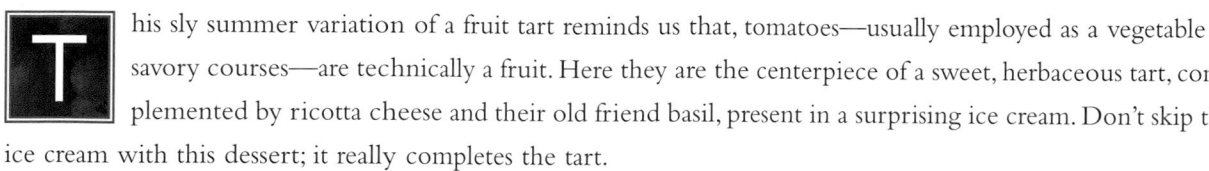

- 1½ CUPS SIMPLE SYRUP (SEE TERMS AND TECHNIQUES)
- 8 POUNDS PLUM TOMATOES, PEELED (PAGE 95), SEEDED, QUARTERED, INSIDES TRIMMED (SEE TERMS AND TECHNIQUES)
- 2 CUPS ALL-PURPOSE FLOUR, PLUS MORE FOR FLOURING A WORK SURFACE
- 10 TABLESPOONS (1 STICK PLUS 2 TABLESPOONS) COLD, UNSALTED BUTTER, CUT INTO CUBES
- ⅛ CUP SUPERFINE SUGAR

- ½ TEASPOON FINE SEA SALT
- 1 LARGE EGG, BEATEN
- ½ TO 1½ TABLESPOONS COLD WATER
- 2 CUPS RICOTTA CHEESE
- 1 TEASPOON PURE VANILLA EXTRACT
- ¼ CUP HONEY
- BASIL ICE CREAM (PAGE 307)
- 4 BASIL LEAVES, FOR GARNISH

PUT the syrup in a medium saucepan and bring it to a boil over high heat. Lower the heat, add the tomatoes, and simmer until tender, approximately 5 minutes, depending on the ripeness of the tomatoes. Use a slotted spoon to remove the tomatoes from the syrup, letting any excess syrup run off, and set them on a wire rack to cool. Reserve the poaching liquid.

PUT the flour, butter, sugar, and salt in the bowl of a standing mixer fitted with the paddle attachment and paddle on medium speed until the mixture resembles coarse cornmeal.

SLOWLY paddle the egg into the flour mixture. Add ½ tablespoon cold water and continue to paddle just until the dough comes together, adding more water in ½-tablespoon increments, if needed, but do not add more than 1½ tablespoons water.

LIGHTLY flour a work surface. Turn the dough out onto the surface, and knead it gently into a ball. Wrap the dough in plastic wrap and refrigerate for at least 30 minutes or up to 24 hours; it also freezes very well for up 2 months.

MEANWHILE, make the ricotta filling: Put the ricotta, vanilla extract, and honey in the bowl of a standing mixer fitted with the paddle attachment. Paddle on medium speed until smooth, approximately 1 minute. Cover the bowl with plastic wrap and refrigerate.

REFLOUR the work surface. Remove the chilled dough from the refrigerator and roll it out to a thickness of ⅛ inch. Cut four 4-inch rounds from the dough. Place four 4-inch pastry rings (¾ inch high) on a parchment paper-lined cookie sheet. Press 1 round into each ring and trim any excess dough. Chill the molds in the refrigerator for at least 30 minutes or up to 24 hours.

PREHEAT the oven to 325°F. Remove the tart shells from the refrigerator. Line each mold with parchment paper, extending the paper ¼ inch over the top of the molds. Top with pie weights or dried beans. Blind bake the shells in the oven until golden-brown, 8–10 minutes. Remove from the oven and let cool; remove the weights and parchment paper.

TO serve, spoon the ricotta filling into the molds three-quarters of the way up the edge of each tart shell. Divide the tomatoes evenly among the shells, overlapping the pieces in a circular pattern as neatly and uniformly as possible, and place a tart on each of 4 plates. Top each tart with a scoop of basil ice cream and drizzle some poaching liquid over and around the tart. Garnish with a sprig of basil and serve.

TERMS AND TECHNIQUES *Simple syrup:* To make 1½ cups simple syrup, pour 1 cup of water into a small saucepan and stir in 1½ cups sugar. Bring to a boil over high heat. Cook, stirring until the sugar dissolves and the liquid becomes a clear syrup, 2 to 3 minutes, then simmer an additional 2 to 3 minutes. Remove the pan from the heat and let cool.

Making tomato petals: To create smooth, clean "petals," lay each tomato quarter on your cutting board with the inside facing upward and run a sharp paring knife along the "rib," removing it.

Shaping dough to a tart shell: If you have any excess dough, roll it into a small ball and use the dough ball to shape the dough to the tart shell. This will avoid leaving fingerprints in the dough and also help prevent you from tearing the dough.

THE REASON *The dough is chilled:* Chilling doughs before rolling and baking them helps them maintain a uniform texture and prevents shrinkage.

FIG FINANCIER TART

MAKES ONE 10-INCH TART, ENOUGH TO SERVE 6 TO 8

I love fresh figs, on their own, as an accompaniment to cheese, or in a dessert that celebrates their flavor. This tart is a convenient way to make a fig dessert by arranging the fruits in a tart pan, pouring a simple batter over them, and baking it. Keep it in mind for a last-second indulgence: if you have all the ingredients on hand, it can be prepared and cooked in about 25 minutes.

½ CUP (1 STICK) UNSALTED BUTTER, PLUS MORE FOR GREASING A TART PAN

3½ CUPS CONFECTIONERS' SUGAR

½ CUP ALL-PURPOSE FLOUR

1 CUP ALMOND FLOUR

6 LARGE EGG WHITES, AT ROOM TEMPERATURE

24 FIGS, ABOUT 2½ PINTS, HALVED, STEMS REMOVED

PREHEAT the oven to 350°F. Put the butter in a small sauté pan and cook over medium heat until it melts and turns brown, 7 to 9 minutes.

PUT confectioners' sugar, flour, almond flour, and egg whites in the bowl of a standing mixer fitted with the paddle attachment and mix on medium speed until smooth. Add the brown butter and mix well on medium speed. Stop the motor, scrape down the sides of the bowl, and mix again.

BUTTER a 10-inch tart pan and arrange the fig halves, cut side down, in a circular pattern, leaving about ¼ inch of space between fig halves. Pour the batter evenly over the figs.

BAKE the tart until the batter rises around the figs, turns golden-brown, and a toothpick inserted comes out clean, approximately 15 minutes.

COOL the tart. Invert it onto a platter by placing the platter or cake plate over the pan and holding the two together. Invert them to transfer the tart to the plate. Slice into individual portions, and serve warm or at room temperature.

VARIATION This dessert can also be made with berries or apricots.

EMBELLISHMENT Liquefy some apricot jam or jelly with a little water and warm it over medium heat. Brush this over the finished tart to create a glaze. This embellishment can be used to finish any tarts or desserts with exposed fruit. It will make them shine and preserve them longer.

PAVLOVA WITH BERRY COMPOTE

SERVES 4

The pavlova, a meringue dessert topped with fresh fruit and whipped cream, is an innocent-looking dish that has inspired quite a bit of controversy Down Under: Both Australia and New Zealand have through the years tried to lay claim to creating it. What nobody disputes is the origin of the name. The pavlova was inspired by the Russian dancer Anna Pavlova, who toured Australia and New Zealand in 1926.

I first had pavlova at the home of a friend on Long Island. I prefer the version here to the classic French version because the meringue in this recipe is crispy yet chewy, a combination that I find irresistible.

BERRY COMPOTE

- 2 CUPS FRESH BERRIES, SUCH AS RASPBERRIES, BLACKBERRIES, AND BLUEBERRIES (PREFERABLY A MIXTURE OF ALL THREE)
- 1 TABLESPOON FRESHLY SQUEEZED LEMON JUICE
- 1/3 CUP GRANULATED SUGAR
- 1/2 VANILLA BEAN, SLIT LENGTHWISE, SEEDS SCRAPED

PAVLOVA

- 1/2 TEASPOON WHITE VINEGAR
- 2 LARGE EGG WHITES, AT ROOM TEMPERATURE
- 1 TEASPOON FINE SEA SALT
- 6 TABLESPOONS SUPERFINE SUGAR
- 1/2 TEASPOON CORNSTARCH
- CRÈME CHANTILLY (PAGE 299)

LINE a baking sheet with parchment paper. Draw four circles, 3½ inches in diameter each, on the paper, leaving about 2 inches of space all around each circle.

MAKE the berry compote: Put 1 cup berries, the lemon juice, granulated sugar, and vanilla in a medium saucepan. Bring to a boil over medium heat and cook, stirring, for 5 minutes. Remove the pot from the heat and let cool slightly. Stir in the remaining 1 cup of berries. The compote can be cooled, transferred to an airtight container, and refrigerated for up to 3 days.

PREHEAT the oven to 300°F. Pour the vinegar into a bowl and set it aside.

MAKE the pavlovas: Put the egg whites, vinegar, and salt in the bowl of a standing mixer fitted with the whisk attachment. Whisk on high speed until soft peaks are just beginning to form. Gently and gradually sprinkle in the superfine sugar (adding it all at once will cause the eggs to collapse), and continue to beat on high speed just until the whites hold their shape. (The eggs should look almost dull; if they look wet and granular, they've been overmixed and will break down, and you should begin this step over again with new eggs, vinegar, and salt.)

SIFT the cornstarch into the egg-white mixture, folding gently with a rubber spatula until all is incorporated, being careful not to deflate the whites by overmixing.

TRANSFER the egg-white mixture into a pastry bag fitted with the plain tip and pipe four rounds 3½ inches (diameter) by approximately 2½ inches (height) onto the lined cookie sheet, using the diagram as your guide, in a spiral with increasingly narrow circles that taper toward the top. Bake for 25 minutes, then turn off the oven and leave the meringues in the oven for another 25 minutes. Remove the sheet from the oven and let the meringues (pavlovas) cool to room temperature.

TO serve, use a small paring knife to remove a tablespoon-size hole from the top of each pavlova. Spoon some compote into the hole, top with some crème Chantilly, and serve.

THE REASON *Fresh berries are stirred into the compote:* Most compote recipes cook all the fruit. I prefer to add some fresh fruit to the cooked compote for the fresh flavor it adds.

EMBELLISHMENT For a more dramatic presentation, cut the pavlovas in half horizontally with a serrated knife and set 1 bottom on each of 4 dessert plates. Evenly divide the compote among the pavlovas, spreading it out in a smooth layer. Top with the other half and a dollop of crème Chantilly.

BABA au RHUM with CRÈME CHANTILLY

SERVES 4

The baba au rhum is founded on a perfect pairing—a yeasty little cake (baba) is soaked in sweetened rum, drinking in the complexity of the liquor. Cut through your baba with a fork and it emits little tears of rum, a preview of the flavor that dwells within. Serve the baba with summer berries and crème chantilly, but you can leave those out and it will still be delicious.

Classically babas are served cold or at room temperature. Either way, they are doused with the rum and soaked as soon as they come out of the oven.

¼ CUP PLUS 1 TABLESPOON MILK

1¼ TEASPOONS ACTIVE DRY YEAST

½ CUP PLUS 1 TABLESPOON PLUS ½ TEASPOON SUGAR

1 CUP ALL-PURPOSE FLOUR

PINCH FINE SEA SALT

¼ TEASPOON PURE VANILLA EXTRACT

FINELY GRATED ZEST OF 1 LEMON (OPTIONAL)

¼ CUP UNSALTED BUTTER, SOFTENED AT ROOM TEMPERATURE, PLUS MORE FOR GREASING BAKING MOLDS

2 LARGE EGG YOLKS

1 CUP WATER

½ CUP LIGHT OR DARK RUM

CRÈME CHANTILLY (RECIPE FOLLOWS)

POUR the milk into a small saucepan and warm it over low heat just until warm.

TRANSFER the milk into the bowl of standing mixer fitted with the whisk attachment. Add the yeast, ½ teaspoon of the sugar, and ¼ cup of the flour, and whisk until the yeast dissolves. Cover and set aside in a warm place until the yeast becomes frothy and doubles in volume, 10 to 15 minutes.

SIFT together the remaining flour, 1 tablespoon of the sugar, and the salt directly into the bowl with the yeast mixture. Add the vanilla extract, half the lemon zest, if using, 4 tablespoons of the butter, and the egg yolks. Fit the mixer with the dough hook and process the mixture on medium speed until the dough pulls away from the sides of the bowl, 3 to 4 minutes.

COVER the bowl with plastic wrap and set it aside in a moderately warm place until the dough doubles in volume, 25 to 35 minutes.

MAKE the soaking liquid: While the dough is rising, pour the water into a small saucepan.

Add the remaining ½ cup sugar and the remaining lemon zest, if using, and bring to a boil over medium heat. Remove the pan from the heat and set aside to cool.

PREHEAT the oven to 325°F. Butter four 4-ounce baba molds or stainless-steel timbales.

ONCE the dough has risen, divide it among the buttered molds, filling them two-thirds of the way up their sides with the dough, and set the molds on a cookie sheet. Let the dough rise in a warm place until it becomes flush with the rim of the mold, another 15 to 20 minutes.

BAKE the babas until light golden-brown, 12 to 14 minutes. Remove the sheet from the oven and let the babas cool slightly.

STIR the rum into the cooled soaking liquid.

TO serve, remove the babas from their molds, cut them in half lengthwise, and dip each side in the soaking liquid. Put the 2 halves of 1 baba on each of 4 dessert plates and top each one with crème Chantilly. (The babas can also be made ahead of time and served cold or at room temperature.)

EMBELLISHMENTS Serve the babas with fresh berries, currants, or simply with the crème Chantilly.

CRÈME CHANTILLY MAKES ABOUT 2 CUPS

Like so many taken-for-granted condiments, crème Chantilly, a fancy name for whipped cream that dates back hundreds of years, benefits greatly from being prepared from scratch at home. This recipe, which couldn't be easier, will open your eyes to just how refined and satisfying whipped cream can be. Use this vanilla-flavored cream to top any number of desserts.

If you have the time, chill the bowl and whisk attachment before beginning this recipe. It's not essential, but helps the cream thicken more quickly.

I CUP COLD HEAVY CREAM

2 TEASPOONS SUPERFINE SUGAR

½ TEASPOON PURE VANILLA EXTRACT

POUR the cream into the bowl of a standing mixer fitted with the whisk attachment. Whisk on high speed until soft peaks form, then gradually add the sugar and vanilla extract and continue to whisk until incorporated. Serve.

PROFITEROLE SUNDAE WITH CHERRY ICE CREAM

MAKES TWENTY-FOUR 1 ½-INCH PROFITEROLES

Profiteroles are a French classic of vanilla ice cream sandwiched between airy choux pastry and topped with chocolate sauce. I love taking them in a decadent American sundae direction, adding cherry compote, whipped cream, and almonds. This is a very flexible recipe; serve up to 8 people, or serve fewer people and freeze the remaining pastries in a plastic bag.

½ CUP PLUS 1 TABLESPOON UNSALTED BUTTER

¼ CUP PLUS 1 TABLESPOON MILK

¼ CUP WATER

½ CUP PLUS 3 TABLESPOONS ALL-PURPOSE FLOUR

1 TABLESPOON PLUS 1 TEASPOON SUGAR

⅛ TEASPOON BAKING POWDER

4 LARGE EGGS

CHOCOLATE SAUCE (PAGE 315)

CHERRY ICE CREAM (PAGE 309)

CHERRY COMPOTE (PAGE 39)

CRÈME CHANTILLY (PAGE 299)

CANDIED ALMONDS (PAGE 316)

PREHEAT the oven to 375°F. Put the butter, ¼ cup of the milk, and the water in a medium saucepan and bring to a boil over high heat. Turn the heat to low, and add the flour, sugar, and baking powder. Stir the mixture with a wooden spoon until it begins to pull away from the sides of the pan and form a small ball, 3 to 4 minutes.

PUT the dough in the bowl of a standing mixer fitted with the paddle attachment and paddle on medium speed for 3 minutes to cool it. Add 3 of the eggs, one at a time, only adding the next egg after the previous one has been incorporated. Continue to mix the dough until it becomes thick and shiny, 5 to 6 minutes.

LINE a cookie sheet with parchment paper, or use a nonstick cookie sheet.

PUT the dough in a pastry bag fitted with the #5 plain pastry tip. Pipe the dough onto the sheet, forming rounds that are 1 inch in diameter and 1 inch high, leaving ½ inch to 1 inch of space around each piece.

POUR the remaining 1 tablespoon milk into a small bowl. Add the remaining egg and whisk together to make an egg wash. Using a pastry brush, lightly brush the tops of each profiterole with the egg wash.

BAKE the profiteroles until golden-brown, approximately 18 minutes. Remove the profiteroles from the oven and cool on a rack.

TO serve, cut the profiteroles in half crosswise. Put 3 dabs of chocolate sauce on each plate and set a profiterole bottom on each dab. (The sauce will hold the profiteroles in place.) Top with a scoop of ice cream, then with a profiterole top. Put some cherry compote in the center of the plate, and top the compote with some crème Chantilly and almonds. Spoon some chocolate sauce over the profiteroles, or bring the plates to the table and pour the sauce over the profiteroles there.

VARIATION Make this with your favorite ice creams and/or fruits.

GRANITÉS, SORBETS, AND ICE CREAMS

DO YOU KNOW ANYONE WHO DOESN'T LOVE ice cream, sorbet, or granité? Not only are these frozen delicacies enjoyable on their own, they can also be added to other desserts, bringing additional textures and flavors to the plate or bowl. There are a number of effective and very affordable ice-cream makers on the market today, many of which can produce ice cream or sorbet in just about 30 minutes, which to me is an irresistible proposition.

Here are my favorite granités (ices), sorbets, and ice creams. They are all great on their own, many of them are recommended to accompany other desserts in this chapter, and I'm sure you'll find your own uses for them as well.

POMEGRANATE GRANITÉ

SERVES 4

7 OR 8 SMALL POMEGRANATES

½ CUP SUGAR

½ CUP WATER

JUICE OF 1 LEMON

SET a food mill inside a bowl. Roll the pomegranates firmly on your work surface to break their membranes. Quarter the pomegranates. Remove the seeds, reserving about 20 and transferring the rest into the mill, taking care not to pick out all of the white membranes. Process the seeds, being careful not to splash the juice because it stains. You should have 1½ cups juice.

PUT the sugar and water in a small saucepan, stir, and simmer over low heat until the sugar dissolves, 2 minutes. Let cool. Pour the syrup, pomegranate juice, and lemon juice into a 10-inch-square by 2-inch-deep pan.

FREEZE for at least 2½ hours, scraping the mixture with a fork every half hour to break it into ice crystals. When ready to serve, use the edge of the fork to scrape the shavings into a fluffy ice, or scoop the shavings with an ice-cream scoop.

TO serve, divide the granité among 4 bowls and garnish with the reserved seeds. This is especially stunning served in martini glasses.

PINEAPPLE-VANILLA SORBET

MAKES ABOUT 3 CUPS

1 PINEAPPLE, PEELED, CORED, AND CUT INTO LARGE DICE

¼ CUP PLUS 1 TABLESPOON SUPERFINE SUGAR

1 VANILLA BEAN, SPLIT LENGTHWISE, SEEDS SCRAPED

PUT the pineapple, sugar, and vanilla seeds in a standing blender. Puree for 30 seconds. You should have about 1½ cups puree.

STRAIN the puree through a fine-mesh strainer set over a bowl, pressing down on the solids with a rubber spatula or the back of a ladle to extract as much flavorful liquid as possible.

TRANSFER the mixture to an ice-cream maker and freeze according to the manufacturer's instructions.

BERRY YOGURT SORBET

MAKES ABOUT 1 QUART

2 CUPS BERRIES SUCH AS BLACKBERRIES, BLUEBERRIES, AND/OR RASPBERRIES

1 BANANA, PEELED AND MASHED

¾ CUP SUGAR

½ CUP ORANGE JUICE, PREFERABLY FRESHLY SQUEEZED

2 CUPS NONFAT PLAIN YOGURT

1 VANILLA BEAN, SPLIT LENGTHWISE, SEEDS SCRAPED, OR 1 TEASPOON PURE VANILLA EXTRACT

PUT the berries, banana, sugar, orange juice, yogurt, and vanilla seeds in a blender. Puree for 30 seconds.

STRAIN the puree through a fine-mesh strainer set over a bowl, pressing down on the solids with a rubber spatula or the back of a ladle to extract as much flavorful liquid as possible.

TRANSFER the mixture to an ice-cream maker and freeze according to the manufacturer's instructions.

RICOTTA SORBET

MAKES ABOUT 3 CUPS

2 CUPS MILK

12 OUNCES FRESH RICOTTA

½ CUP PLUS 3 TABLESPOONS SIMPLE SYRUP
(PAGE 294)

1 VANILLA BEAN, SPLIT LENGTHWISE, SEEDS
SCRAPED, OR 1 TEASPOON PURE VANILLA
EXTRACT

FILL a large bowl halfway with ice water.

PUT the milk, ricotta, simple syrup, and vanilla in a medium saucepan and whisk over low-medium heat until well incorporated; do not let the mixture boil. Remove the pot from the heat and let steep for at least 30 minutes, or up to 1 hour.

STRAIN the mixture through a fine-mesh strainer set over a bowl, pressing down on the solids with a rubber spatula or the back of a ladle to extract as much flavorful liquid as possible. Set the bottom of the bowl in the ice water and stir the mixture to chill it as quickly as possible.

TRANSFER the mixture to an ice-cream maker and freeze according to the manufacturer's instructions.

CHOCOLATE SORBET

MAKES ABOUT 1 QUART

1¾ CUPS SUPERFINE SUGAR

½ TEASPOON FINE SEA SALT

3 CUPS WATER

12 OUNCES BITTERSWEET CHOCOLATE,
COARSELY CHOPPED

PUT the sugar, salt, and water in a medium saucepan, stir to combine them, and bring to a boil over medium heat. Lower the heat and let simmer for 2 minutes.

PUT the chocolate in a heatproof bowl. Pour the syrup over the chocolate and stir to melt the chocolate and form a smooth, uniform mixture. Let cool at room temperature then transfer the bowl to the refrigerator and chill until the mixture is cold.

TRANSFER the mixture to an ice-cream maker and freeze according to the manufacturer's instructions.

LIME-COCONUT ICE CREAM

MAKES ABOUT 1 QUART

1½ CUPS UNSWEETENED COCONUT MILK

1½ CUPS MILK

1 CUP HEAVY CREAM

6 LARGE EGG YOLKS

¼ CUP SUPERFINE SUGAR

¼ CUP FRESHLY SQUEEZED LIME JUICE

FILL a large bowl halfway with ice water.

PUT the coconut milk, milk, and cream in a large saucepan, stir to combine them, and bring to a boil over low-medium heat.

MEANWHILE, in a separate bowl whisk the egg yolks and sugar together until pale yellow ribbons form.

POUR ⅓ of the milk mixture into the yolks and whisk just to combine. Pour the mixture back into the milk mixture and cook over low-medium heat until the mixture thickens enough to coat the back of a wooden spoon, 6 to 8 minutes. Do not let the custard boil at any time.

STRAIN the mixture through a fine-mesh strainer set over a bowl, pressing down on the solids with a rubber spatula or the back of a ladle to extract as much flavorful liquid as possible. Set the bottom of the bowl in the ice water and stir the mixture to chill it as quickly as possible. Once the base is cold, add the lime juice.

TRANSFER the custard to an ice-cream maker and freeze according to the manufacturer's instructions.

EMBELLISHMENT In my restaurants, we infuse ½ stalk chopped lemongrass to the cream mixture, for a more complex flavor.

BASIL ICE CREAM

MAKES ABOUT 3 CUPS

1½ CUPS MILK

½ CUP HEAVY CREAM

1 CUP SUPERFINE SUGAR

½ VANILLA BEAN, SPLIT LENGTHWISE

½ CUP THINLY SLICED BASIL

6 LARGE EGG YOLKS

FILL a large bowl halfway with ice water.

POUR the milk and heavy cream into a saucepan. Stir in ½ cup sugar and the vanilla and bring to a boil over medium heat. Remove the pan from the heat, add the basil, blend with an immersion blender, and let steep for 10 minutes.

PUT the egg yolks and remaining ½ cup sugar in a separate bowl and whisk them together until pale yellow ribbons form. Slowly pour the milk mixture into the egg yolk mixture and whisk well. Pour the mixture back into the saucepan and cook over low-medium heat until the mixture thickens enough to coat the back of a wooden spoon, 6 to 8 minutes. Do not let boil.

STRAIN the mixture through a fine-mesh strainer set over a bowl, pressing down on the solids with a rubber spatula or the back of a ladle to extract as much flavorful liquid as possible. Set the bottom of the bowl in the ice water and stir the mixture to chill it.

TRANSFER the custard to an ice-cream maker and freeze according to the manufacturer's instructions.

PLUM-TEA ICE CREAM

MAKES ABOUT I QUART

1 POUND DARK-SKINNED PLUMS, HALVED, PITTED, AND CUT INTO 6 OR 8 WEDGES EACH

½ CUP PORT

½ CUP PLUS 2 TABLESPOONS SUPERFINE SUGAR

¼ TEASPOON FINE SEA SALT

¼ CUP PLUM-TEA LEAVES

1 CUP HEAVY CREAM

½ VANILLA BEAN, SPLIT LENGTHWISE, SEEDS SCRAPED, OR ¼ TEASPOON VANILLA EXTRACT

2 LARGE EGG YOLKS

PUT the plums, port, 2 tablespoons of the sugar, and the salt in a medium saucepan and bring to a boil over medium heat. Lower the heat and let simmer, stirring frequently, for 15 minutes. Remove the pan from the heat and let cool.

PUT the plums in the bowl of a food processor fitted with the steel blade and process until the plums are coarse in texture. Cover and refrigerate until cold, approximately 1 hour.

PUT the tea leaves and cream (and vanilla, if using the bean) in a saucepan and bring to a boil over medium-high heat. Remove the pan from the heat and let steep for 15 minutes.

MEANWHILE, combine the egg yolks, remaining ½ cup sugar, and the vanilla (if using the extract) in a medium-size bowl. Whisk until pale yellow ribbons form.

FILL a large bowl halfway with ice water.

STRAIN the cream mixture through a fine-mesh strainer set over a bowl and return it to the saucepan. Bring it to a boil over low-medium heat, then remove the pan from the heat.

ADD one-third of the boiling cream mixture to the egg yolk mixture and whisk. Add the egg yolk mixture to the remaining cream mixture in a slow, steady stream, while whisking vigorously. Pour the mixture back into the saucepan and cook over low-medium heat until the mixture thickens enough to coat the back of a wooden spoon, 6 to 8 minutes, careful not to let the mixture boil. Immediately remove the pan from the stove. Strain the mixture through a fine mesh strainer set over a bowl. Set the bottom of the bowl in the ice-water and stir the mixture to chill.

WHISK the plum puree into the cream mixture gently.

TRANSFER the mixture to an ice-cream maker and freeze according to the manufacturer's instructions.

CHERRY ICE CREAM

MAKES ABOUT 1 QUART

1½ POUND BING CHERRIES, HALVED AND PITTED

½ VANILLA BEAN, SEEDS SCRAPED AND RESERVED FOR ANOTHER USE

¼ CUP PORT

1¾ CUPS MILK

1¾ CUPS HEAVY CREAM

2 CINNAMON STICKS

8 LARGE EGG YOLKS

½ CUP SUPERFINE SUGAR

2 TABLESPOONS KIRSCH (OPTIONAL)

PUT the cherries, vanilla bean, and port in a medium saucepan and set over medium heat. Cook, stirring frequently, for 15 minutes. Remove the pan from the heat and set aside.

FILL a large bowl halfway with ice water.

PUT the milk, cream, and cinnamon sticks in a medium saucepan and bring to a boil over medium heat.

IN a separate bowl, whisk the egg yolks and sugar together until pale yellow ribbons form.

POUR one-third of the hot cream mixture into the egg yolk mixture and whisk. Pour the egg yolk mixture into the rest of the cream mixture. Pour the mixture back into the saucepan and cook over low-medium heat until the mixture thickens enough to coat the back of a wooden spoon, 6 to 8 minutes.

IMMEDIATELY remove the pan from the stove. Strain the mixture through a fine mesh strainer set over a bowl. Set the bottom of the bowl in the ice-water and stir the mixture to chill. Stir in the cherry puree and Kirsch, if using, and mix thoroughly.

TRANSFER the custard to an ice-cream maker and freeze according to the manufacturer's instructions.

RED WINE–PORT ICE CREAM

MAKES ABOUT 1 QUART

2 CUPS FULL-BODIED, BUT NOT TOO TANNIC RED WINE SUCH AS MERLOT

2 CUPS PORT

1½ CUPS SUPERFINE SUGAR

1 TEASPOON FINE SEA SALT

2 CUPS HEAVY CREAM

2 CUPS HALF-AND-HALF

1 VANILLA BEAN, SPLIT LENGTHWISE, SEEDS SCRAPED

12 LARGE EGG YOLKS

FILL a large bowl halfway with ice water.

POUR the wine and port into a medium saucepan and bring to a boil over high heat. Continue to boil until the mixture is reduced to 1 cup, approximately 15 minutes. In the last 2 minutes of reducing, add 1 cup of sugar and the salt and stir to dissolve them.

MEANWHILE, put the heavy cream, half-and-half, and vanilla bean in a separate large saucepan and bring to a boil over low-medium heat. Remove the saucepan from the heat.

PUT the egg yolks and remaining ½ cup of sugar in a bowl and whisk until pale yellow ribbons form. Add one-third of the cream mixture to the yolks and mix well. Pour the yolk and cream mixture into the saucepan with the remaining cream mixture. Add the wine mixture to the saucepan. Whisk thoroughly.

RETURN the saucepan to the stovetop over low heat. Stir constantly until the custard thickens enough to coat the back of a wooden spoon, 6 to 8 minutes. Keep the custard just under a simmer, not letting it boil at any time.

STRAIN the custard through a fine-mesh strainer set over a bowl. Set the bottom of the bowl in the ice water and stir the mixture to chill it.

TRANSFER the custard to an ice-cream maker and freeze according to the manufacturer's instructions.

EMBELLISHMENTS Serve this ice cream with Poached Fall Fruits (page 284), Fig Financier Tart (page 295), or Chocolate Soup with Orange Curd Napoleon (page 313).

SALTED CARAMEL ICE CREAM

MAKES ABOUT 1 QUART

½ CUP WATER

1½ CUPS SUPERFINE SUGAR

2 CUPS HEAVY CREAM

1½ CUPS MILK

1 VANILLA BEAN, SPLIT LENGTHWISE, SEEDS SCRAPED

10 LARGE EGG YOLKS

1 TEASPOON FINE SEA SALT

FILL a large bowl halfway with ice water.

POUR the ½ cup water into a tall pot, add the sugar and stir. Bring to a boil over high heat and cook until the mixture achieves a dark amber color, 8 to 10 minutes. As it cooks, set a small pot of water to a simmer on another burner and brush down the sides of the caramel pot with a 1-inch to 2-inch pastry brush to keep the sugar from sticking to the sides of the pot.

MEANWHILE, pour the heavy cream, milk, and vanilla bean into a small saucepan and warm over low-medium heat. Remove the caramel from the heat. Pour the warmed heavy cream into the caramel, ¼ cup at a time to keep the mixture from darkening, and whisking constantly to combine them. (Be very careful; the caramel will bubble up very aggressively and is extremely hot. This is why a high pot is essential.)

PUT the egg yolks in a separate bowl and whisk them together. Pour one-third of the custard mixture into the egg yolks, whisking constantly. Whisk in the remaining custard mixture and the salt. Pour the mixture back into the saucepan and cook over low-medium heat until the mixture thickens enough to coat the back of a wooden spoon, 6 to 8 minutes.

STRAIN the custard through a fine-mesh strainer set over a bowl, pressing down with a rubber spatula. Set the bottom of the bowl in the ice water and stir the mixture to chill it.

TRANSFER the custard to an ice-cream maker and freeze according to the manufacturer's instructions.

EMBELLISHMENT This is delicious with chocolate or pineapple, and sprinkled with coarse sea salt.

CHOCOLATE SOUP WITH ORANGE CURD NAPOLEON

SERVES 4

f you love chocolate-dipped orange peels, this is the ultimate variation on that theme.

The tried-and-true combination takes a unique twist with the orange present in a miniature napoleon and the chocolate in a soup.

NAPOLEON

3 LARGE EGGS

2 LARGE EGG YOLKS

½ CUP SUGAR

¼ CUP FRESHLY SQUEEZED ORANGE JUICE PLUS 3 TABLESPOONS FINELY GRATED ORANGE ZEST

2 TABLESPOONS FRESHLY SQUEEZED LEMON JUICE

1 CUP (2 STICKS) UNSALTED BUTTER, SOFTENED AT ROOM TEMPERATURE, PLUS ½ CUP (1 STICK), MELTED

4 SHEETS PHYLLO DOUGH, 12 INCHES BY 17 INCHES EACH (IF FROZEN, LET THAW TO REFRIGERATOR TEMPERATURE)

¼ CUP POWDERED SUGAR

CHOCOLATE SOUP

8 OUNCES BEST-QUALITY BITTERSWEET CHOCOLATE, FINELY CHOPPED

PINCH FINE SEA SALT

2 CUPS MILK

1 VANILLA BEAN, SPLIT LENGTHWISE, SEEDS SCRAPED

MINT SPRIGS, FOR GARNISH

FILL a large bowl halfway with ice water.

PUT the eggs, yolks and sugar in a bowl set over a pot of simmering water. Whisk until pale yellow ribbons form. Add the orange juice, orange zest, and lemon juice. Whisk constantly until the mixture thickens, approximately 6 minutes. Do not let the mixture boil at any time. Whisk in the 1 cup butter just before removing the pot from the double-boiler, continuing to whisk until incorporated.

IMMEDIATELY remove the pot from the heat and strain the curd through a fine-mesh strainer set over a bowl. Use the back of a ladle to push the most flavorful liquid through. Set the bottom of the bowl in the ice water and stir to chill the curd.

GENTLY press a piece of plastic wrap directly on the surface of the curd and refrigerate until cooled completely, or overnight. The curd can be refrigerated for up to 3 days in an airtight container.

PREHEAT the oven to 350°F. Put 1 layer of phyllo onto a flat surface. Use a pastry brush to brush sparingly with melted butter, making sure to lightly coat the corners. Top with another sheet of phyllo and brush with butter. Repeat with the remaining sheets of phyllo, making a single stack, but do not apply butter to the top of last phyllo layer. With a sharp knife cut the phyllo into twelve 2½-inch squares by cutting four 2½-inch strips from top to bottom and three 2½-inch strips across those. (You will not use all the pastry.).

SPREAD half of the powdered sugar evenly onto on a parchment paper–lined cookie sheet. Place the phyllo dough on top of the sugar. Sprinkle the top of the dough evenly with the remaining powdered sugar.

BAKE in the oven until golden-brown, approximately 8 minutes. Remove the phyllo from the oven and let cool on the sheet. Once cool, set it aside or store in an airtight container at room temperature for up to 24 hours.

PUT the chopped chocolate and the salt in a small bowl.

POUR the milk and vanilla into a small saucepan and heat it over medium-high heat, stirring it occasionally (do not let it boil). Pour $\frac{1}{3}$ of the hot milk over the chocolate. Gently whisk in the remaining milk. Carefully scrape the bottom and sides of the bowl with a rubber spatula to make sure all of the chocolate has been incorporated. Chill.

TO serve, put 1 teaspoon of orange curd in each of 4 shallow bowls. Put 1 phyllo crisp on top of the orange curd, and top with a heaping tablespoon of orange curd and another phyllo crisp. Repeat this process one more time. Pour chocolate soup around the "napoleon" in each bowl and garnish with a sprig of mint.

EMBELLISHMENT Garnish each serving with orange segments.

CHOCOLATE SAUCE

MAKES 2 CUPS

LIKE THE CRÈME CHANTILLY on page 299, this is a dessert staple that's good to have around. Keep this sauce in your refrigerator and a great dessert will never be more than a spoonful away.

6 OUNCES BITTERSWEET CHOCOLATE, COARSELY CHOPPED

3 TABLESPOONS UNSALTED BUTTER, AT ROOM TEMPERATURE

⅓ CUP HEAVY CREAM

⅓ CUP SUGAR

⅓ CUP LIGHT CORN SYRUP

PUT all ingredients in a double-boiler set over simmering water and cook over low heat, stirring with a rubber spatula, until the chocolate melts and the sugar dissolves.

THE chocolate sauce can be cooled, transferred to an airtight container, and refrigerated for up to 1 week.

CANDIED ALMONDS

SERVES 4 AS A GARNISH

USE THIS HOMEMADE dessert topping on just about any sundae you like.

1 LARGE EGG WHITE

1 CUP SLICED ALMONDS

3 TABLESPOONS SUPERFINE SUGAR

PREHEAT the oven to 325°F. Put the egg white in a small bowl and whisk until frothy. Add the almonds and toss with a rubber spatula to coat the almonds with the egg. Sprinkle the sugar over the almonds, stirring to coat them evenly with the sugar.

SPREAD the almonds out in a single layer on a baking sheet and cook in the oven for 4 minutes. Toss the almonds with a spatula to ensure even coloring, and cook another 4 minutes until golden all over.

TRANSFER the almonds to a clean, cool, dry surface and let cool.

THE almonds can be used right away, or transferred to an airtight container and kept at room temperature for up to 3 days.

PECAN SHORTBREAD COOKIES

MAKES EIGHTEEN 2½-INCH COOKIES

THESE ARE ANOTHER fine companion to chocolate fondue.

I CUP UNSALTED BUTTER, SOFTENED

I CUP POWDERED SUGAR

I TABLESPOON GROUND CINNAMON

I½ CUPS ALL-PURPOSE FLOUR

I LARGE EGG

½ CUP FINELY CHOPPED PECANS

PUT the butter and powdered sugar in the bowl of a standing mixer fitted with the paddle attachment and paddle on medium speed until smooth, approximately 3 minutes. Add the cinnamon and flour.

USING a rubber spatula, scrape down the sides of the bowl. Add the egg and continue to mix for 1 minute. Add the pecans and mix to incorporate.

FORM the dough into a ball and wrap it in plastic wrap. Refrigerate for at least 1 hour or up to 3 days, or freeze it for up to 3 months.

WHEN ready to proceed, preheat the oven to 325°F. Flour a work surface. Roll the dough out with a rolling pin to a thickness of ⅛ inch. Using a 2½-inch round cookie cutter, cut out 18 cookies, arranging them on 1 or 2 cookie sheets. Bake the cookies until set, 11 to 12 minutes.

LET the cookies cool in the pan. Serve, or store in an airtight plastic container at room temperature for up to 3 days, or freeze in the container for up to 3 months.

SOURCES

ARTISANAL PREMIUM CHEESE
More than 300 of the world's finest cheeses, aged to the peak of flavor.
877-797-1200 (toll free)
www.artisanalcheese.com

BROWNE TRADING COMPANY
Fish and shellfish, as well as specialty items such as crème fraîche, oils, vinegars, spices, and salts.
800-944-7848 (toll free)
www.browne-trading.com

THE CHEF'S GARDEN
Micro-greens, micro-herbs, and specialty vegetables.
800-289-4644 (toll free)
www.chefs-garden.com

CHEFS' WAREHOUSE
Specialty items, including olives, capers, oils, and special butters, chocolates, and flours for baking.
www.chefswarehouse.com

D'ARTAGNAN
Duck and duck products such as confit duck legs and duck fat, game, game birds, mushrooms, poultry, rabbit, smoked and cured meats, truffles.
800-327-8246, ext. 0 (toll free)
www.dartagnan.com

JAMISON FARM
Lamb and lamb products.
800-237-5262 (toll free)
www.jamisonfarm.com

JB PRINCE
Kitchen equipment.
800-473-0577 (toll free)
www.jbprince.com

KALUSTYAN'S
Beans, honeys, legumes, nut flours, oils, salts, spices, tahini, verjus, and vinegars.
800-352-3451 (toll free)
212-685-3451
www.kalustyans.com

LOBEL'S OF NEW YORK
Online butcher shop offering steaks and other meats.
877-783-4512 (toll free)
www.lobels.com

MARCHE AUX DELICES
Delicacies from the farm, woods, and sea such as mushrooms, sea salt, and seasonal fruits and vegetables.
888-547-5471 (toll free)
www.auxdelices.com

NIMAN RANCH
Beef, pork, lamb, and double-smoked bacon.
866-808-0340
www.nimanranch.com

SALUMERIA BIELLESE
French and Italian charcuterie.
212-736-7376
www.salumeriabiellese.com

SHERRY-LEHMANN
Fine wines from around the world.
212-838-7500
www.sherry-lehmann.com

THE TASTEFUL GARDEN
Herb and vegetable plants to be grown or maintained at home.
www.tastefulgarden.com

INDEX